PENGUIN BOOKS

# Wife in the North

Judith O'Reilly is a former journalist with the *Sunday Times*, ITN and the BBC. She now works freelance. She is married with three children.

D1322512

# Wife in the North

JUDITH O'REILLY

PENGUIN BOOKS

PENGUIN BOOKS

Published by the Penguin Group
Penguin Books Ltd, 80 Strand, London WC2R ORL, England
Penguin Group (USA), Inc., 375 Hudson Street, New York, New York 10014, USA
Penguin Group (Canada), 90 Eglinton Avenue East, Suite 700, Toronto, Ontario, Canada M4P 2Y3
(a division of Pearson Penguin Canada Inc.)
Penguin Ireland, 25 St Stephen's Green, Dublin 2, Ireland (a division of Penguin Books Ltd)
Penguin Group (Australia), 250 Camberwell Road, Camberwell, Victoria 3124, Australia
(a division of Pearson Australia Group Pty Ltd)
Penguin Books India Pvt Ltd, 11 Community Centre, Panchsheel Park, New Delhi – 110 017, India
Penguin Group (NZ), 67 Apollo Drive, Rosedale, North Shore 0632, New Zealand
(a division of Pearson New Zealand Ltd)
Penguin Books (South Africa) (Pty) Ltd, 24 Sturdee Avenue,
Rosebank, Johannesburg 2196, South Africa

Penguin Books Ltd, Registered Offices: 80 Strand, London WC2R ORL, England

www.penguin.com

First published 2008
3

Set in Monotype Bembo
Typeset by Rowland Phototypesetting Ltd, Bury St Edmunds, Suffolk
Printed in England by Clays Ltd, St Ives plc

ISBN: 978-0-141-03343-3

www.greenpenguin.co.uk

Mixed Sources
Product group from well-managed
forests and other controlled sources
www.fsc.org  Cert no. SA-COC-1592
© 1996 Forest Stewardship Council

Penguin Books is committed to a sustainable future
for our business, our readers and our planet.
The book in your hands is made from paper
certified by the Forest Stewardship Council.

For Alastair and the children

## Tuesday, 23 August 2005

### Road rage

As we drove out of the city's fabulous sprawl last night, I wondered whether I could kill my husband and plead insanity. I knew it would be slightly unfair – I had agreed to the move, although I had not meant it. 'Hormones ate my brain, Your Honour.' Might work. Or I could try: 'He beat me for years, Your Honour, but it entirely slipped my mind. I suddenly remembered in the car and snapped.' In truth, the only abuse I have ever suffered is his music collection and the fact he can only cook two meals – fish pasta, and bacon and leek pasta. I am not sure that would be considered adequate grounds for murder. Particularly if the jury insisted on sampling them, because they are really rather nice.

We have been married so long, and it turns out that after all these years he wants something entirely different from what I want. He wants to live in the country. Cor blimey. What possessed me to agree to such a ridiculous idea? If my cousin the priest had said: 'Do you, Wifey, take him over there in sickness and in health, for richer for poorer, up in the North and down in the South,' I would have said: 'Hang on a minute, a poverty-stricken invalid's one thing . . .' I never, ever thought he would pack us all up and carry us away with him. I did not think he had it in him to make me leave London, still less for the northern wastelands. Who wants to live up north? Northerners. But not me – I stopped being a northerner a long time ago. I love London – it is where I want to be. He suffered it; he thinks we will move to Northumberland and life will be perfect. Life is never perfect.

Outside, it was all speeding cars and sodium lights strung

along the highway; inside my head, a blur of resentment and tail lights. I rested my hands on my pregnant belly and turned my head away from him. I stared at the fake diamond of my engagement ring, nestled next to my wedding ring, which is missing a diamond chip. I thought: 'If I kill him, how will I explain it to the children? "Boys, the good news is we are going back to London; the bad news is your father is staying here. In this lay-by, just under that bush. Look, we'll tie a bunch of flowers to the fence. Wave bye-bye to Daddy now."'

The bloody A1 did not help my mood. There are signs along it. Signs like '168 casualties, 3 years' and 'Next 7 miles 42 casualties, 3 years'. Presumably they are there to make you think when you arrive: 'It could be worse: I could be dead.' It is true to say that I have never liked road movies – the endless journeying, the deep and witty conversations en route to the wherever place the hero is headed, the quirky destination itself – and it was something of a shock to find myself in one. I felt like abandoning my popcorn and going to watch something else entirely – possibly something with graphic sex and hard-core violence in it; definitely not a romantic comedy where two goofy nobodies ended up married. 'Maybe I should try *Star Wars* now the two-year-old and four-year-old have fallen asleep,' I thought. Then again, I did not want to watch anything where a hero fulfils his destiny. I was feeling like a bit player in my own life – that could not be good and the pay would be terrible.

Awkwardly I reached through the gap between our seats to turn off my boys' DVD players blazing intergalactic war, and as the silence introduced itself to darkness, my husband glanced across and gave me a sweet and joyful smile. It reminded me that I loved him and he did not even have to speak. I thought: 'I hate it when you do that.' My life was in a removal lorry with a man in overalls and an interest in martial arts. I was a fat woman in a car heading nowhere I wanted to go with a husband, two small boys, a foetus and a cat. 'Repeat: I am not fat, I am pregnant.' If I had not been pregnant I would never have agreed to this ridiculous experiment in country living. I sincerely hope I do not resent this baby – it might get in the way of my resenting my husband.

He looked back to the road, checked his mirrors, pressed lightly on the indicator and pulled out into the fast lane. I felt the car pick up speed as we drove alongside and then left behind an Eddie Stobart lorry, its headlights blazing. 'How are you feeling?' he asked. My stomach muscles were in spasm; my feet had pins and needles and I could not reach them to rub; I had been crying on and off since we left. I scrupulously folded up my ancient black silk jacket to make a pillow, rested my head against it and closed my eyes.

Twenty-odd years ago, my husband and I were in the same American Politics seminar group at university. I remember him because he would tilt and balance on the back two legs of his chair and never knew the answer to a question. He has no memory of me as I sat four-square and eager to impress. Studies over, we met again in Newcastle, where I trained as a journalist on a regional morning paper. I cannot remember enjoying a day out in Northumberland – unlike my husband, who loved the North-East from the start. As soon as I could, I went down to London and, love-struck, he followed.

I do not care that much for holidays, all that expectation and dislocation, but he does. Every year we would take a cottage in Northumberland for a week. On one of those holidays, nearly five years ago, he saw an advert in the paper: 'Cottage for Sale'. A farm had been bought by a farmer who also owned the local castle. This King of the Castle wanted the cropped fields around the farm and the great barn behind it. He was keeping Number 1, a tenanted cottage which was still home to the former farm manager and his wife, but selling the empty cottage adjoining theirs. It was a rain-sodden day in December, grey clouds papering the endless skies. The slate-roofed cottages, built of whinstone and sandstone, stood in a row of eight, on a slight rise overlooking hedged fields. To the left, a dark bank of trees protected them from the north winds, while an access road in front separated the houses from bunched coal sheds and gardens beyond.

The former farm manager gave us the key to look around. There was no view from the sitting-room window other than of the coal sheds, but from the bedrooms there was glory: land and sea and sky stretching to for ever. We stood together in the empty master bedroom, looking out into the twilight and towards the striped, blue-grey horizon. My husband said: 'Let's do it. After everything we've been through, let's just do it. We promised ourselves we'd do things differently.'

The light had gone from the day by the time we went back into their house to return the keys. The sitting room was dark and snug, watchful with china birds and photographs of grandchildren hanging on the walls. His little old lady wife made us tea and we ate fruit cake in front of their coal fire. My husband was lying back into their sofa, his long legs splayed out, his knees pushing against their coffee table, laughing at a story the man was telling. They looked like they had known each other for years. 'Is it all right if we try and buy next door and come up here on holidays?' I asked. 'We wouldn't be here all the time.' He smiled at us. 'That's the way of things,' he said. It turned out that only the retired couple and one other woman lived in the row: the other cottages were all second homes.

Buying the cottage stretched us; it meant we could not afford a bigger house in London. I agreed to it because it made him happy. I was pregnant then, too. My brain must shrink to the size of a walnut when I am pregnant. I remember the exact words my husband used. He wrapped his arms around me and said: 'Don't worry. This is not the thin end of the wedge. I'm not going to ask you to live here.' Hah.

Sometimes when you are drunk, you comment on the lives of friends. You would never want them to hear you; if they did, they would not want to be your friend any more. You predict who will divorce, who will stay together. Smug. You include yourself in the ranks of the gloriously and utterly committed and you can feel foolish if the game runs its course and leaves you in an altogether different category. There are variations on the game: 'Whose Children are Monsters?', 'Who Earns the Most?', 'Who Among Us Will Die First?' You play the last one when you are old enough to care. But I always thought the least interesting game to play was 'Who Will Move to the Country?'. Even worse, we just lost that round.

We used to go to a therapist in London. I would go in; my husband would sit outside in the car and sleep. I would come out. Cry sometimes. We would drive to an East End café for large yellow cups of coffee, warm ciabatta and sweet berry jams baked in the oven. That would make me feel better. My husband would say: 'I can't believe you pay someone to make you cry' and 'If you didn't go for therapy, you wouldn't need to make yourself feel better after it.' I would laugh. I would feel better because he made me laugh, not really because I liked the oven jams. Though they were good.

One day in February, I came out from my appointment to find him drawing pictures. Large pencil pictures of his dream house: our Northumberland holiday cottage knocked through to the one next door to make a family home. My husband had heaven on his mind. I thought: 'Bollocks.' I stood on a dirty North London street, the large Edwardian terraces stretching either side of us, thinking what I would do, what I would say. I looked in through the open window to see the sketch resting against the steering wheel, my husband so intent on scribbling in a bathroom that he had not heard me trip-trap up to the car. I knew what he was sketching out – his dream and my future.

We drove to the café and sat in the back, warming ourselves

over the coffee. A budding yellow rose on the pressed aluminium table gritty from a legacy of a stranger's sugar. Trendy, haggard mothers let toddlers wander while they jolt-started their day among other trendy, haggard mothers. A few weeks before, my husband had said to me: 'The good thing about our relationship is that we always put the other person first.' I had thought to myself: 'You do. I don't,' then shrugged away the guilt. I sipped at my cappuccino: 'Talk me through this house then.' When we got married after ten years together I did not think marriage would make a difference. I was wrong. Marriage, the everyday everything of family life, melted us one into the other – no one warned me that was the way of it. My husband looked up from stirring his coffee, the black water crashing into the suddenly still spoon. 'Let's do it,' I said. I thought: 'I am tired of standing on your dreams.' I thought: 'Don't expect me to like you while I'm doing this.' He did not say anything at all. He put the spoon carrying a tiny pool of coffee in its bowl safely down on to his saucer. He reached for my hand and held it.

## Wednesday, 24 August 2005

### Holiday home

We arrived in the early hours of Tuesday, unloaded the boys into their small bedroom, let the cat out of her box in the kitchen, carefully shut the door behind us and crawled up to our room. I did not expect to sleep. I never do when I am pregnant. Too hormonal, uncomfortable and stressed. I surf sleep instead, taste it then spit it out again; I was not helped then or last night by the fact the curtains need a blackout lining. We are two miles from the sea across fields, and every twenty seconds the light from a lighthouse on the Farne Islands raps against the window then sweeps round, back and away again to sea.

The cottage is nearly 350 miles away from London. So far away that although the removal van set off on Monday, it only arrived yesterday as we were clearing away the breakfast. The gaffer climbed down from the cab and came in from the sheeting rain; he wiped his boots on the mat and poked his head into the small sitting room. 'You've already got furniture in here then?' he said. We all looked into the small room at the three-piece suite, oak table and two chairs, pine dresser and TV. 'This was our holiday cottage.' I could hear his mate outside swinging open the metal doors and fixing the steep ramp between the van and the threshold. The gaffer rubbed his large, calloused hands together. I think he was looking for a place to put things. There was no place. Being a removal man must put you at risk of a hernia and too much insight into the human condition. People move up the property ladder or slide down it. Full of newly married hope or divorced despair; keen to impress each other and their neighbours, at the start of new lives. Convincing themselves that the sun will shine brighter, their wife love them more; that they can be happier in this house than they were before. I wondered what they thought of us. Then I thought: 'I don't want to know.' 'Kids, let's get you dressed,' I said. 'We're going out.'

## Friday, 26 August 2005

### His dream, my future

Unpacked so far: knickers; cat (about as relaxed as I am); the feeling I have made the biggest mistake of my life; thirty-four black bags (thirty-three of them belonging to the children); twelve plastic boxes of toys (not so much 'unpacked' as put on a shelf so the children can't get them – who needs more mess?); maternity notes (in case of emergency; already lost); Gaggia coffee-maker (a going-away present from London friends who doubt Northumberland café society); Colombian coffee (similar); wine glasses; a packet of photographs tied with a narrow black ribbon; my address book with all my friends' phone numbers (if I lose this book, my life ends); mobile phone (no signal: so much for the address book); digital radio (no signal: good grief).

## Sunday, 28 August 2005

### Thin end of the wedge

I had to get away from the chaos for half an hour. I drove along the road which borders the dunes, parked up, then climbed carefully down through the marram grass to the beach. I sat on a rock and watched the shivering sea and the islands that litter it. My bones felt cold. If Northumberland does not work out for us, if it is not a 'fit', the deal is this: we go back to London, go back home. D-day is 31 December 2007, when we make our decision to stay or go. I said out loud: 'I am never going to get out of here. He is never going to let me leave.' He must have slipped some date-rape drug into my latte, but he did not want to remove my panties, he wanted to remove my life. The problem is, he loves Northumberland and I do not. He thinks it is his spiritual home while I think it beautiful but bleak and chill and nowhere that I want to be. And yet I love him and he wants this chance so badly – for all of us to make a life away from noise and city strife, the smell of dirty streets and hostile strangers. I told myself: 'This is what marriage is – a question of loving, honouring and compromise.' I am compromising right now on where I want to be. I do not know how good I am at compromise. I thought I heard a child laugh behind me – there was no one there. The beach was all but empty: a few walkers, a man throwing a hard rubber ball into the waves for his dog to fetch. No laughing child and no escape route.

If you close your eyes, then open the green one on the left and squint a bit, in a dim light my husband looks like a Hollywood star. The kind who wears a Smith & Wesson slung round snake hips, sports a woollen poncho and chews a cigarillo. The kind that spits in the dust then kills you. There are all sorts of red-rose reasons he deserves his shot at happiness, not just the cowboy charm and spurs. Every other month, he will say something to make me laugh so hard I fall off a kitchen chair. I am not sure who else could make me laugh like that now Benny Hill is dead. In any case, the boys look like him, so I could not forget the man, and I have grown to love the sad, plastic-wrapped garage flowers he rescues from the forecourt buckets of petrol stations and which he carries in with care. To which I say 'Thank you' and 'I'll put these lovely turquoise chrysanthemums in a vase.' Then drop them in a bin.

## Monday, 29 August 2005

### Sick and tired

One day you wrap, in acid-free tissue layers, the daughter in you. You admire it as you put away its girlish chiffon colours, you mourn its passing as you stand on tiptoe to store it on the very highest shelf. From a hanger, you take off and shake out the sensible navy role of mother and slip it on. Mother not only to your children but to your own mother. I am at that moment.

My mother was very sick this summer. I thought she would die when she was suddenly struck down by rheumatoid arthritis. One of those diseases which leaves you in so much pain, you close your eyes and rest your head upon the pillow. Still. You take a moment. You ask yourself: 'Shall I go on?' Another breath. 'Can I go on?' She is over the immediate crisis but still infinitely frail. In my head, she is a pretty forty-two; in reality, she is still pretty but cannot manage stairs. One of my part-time neighbours came up for a couple of days and popped in to see how I was getting on. She is a hospital consultant. She sat down in a rocker by the door and gave me a warm smile. 'How are you?' she asked. I am enormously pregnant, cumbersome, shattered, old, tired beyond belief. I have abandoned the city of my heart. We have cleared the sitting room; it now has a single bed against the back wall which I have made up so that it is ready for my mother, who is arriving tomorrow. My dad is going in the cottage next door. I am sitting on the single bed because there is nowhere else to sit. My husband is about to leave to go back to work in London. He has not yet left and I am already as lonely as I have ever been. I cry. Loudly. I cannot find the words. The Consultant comes over and sits next to me on the bed. I think: 'I am ridiculous.' I think: 'I am *not* ridiculous' and cry some more. There is a sympathy between women which does not need to hear the words to feel another's hurt, to try to ease the pain as best they can. She rubs my back, says: 'There, there.' And I feel better.

All told, it has been a damnable summer. Over the past few months, between arranging the move from one end of the country to the other, working, looking after a four-year-old, a two-year-old and being pregnant, I have been up and down to Yorkshire hospitals and moved the entire family to North Wales for ten days when my mother took up convalescence with her niece. I did not want to spend that much time away from the children, so my husband came too. Every day, he would take the boys on expeditions to the beach or adventuring while I was with my mother. Every night, he would clear the knives and forks and marmalade pots from the table in the dining room of the bed and breakfast where we were staying to do his work on his laptop, then come to bed at three.

We had been back from Wales a week when we moved

house. I am an only child. That was bad planning on my part. I was utterly and entirely grateful to my cousin for stepping in to care for my mother, whom I know she loves. But another reason I agreed to the move is that *I* need this chance too. In London, it would be difficult to afford a house which could have a comfortable set-up for my parents, room for three children and an office for us. In Northumberland, it becomes a runner. When illness and age strikes again, my mother can come to me. My husband lives where he wants to live; the children get small classes and large beaches; my parents get space in our house when they need it. All I have to do is hold it together long enough to have a baby and create a new life for everybody. If this move does not work, I am busted.

## Tuesday, 6 September 2005

### Park and ride

My four-year-old's first day in the reception class at his new school. It is a small school on the outskirts of a stone-built village, set next to grazing sheep and across the fields from a spired church. It has a pupil roll of around forty. His London school, where he was in the morning nursery class, had a roll of 400. I loved the London school. The only problem: I was old enough to have given birth to the other mothers. Not insurmountable. I wore more lipstick. That solves more problems that you would think.

In London, we would walk him along a canal and through a park to school. In the country, we drive. About a mile into the journey, my four-year-old said: 'I liked my old school.' 'I'm sure you'll like your new school too, darling,' I replied. He kept looking out of the window. 'Look, there's a horse,' I said. He harrumphed. 'Why do I have to go to school anyway?' 'And a chicken,' I said. 'They have chickens up here, too.

Hello, chicken.' He harrumphed again. My two-year-old piped up: 'I like the soldiers. Where are the soldiers?' My two-year-old is obsessed with the Changing of the Guard. I said: 'The soldiers are in London, darling.' He started to cry.

When we got back, I said to the two-year-old as we got out of the car: 'Shall we go for a walk in the woods?' Next to the cottages and across the road there is a steeply sloping wood of huge beech and sycamore trees. He shook his head. 'Bears might eat me.' 'There are no bears,' I said. I stroked his hair, crouched down, asked: 'Are you OK with the move, with living here?' He shook his head again. 'Bears might eat me.' 'There are no bears,' I said as I looked into the darkness and the growling started.

## Wednesday, 7 September 2005

### Kiss and make-up

Yesterday afternoon, when I picked up the four-year-old, I said: 'How was it then?' 'Can't remember.' 'Did you play with anyone?' 'Can't remember.' Later, slumped against my mother in her chair, his arms around her, I heard him confide: 'I don't have any friends.' 'You will,' she said, 'it takes time.' He thinks he has it bad making new friends in school. Life in London was simpler in many ways. Cafés knew how to make a decent skinny latte with an extra shot, muddy wellies weren't de rigueur and most importantly I had friends. Quite a few of them. Those who had children juggled their responsibilities, adjusted their career expectations and got on with it. Those who didn't tried not to talk too much about the exotic holidays and how long they spent in bed on a Sunday. I had things in common with my friends: work, children of the same age, an outlook. Now I have to start again. I said to my mother: 'I don't have any friends either.' She patted my arm, said: 'Give it time.'

This is me at the school gate. Hand extended for warm, professional handshake. Big smile. It says: 'Trust me. I'm a mother. Just like you.' The fact I am shaking hands at all, however, is a giveaway. Shaking hands is something you do in an office. Or to a stranger. I tend to do it to men. 'Do you shake hands with other women out in the real world?' I suddenly wonder. They do not know this, but it could be worse. I could be doing that metropolitan swoop to air-kiss their cheeks. A blur of women shake my outstretched hand. A few look like they might even have done it before. Some of them wear gilets. Some wear wellies. One looks like she climbs off a horse to get into her 4×4, picks up her child, drives home, then climbs back in the saddle. Another wears tweed and a strange furry hat. Her husband farms oysters as well as cows. She used to teach mathematics in secondary school and has a very 'County Set' accent – an intimidating combination. Hardly anyone seems to wear make-up. Do they have natural make-up down to such a fine art that I cannot spot it? It takes me an hour and a half to look as if I am not wearing any. No one took it upon themselves to introduce themselves to me. Perhaps I just leapt on them with my class-president campaign buttons a little too early.

## Thursday, 8 September 2005

### Have you heard? Love is blind

My mother is registered blind. Macular degeneration affects the central vision of the eyes and is the most common cause of blindness in the UK. Fragile capillaries grow underneath the 'macula', the central area of the retina at the back of the eye. In my mother's case, they have leaked and bled, leaving her with peripheral vision – the edge of things. My mother, who can see to the heart of the matter in moments, now lives at the margins. I find it almost unbearable to see her hold a grandchild's face between soft palms and turn her head this way and that to snatch at what is hers by right. Later, she sits sideways pressed against a television screen, squinting hopelessly at a letter tilted and close against her eyes, struggling to find her way in a place of darkness and fighting it every moment.

Deafness makes it worse. She cannot hear you in a crowded room. Cannot hear you in a room with the two of you unless she concentrates. Unless you are saying something you do not want her to hear – that she can do. Two hearing aids help her get by. She buys a watch for the blind and has to lift it to her ear to hear the voice. She buys scales for baking, made especially for the blind. The scales, too, have a voice. They ring out: 'One pound and seven ounces.' 'What was that?' she asks, and presses it again. 'One pound and seven ounces.' 'No, didn't get that,' she says, and presses it again. As for me, I laugh, and she laughs herself and says: 'Don't laugh,' and, helpless, I say: 'I'm not laughing,' and I am not laughing – inside I am weeping, it just looks like laughter.

I watch her face sometimes. In company, she sits too quietly, smiles a moment late, nods when she should shake her head. She misses the beat. You accept the rebukes when she says you do not speak clearly enough, speak too fast, sit too far away. You move closer, speak more slowly, raise your voice. Even as my father holds her hand, age isolates her. Age is terrible. I am not signing up to it. God is an ingrate. My mother's goodness and her Catholic reverence brought her decay and sickness. She got old, blind, deaf. These are sins to be reckoned with. These are sins he should forgive. Step up to the mark, Jesus. Lay on hands. Heal the sick. It's been a while.

## Friday, 9 September 2005

### Haunting houses

I am down in London for work – two nights away for a media consultancy job, then back to Northumberland on Saturday morning. Our London house is nothing special apart from the fact it was ours. End of terrace, Victorian. It looks as if it suffered some damage during the Second World War when bombs rained down on the East End. It has a kitchen with wooden cupboards and a faux stable back-door into a paved garden with Peace roses and a frenzied Russian vine. The wall between the sitting room and the dining room was replaced by shuttered doors, which we pulled across to make a downstairs office. I covered them with charcoal and pencil nudes from my life-drawing class. When I needed inspiration I would look across from my computer and think: 'I should really lose some weight.' The house has a cellar we filled with junk, stripped floors, a small bathroom with antiqued gold taps, and three bedrooms – just enough for who we were. At night we would fall asleep to the sound of police sirens and other people's conversation as they staggered home. We could walk to a good school, a market and the library, catch a bus to Canary Wharf or a tube to the West End. I felt safe, alert, busy. I loved my London life. I never went to clubs, never danced till dawn; I gave birth, drank coffee, spent hours in parks and far too long at work. But this book shop here I love, this shop for clothes, and this bridge lifts my heart whenever I cross the river. I had some fancy jobs and met some fancy people, but I never did anything extraordinary. It is London which is extraordinary: the teeming, urgent streets; palaces; power; the history of a nation, casual, standing with pigeons on a plinth.

I do not want to sell the house until we decide whether the move north is a permanent one. The plan is to start renting it out early next year. We cannot do it before because we need somewhere to come back to after I give birth – then we will buy furniture and get it ready for tenants. When I visit it like this, the city itself seems strange. As for what was my home – I know how it is to haunt a house. You move around it in silence. You look into unfamiliar rooms emptied out of the people who once lived alongside you. Disconnected and unseen. It has nothing for you unless you count dustballs and memories.

## Monday, 12 September 2005

### Careering out of control

In London, when I worked full time in a newsroom, I had a professional nanny with a degree and a reasonable wage. That is to say, I signed over virtually everything I earned to her and her best friend, the taxman. When I freelanced from home and worked less, I kept my nanny but she worked fewer days. I have thought about it but there is no way I can look after everyone, organize the house, be this pregnant and do any work at all. I know some women could, but they are better women than me. I am permanently exhausted and enormous. When my husband goes back down to London, it will get worse. We advertised in the local newspaper. I admit it: I need help.

One applicant, a sales rep, told me: 'I want to come in off the road – I've just had a really bad car smash. I have a permanent headache and a ringing in my ears.' I liked her, but I thought: 'A "permanent headache" and you want to work with children?' One had removed a nose ring for the interview. I do not want to think about how she did that. Another honest applicant told me as she drank my tea: 'I don't know why I've applied.' I liked her too, but thought: 'Well, if *you* don't know, how am *I* supposed to?' My mother and father are still with me. Deaf as she is, my mother misses nothing. If you did not know her, you would see her sitting with a blanket round her knees, hearing aids, white stick by her side and enormous black glasses perched on her tiny nose and think her an entirely harmless old lady. But as each candidate left, my mother's mouth turned down and she shook her silver, permed, curl-perfect head. 'Absolutely not,' she would say. A hanging judge.

Then the Dairy Farmer's Wife appeared. Long, glossy hair with a fringe and an auburn tint. She has a trim, curvy figure; girlish-looking, despite the fact she is two years older than me. She had seen the advert but already knew about the relocating Londoners courtesy of the local farming grapevine. She laughs easily, which I always like. She told me she was married at twenty-one and has three girls of her own, a twenty-year-old at university, an eighteen-year-old about to go and a thirteen-year-old. All privately educated. A swimming pool. Milking 150 cows. She is going to do three days a week for me because she wants to do something out of the house now the family is grown — I think perhaps she does not feel as needed as she once did. She makes me feel embarrassed to be pregnant at my age. Makes me think: 'What have I been doing with my life?' Women look at other women. They think: 'Nice legs. Good teeth.' They think: 'Could I be her? Should I have trod her path? Was her way the better way to go? If I had gone this way as she did, not that way when I did, would I be happier today?'

I have a friend. This one a perfect mother. She too stayed looking young — perhaps because she did it right: had her kids early, sidelined the nursing career, made family her life. Her children are adolescents now. She knows what to do when they are knocked or sick or broken up; lets them have hairy pets; cooks meals from scratch. I wonder whether she, too, looks at me and thinks: 'What has she been doing with her life?' OK, I have had a career. Marvellous while it lasted, but what after all *is* a career and where did it get me? I am a geriatric mother.

I am clever, or so I thought. I said: 'I know I will shape my brilliant career to fit my life as a mother. I will give up my well-paid, glamorous, high-status job. I will cut my days and free-lance from home. That way, I can exercise my brain, take back control of my life and see more of the children.' How stupid can a well-educated woman be? Look where I am. An old mother, struggling to keep up with two small boys and about to have another baby. No figure. No 'career'. No time to make another. No salary and no status. Without a salary and an office, I could not defend myself from pleas to relocate. I am a has-been living in a world which thinks I am a never-was.

## Tuesday, 13 September 2005

### Absent with leave

My husband left for London for two weeks. Let me see, how long have we lived here? Oh yes, three weeks. How pregnant am I? Seven months. How many children do I have? Two and a bit. Do I want to be here? No. Excellent. He has a deadline. He always seems to have a deadline. He is the one who wants to live up here, yet he is the one who has to work away for weeks at a time. I knew he would have to go back soon after we moved: he can do part of his job down the line but not all of it. Seeing him go – not having him here – is about as hard as I thought it would be. He called me. He said: 'I miss you.' I gripped the phone, said: 'If we lived in London, you wouldn't have to miss me.'

Real friends I count like beads on a rosary. Among them, my Best Friend From School, who knows the worst of me and still loves me. My Gay Best Boyfriend from university – the one who knew that guy I liked was gay before I did. London Diva, ahead of me in wisdom and in life; the Perfect Mother I turn to for advice; and Islington Beauty, a fellow working mother.

You do not keep every friend you ever make. If you are lucky, you keep one or maybe two from the pigeonholes of life: study, jobs, children. One of the best places for making friends is, of course, the office. I have friends from all of the places I have worked: newspapers and TV. If you invest wisely, you double them as they grow old and marry. Some friends become another family. Some friends you talk to once a year. A few are there in every crisis and extremity. You hurt when they hurt. There are times when you put down a phone after they have read you the latest chapter of their life, and you weep for them. Some, occasionally, disappoint. Occasionally, you disappoint back. You try to listen. In sadness and disaster, you say: 'I love you' and hope they can hear between their shouts of pain. You say: 'I'm here for you' and hope they can see you in their darkness. It seems the least that you can do.

My friends. Each precious and shiny to me. They have two things in common: they love me back and, apart from my Best Friend From School, they tend to live in London. Bastards all, those London livers. I have betrayed them. I have challenged them and I do not want to challenge my friends. I want to get drunk with them on expensive wines that taste of sunshine. I want to tell them: 'Whatever you do is fine with me.' I want them to say the same to me. I have let the side down. My friends would not have approved if we had moved to suburbia. You can at least explain an escape to suburbia. You can shrug your shoulders and show them the palms of your hands. Sorrowful. You can tell them: 'The children. Schools.' You can look sombre. 'Fees.' You can shake your head. 'Just not possible.' Try telling a serious career woman who does something indescribably complicated with television satellites the same in husband-speak. Try saying: 'My husband. His dream.' Her diva blue eyes narrow. Try saying: 'Love. His happiness.' Try saying: 'Northumberland. It's not far – you can visit.' She spits on your stripped and polished floor.

## Wednesday, 5 October 2005

### The kindness of strangers

Northumberland is considered by many to be the cradle of English Christianity, courtesy of the saints and holy men who once lived on its rocky outcrops among the seabirds and the seals. It seems fitting then, somehow, that so many people we meet appear to be so very faith filled. The school community, at least, seems very religious; Church of England, although many of those connected with it worship at a Baptist church. I asked one volunteer who plays the guitar and wears small Jesus fish for earrings how she came to be at the school. She smiled and said: 'The Lord wants me here.' At toddler group the other morning, I admired the child-crafted art on the walls. Then looked again. I asked Guitar Girl: 'Are the little cut-out people being burnt up by the flames of hell?' (My Catholic interpretation of red and licking fire.) It was nothing so infernal – Pentecostal art, apparently. Tongues of flame come down from heaven to lend the silhouettes the power of babbling speech, not to burn up paper toes.

Moving after the baby was born would have meant making my four-year-old start school in London in September and then start another school a few months later in Northumberland. It did not seem fair to him. But moving when we did has made me more reliant on the kindness of these devout and earnest strangers. Three women linked to the school, the Head Teacher, the Evangelical Woman who chairs the governing body and Guitar Girl, have all told me to call them if I need help while my husband is away. I waddle into school with my enormous pregnant belly, my mother's arm tucked in mine, she tip-tapping with her dark glasses and her white stick, with the two big-eyed boys clutching at my knees. These people are Christians. Naturally they want to help me. I am amazed they have not had a sponsored walk on my behalf. They make me tea at toddler group on Monday mornings and thrust scraps of paper with telephone numbers into my hands. 'For emergencies,' they say, 'or any time.' I am a stranger come among them to live in barley fields. In London, I do not think anyone would have noticed had my husband been away. Of course, the need would not have been there either. I gratefully nod my thanks; I drink their tea; I cannot remember where I put their numbers.

## Monday, 17 October 2005

### Tears for fears

I read to the boys last night and then could not get off my bed for the next hour and a half. I kept trying different ways to roll on one side and then up, but it was all too excruciating. My ligaments have softened. The boys got so bored they wandered off and put themselves to bed. We are going down to London in a week's time. I lay there, thinking: 'I am sooooooooooooooo looking forward to the journey.' Clambering on the train, nearly nine months pregnant. Settling down with the snacks and colouring books. Only three and three-quarter hours to go before dear old London town. I am not entirely sure I can fit into a railway seat, or, for that matter, whether I will be able to get out of it if my back goes. Baby induction date: Friday, 4 November. The children were so good last night and I am utterly bad-tempered with them both. I am unhappy, and if I were not so damned busy I would be frightened about what we have just done and what might be yet to come. This morning, I sat on the bed and sobbed. The boys climbed on to the bed and held on to me. I had to do that 'Mummy's fine. Mummy's just a bit tired' thing you do to avoid them knowing that Mummy is a lunatic.

## Tuesday, 18 October 2005

### Womb with a view

Feeling absurdly abandoned. My husband came back, flung out his arms and said: 'Beautiful, isn't it?' Then set off again for London. But two young rampaging hearts, all boy and breathless haste, beat along the corridor from me. I have them both and, though not yet born, I have the baby with me. At night, before I try to sleep, I breathe in and down, imagine myself sinking through my body to reach the life inside. I see the golden baby through the darkness, move closer to chalice the child in my arms, pouring my blood love into and through the light. I think: 'If, by some dark chance, we never get to meet, if I never get to hear your voice or you never see me smile, know this: your mother loved you.'

## Wednesday, 19 October 2005

### Best-laid schemes

I am hoping desperately I do not give birth when my husband is away in London. I have a very complicated table of arrangements designed to kick in if I go into labour. Courtesy of living remotely, I am advised the ambulance might never find me. And, if they did, it might be too late to move me. I need volunteers to look after the boys and others to take me into hospital.

An accountant lives in the farmhouse along the road. He used to work in the City. I know him slightly from our holidays here. I asked him whether he would drive me the hour to hospital if I go into labour. The Accountant is not a complete stranger, but neither is he the father of my baby. He did not look keen. 'I think I'm busy that day,' he said. 'You don't know which day it will be,' I replied. 'No,' he said, 'but I'm almost certainly busy.' He finally agreed but later arranged some complicated swap on the A1 with the Dairy Farmer's Wife. He would take the kids and I could go with her. He is divorced, does not have children of his own. He has no idea that a labouring woman would be much less trouble than my two boys, even if he ended up pulling into a lay-by, erecting a warning triangle behind the car and biting through the umbilical cord.

## Monday, 24 October 2005

### Straight down the line

We have had to come down early on the instructions of the obstetrician. She said if I wanted to be sure the baby was born in London, I could not leave it up to the wire. But because I am living in Northumberland, I was required to book in locally in case of emergency. The two-year-old was amusing himself with the midwife's toys while she filled out the paperwork. I do not know what they would do if I went into labour and they did not have a completed form – presumably drive me to the county border in an open pick-up truck. She was running through questions on her booking-in form when she casually enquired: 'Are you and your baby's father blood relatives?' I thought: 'You mean, is he my brother?' I sat up straighter. 'No. Why?' I swallowed. 'Does that happen often up here?' 'No,' she said reassuringly, her head bent over my notes, 'not now.'

The Dairy Farmer's Wife drove us to the railway station. She looked more relieved than I was to see me climb on to the train with the two boys, two cases and a buggy. I also carried a bin bag of toys wrapped in newspaper and a huge picnic lunch. This is not because I am a particularly good mother. It is because I was scared. Four hours on a train in my present state

23

with two excitable children could well induce labour. My two-year-old abandoned me to sit on the floor of the luggage space. I decided that was all right. My four-year-old slithered underneath the table. I decided that was all right, too. At any given moment, one or other of us wanted to go to the toilet. I would brush aside the crumpled sheets of newspaper, cheap toys, sandwich remnants, apples, raisins and water bottles, not to mention the comics, pads and crayons, and ease myself out from the table. We rollocked along the corridor to the toilet, where I would propel the little one in to one side of the cubicle, push him under my belly and across to the other side, shuffle in myself, then reach out a hand and haul the four-year-old in after us. Remembering to lock the door.

My fellow passengers watched from behind their books and laptops as first the food mountain and then the parcelled toys came out. When strangers disapprove of your parenting, you can virtually chew the air between you. Every time my eyes met those of another passenger, I would smile like a Madonna, like the sort of woman who thinks nothing of spending four hours on a train, nine months pregnant, with two small boys. I looked like the sort of woman who likes children. I do not like children. I make an exception for my own. I suspect my fellow passengers were thinking: 'Those children are going to grow up obese', 'That woman spoils those children' and my personal favourite: 'She's making a rod for her own back there.' I did not care. I had given up caring when we reached Doncaster. By which time it was a question of survival. Would I get through the journey without losing my mind? I am not sure I made it. The journey lasted three and a half years.

## Tuesday, 1 November 2005

### Chim-chiminey

In for a sweep. This is not a good thing. This is not: 'Would you mind popping round and clearing out the bird nests?' At least, I hope not. It is a grit your teeth while another woman does something to the neck of your cervix which, if not illegal, should be. The obstetrician said: 'Try to relax.' How can you relax when it feels like someone wearing costume jewellery is reaching for your lungs to pull them out through your vagina? The idea behind the sweep is to start things off 'naturally' and to avoid if possible an induction with pessaries and a drip when labour can build very quickly. A sweep is exquisitely uncomfortable and it is impossible to know if it will work. Infinitely better than the sweep was the frighteningly expensive haircut I just got. Amazing what a good haircut will do for you. I am hoping it will take people's mind off my nether regions when I am having the baby. It can all get a bit: 'Come in. Make yourself at home. Have you seen my fanny?' This way, I stand a chance of: 'Hello. How are you getting on, dear?' She might pause long enough to say: 'I like your hair.' Back to business. 'Would you mind if I had a look at your fanny?'

## Thursday, 3 November 2005

### Operation New Baby

We have been staying in the London house since we got down. Anything personal was shipped up to the house I now pretend to consider home. The sofa, an armchair, an old TV and three beds are all that is left, along with four plates, four mismatched cups, four sets of knives and forks and enough bedding to see us through the birth.

It was quarter to six in the morning when my waters broke. I was on my own. When I say 'on my own', that generally translates to 'surrounded by small children'. My husband was working overnight on another deadline. I rang him in the office. I told him I thought it would be a good idea if he came home. It looked as if I was having the baby. He agreed. He tried saying: 'I'll just finish . . .' Slowly and calmly, I said that sometimes you had to meet a deadline and sometimes you had to have a baby. He muttered something. It may have been: 'Quite right, darling, I'll be straight home.' It may have been: 'It will only take twenty minutes.' When I was pregnant with my four-year-old, things started to move during an episode of *The Sopranos*; my husband kept watching. He is a big fan. I shouted at him so loudly he decided he would buy the boxed DVD collection.

There are logistical complications giving birth in London. My parents live in Yorkshire. Anyway, they are too old and frail to look after both boys, though my mother said 'We can manage one of them.' I am not sure what I was expected to do with the other. Up to now, I have always been able to buy myself out of a crisis with childcare. A crisis like going into hospital to have another baby. These days I have coping strategies to get me from one crisis to the next. I might as well be in the Territorial Army. Who is going to be at Foxhole A when I am at Dugout B? How will I get between A and B? Do I have adequate supplies for Operation New Baby? Who will rescue me when I am pinned down? How will the helicopter gunships get through?

I had organized cover for the boys to sleep over with London Diva and her husband, the four-year-old's godfather, if I went into premature labour at night. During the day, when I was due in for induction, I had arranged for one of my ex-nanny's friends to take them. They knew her and liked her.

The problem was I started labouring in a limbo time and a limbo place.

After I made contact with my husband, I scrambled into my clothes – if a nine-month-pregnant woman can be said to move fast enough to merit the term 'scramble'. I tiptoed down the staircase of the emptied house, trying not to wake the boys. The sitting room has wooden floors and shutters, and without any of our effects felt like a crate. I was calling in the gunships to take my two boys to safety. It was still dark outside and I waited for the minutes to move on from the 'What fucking time do you call this?' zone into the respectable 'I know it's a tad early' zone.

5.55 a.m. I rang London Diva. She was away on business in Washington. I immediately felt parochial. The Godfather was in charge. I explained the early shout. 'Are you OK to take the boys till nineish when the nanny will take over?' I asked – not so much asking a question as sounding the alert. 'No,' he said, 'that would be difficult.' I love my friend's husband a lot. At that moment, I loved him slightly less. He had to take his own daughter to school. Dawn bleary, he could not compute. I did not try to persuade him. I thought cheerfully: 'You are so going to get it in the neck when your wife gets home and you tell her what you just did.'

5.57 a.m. I had a moment while I thought: 'Oh my God. What do I do now?'

5.58 a.m. I rang our old nanny's friend. Her husband answered the phone. He seemed unaware that we were in the 'respectable' zone. He did not sound keen to hand the panting stranger over to his wife, but did. I burbled about waters breaking and being on my own, asking: 'Would you mind?' and 'How soon could you possibly . . .?' and 'Would you say sorry to your husband?' She was not my children's nanny but she has a baby of her own and understood that another woman was in a fix. She said: 'Fine. I'll come over.'

In hospital, we went straight from the 'We're having a baby right this minute' crisis to zip. Nothing moved. Midwives said things like: 'Let's see how it goes ... Maybe you should go home ...? We don't have a bed right now and nothing seems to be happening.' I smiled and nodded at them agreeably. I thought: 'If you think I am going home, letting my husband go back to work and unpicking my childcare arrangements, think again. This baby is coming out. Just watch.' They sent me off for a walkabout and we went down to the coffee shop in the ground-floor foyer. We sat with our coffees; my husband tried to look as if he was not thinking about everything he could be doing back in the office. I had a colleague who filed a news story as his wife was giving birth. The journalist, not the labouring mother, in me could appreciate his professionalism. The labouring mother in me watched my husband and thought: 'If you make a move for your mobile phone, I am drowning it in my cappuccino.' Suddenly, I felt more waters gush out. I thought: 'I have a choice between free Subway sandwiches for life or a long wet walk back to the ward.' I am British. I do not like to look as if continence is an issue, but I liked the idea of giving birth next to a tuna baguette even less.

Labour took an incredibly smug two hours. It never takes me two hours. It takes me aeons. I hate women who say it took them three minutes to have their baby and they never felt a thing. It was too fast even for drugs. I hate that too. Mind you, it is probably because my pelvic floor is not what it was. God, I will have to lie about how long it took in case everyone labels me a Slack Alice. Did manage the gas and air, which is like drinking gin and tonic very quickly. It made me sick. Which is also like drinking gin and tonic very quickly. Hurt like bejesus. That moment when the baby's head crowns and that part of your mind which is still coherent asks the eminently rational question: 'Can I manage the rest of my life in two pieces?' When that ripping, burning scream between your legs goes on.

You decide: 'Yes, I can manage that.' You think there will be little alternative. There is a moment of pain-soaked relief when the baby's head makes it out. Then the thought: 'Does the baby really need shoulders? Can't it make do with a head? I will buy it shoulders on eBay.'

I heard the baby cry. The midwife handed the slimy morsel across to my husband. He laid it warm and slippery on my breast. The child heat was enough to sear straight through my skin and mould the babe on to my ready heart. I held the warm skin bundle close. The tiny boned head and pink ribbed face. I thought: 'Ah. Child of mine.' Beauty in an instant. I never thought to ask. My husband whispered: 'She's a girl. She's a girl.' I have a daughter. My first, last and only daughter. My beloved.

### Friday, 4 November 2005

### Girl power

My husband brought the boys in yesterday afternoon. 'Daddy', ga-ga with the thought of a daughter. The boys were desperate for a girl. I think they would have insisted I sent back a tiny, rival brother. Generous, they forgive a sister. My four-year-old looked at his sister – soft-smiled, enchanted, in love with her already. That is how long it took. A moment.

We generally to and fro on names. It took us three weeks to decide on our four-year-old's name. Not my baby girl. We are naming the baby after my Best Friend From School. My friend is always there for me in every way a friend can be. A business tycoon in the West Midlands, she is everything I am not: optimistic, positive, dynamic, efficient, organized, good with numbers, sporty, child-free. She did her own multi-million-pound management buyout and runs a company that makes car cleaning products. She visits. When she thinks my house smells bad, she delves in her car boot and pulls out large plastic bottles of bright blue liquids. She says: 'I think you should use this.' And I do. She never wanted a child of her own, preferred a career. In a name, she can have a little bit of one of mine. I regularly say to her: 'Being a mother is bloody awful.' I want to say to her: 'Being a mother is bloody amazing.' The warp and weft of motherhood, a cloth she will never feel. One time, I wanted to say: 'Have a child. Have a child, do.' But it is not my place. In a way, I feel the loss of her child more than she does herself. I would have watched her child grow and smile, would have looked into a cherub's face for another her.

## Monday, 7 November 2005

### Tits oot for the lads

My husband and boys are driving up to Northumberland while the baby and I catch a train back to the home which isn't a home. The train journey was all right. Men with glazed expressions and lager cans swallowed down their belches to coo over the tiny newborn as I passed them in search of black coffee and chocolate bars.

The hospital where I had her is directly opposite the Houses of Parliament, an old stomping ground when I reported on politics. While I was in there, I kept thinking: 'I could call such and such an MP, they could come over and see me. We could talk politics.' I realized they would perhaps be slightly reluctant to visit a maternity ward in case anyone thought the baby was theirs. The baby would want feeding while they were there. I would have to get at least one enormous wet breast out. I do not think you should get your breasts out in front of Members of Parliament. Unless the story you are trying to obtain is a particularly good one. I felt the same way on the train. It is slightly complicated trying to feed a baby on a train and not reveal too much of your aged breasts to the men with the lager cans, although I am not convinced they could have focused on my breasts anyway. They probably thought I had twins and four breasts. In any event, none of them put aside their can and attempted to join the fray.

## Wednesday, 9 November 2005

### My unfeasibly large nipples

Our cat has had the good sense to bugger off back to London. At least I am hoping that is where she has gone. I suppose she could have gone native. She could be chasing a fox and licking leek and potato soup from her whiskers as I pack away her plastic bowls. She was staying with the Dairy Farmer's Wife while we were in London, and has disappeared. I do not want to tell the boys; I think she may have been eaten by a cow.

I miss the cat not at all. My baby is perfect. I look at her and think: 'You are perfect.' When you have two children already and another is born, there is always a slight 'So whatish?' about it all. I believe that to be as true in London as here. But in London, a few friends, at least, would have dropped by. Here, there are no old and good friends to murmur their marvel. Strangers admire her in passing as I drop off my four-year-old at school, and again when I pick him up. I will accept that currency, the admiration of a stranger. I will bite down on it and find it sound enough to trade a smile. But I would rather trade in more familiar coin.

A bigger problem is that my nipples may be about to drop off, and good riddance. Breastfeeding is agony. I knew it would be. I count on a biblical forty days of suffering before passing through to the Promised Land. A nice midwife came. She said: 'Mmm, that looks like it hurts,' as I struggled to attach the baby. That made me feel much better.

Together, we kept taking the baby off and then running her at the breast. I think the theory is that a rapidly approaching engorged breast makes the baby want to open her mouth for a Hammer horror scream. Then you clamp her on to muffle it. I was once told by a breastfeeding counsellor in London that my nipples were too big. This is not the most helpful thing that has ever been said to a woman attempting to breastfeed a new baby. If my nipples had been spider-legged, they would have clambered off my breasts, scuttled across the floor and kicked her in the shins, at least eight times. I do not think it can be true. I think her judgement may have been warped by her own freakishly small nipples. In any event, there is not a lot you can do about Super Size Me nipples. My attitude since then has been to accept that this is going to hurt. The pain does not last for ever, it just seems that way – but the convenience goes on for months. Either the baby's mouth grows or your nipples shrink. You hang on, and occasionally you scream. Occasionally, as she sleeps, the baby screams. I presume a giant breast with a psychotic-looking nipple is chasing her through the woods. I am living among hazy days of toe-twirling and hazier nights of whirling, broken sleep. Somewhere I have other children. Hope they remember me. Hope I remember me too. Who am I again?

## Saturday, 3 December 2005

### Brothers in arms

We drove south and my parents drove north and we met at a garden centre. I had the baby in the sling and was talking to my mother when I heard the two-year-old let out a wail. It looked as though a bigger boy had pushed past him, knocking him to the ground just as he was about to climb a ladder on his way to a slide. My husband put a hand on my arm. The two-year-old did not require my services. My four-year-old was already there helping his brother to his feet. He said: 'You go up the ladder – I'm right behind you.' The wailing stopped and first one, then the other, climbed the ladder and came down the slide. Later, over tea and cake, my four-year-old said: 'I didn't say anything to that horrid boy, Mummy, but I gave him a proper look.' 'Good for you,' I said, 'sometimes that's all it takes.'

## Monday, 5 December 2005

### Welcome to the deserted village

Northumberland is the northernmost county in England – the sort of place you go to get away from it all. But what if you do not want to get away from it? What if you like 'it' just fine? I never would, never could, say that it is not beautiful: the air cut with lemon, the skies thick with light and cloud, the rise and fall of green fields, hills and moorland, the sweep of empty sands with a history of Romans and Vikings and bloody battles with the Scots. I like its grandeur and its story – I just do not think I want to live in it.

My husband loves it. More particularly, he loves it right here, nudging against the North Sea, in the far north-east corner of this north-east county. He likes to look at the lighthouse and that particular field from this very spot. Just where he stands. He is in love with this steading. No other house in no elsewhere place would do for him. This is a man where he is meant to be; at the very moment, in clock time. Here. He stands. Right here. The idea of here and now is everything to him. Apart from us, of course, his family. We are his all in all. He tells me so. He says: 'You are my world.' He means it, too. I *am* his world. Right here. It is convenient I am his world and I am where he wants me to be. It must be a man thing, this identification with one piece of land. I tell him: 'This is how wars start.' He laughs at me. I mean it.

We have finally taken possession of Number 1, the cottage next to ours. Number 1 was home to the Little Old Lady for forty-seven years as wife and, more lately, widow. Before she lived in that house, she lived in another house along the row for seven years. A creature of happy habit is my friend. My hope: I grow like her. Not discontented and perverse, which, I suspect, is my more natural path. I admire her and admired the husband she lost, a straight and gentle man who made the earth grow round about these houses, who sprinkled favours and saw them as no more than your right. We made a special journey up to say goodbye to her husband as he lay on his sickbed. She said: 'Go up. I'll make some tea.' I sat on a chair by his bed and held his warm and papery hand in mine while his mind slipped in and out of where we were. I smiled into and around my friend, whom I would not see again. I stroked his hand as the roses climbed the wallpaper around us, tightly gripped back a grimace of tears to smile again at him, reeling him into me from his fantastic troubles. I said: 'It's been an honour.' Now I walk into the bedroom which was theirs and think: 'I hope he doesn't mind that she has gone, that he welcomes my children's laughter and noise where once there was his.' Any which way, I do not think he haunts his house. I think, if anywhere, he haunts the garden. At least, I like to think he does.

Their cottage was tied to the farm. When he retired they stayed on, as happens hereabouts. When he died, she stayed a few more years but did not want to live out her days here. Widowhood is woman's shadow and her fate. I think on mine, how it will be to sit as a silent widow in the same chair, the same room, as you have done night after night, but without him. You must look up expecting to see him, you must think you hear him moving about upstairs, but it is just you and your library book. My Little Old Lady laid a coal fire every day, fed a blackbird and a modest blackbird wife with raisins, let in the meter men to the empty cottages roundabout and made tea and coffee twice a day, 10 a.m. and 4 p.m., for old friends who called by for bourbon biscuits and occasional cherry cake with occasional cherries.

But she does not drive. It is lonely here. In the same way as my own mother, she 'didn't want to be a burden'. She wanted her independence, to catch a bus, to shop, to run an errand, and moved into a new-build house in the village. She assures me that she does not miss the cottage that was hers so long. I drive down to the new estate where she lives in a warm and cosy bungalow and I drink her tea and eat her cherry cake, her puzzle books resting by my plate on the tiled coffee table.

You see stone-built, flat-faced rows like ours scattered across the county. They look out on to sheep-pocked fields, hills or across to the sea. Farm workers used to live where they worked. Farm workers do not live in rows like this any more. Machines have taken their jobs; second-home owners, their homes. Hundreds of acres are now worked by one or two men; livestock, the same. Farmers sell off their cottages in the same way they sell off their crops. Of course, cottages do not grow back. Instead of agricultural labourers keeping pigs and growing vegetables, living where they worked, second-home owners 'up for half-term' from northern cities enjoy barbecues and cycle rides.

Not me. I live here 24/7. But further back even than the farm workers, this was a settlement. There is reported to be a burial mound behind the woods where they buried lepers, and it had its own gallows in the thirteenth century. (I do not think I would have liked it then either.) I suppose I could take comfort in the fact I am repopulating what historians call a 'deserted medieval village' – the site believed to be covered by farm buildings and plantations. Records show that once there was a hamlet where tenants farmed strips of land scattered through common fields, and it was significant enough to be marked on a map as early as 1610. Its high point was 1831, when the census indicates there were 149 people living hereabouts, many of them agricultural labourers. All that is left, aside from the holiday cottages, are a retired couple who once farmed here and live in a Sixties bungalow behind the barn, the Accountant and his elderly mother, and my own little family.

Number 1 has electrics that date from just after the war, damp, asbestos ceilings and an avocado bath suite. I am supposed to cheer. It is a good thing, is it not, for my husband's dream to move ever closer? Who would not cheer at that thought? Hurrah! Hurrah! Hear my shout. On the other hand, it would have been simpler not to buy it. We could have sold our own cottage and bought a ready-made family home: a vicarage, a farmhouse, a new-build 'Georgian' pile. We could have had next-door neighbours, maybe even a conservatory. But why would we want to do that? That would have been far too straightforward. Let's go the whole hog. Let's take two handfuls of houses and crash them together, mould the melted stone and make one house in a nowhere place. Damn the mess. Damn the cost. Damn the wife.

### Tuesday, 6 December 2005

### King of the Castle

Northumberland's history is everywhere: the stones of an old barn, limekilns in the harbour, hedged fields around. It also has more castles than any other county in England. The closest is built on an immense rocky crag, high above a stretch of golden sands, and was once a fortress and the home of Northumbria's kings. Its grim and massive beauty dominates the coastline.

There was a knock on the front door. A giant stood there in a plaid shirt with rolled-up sleeves and mud-splattered work boots. He was smiling broadly as he held out a bottle of champagne. He introduced himself. I thought: 'Ah. The King of the Castle.' Then I thought: 'My God, do they still have some sort of droit de seigneur round here? Has he come to collect his due? I was awake with the baby most of the night – I don't think I'm up to it.' He said: 'To celebrate the baby and your purchase of the cottage.' My husband reached past me for the bottle and shook the huge, outstretched hand, saying: 'Thank you, how very kind of you.' I fought off the urge to bob a curtsey. 'Nice castle,' I said. 'Thank you,' he replied. 'We like it.'

## Monday, 19 December 2005

### Weapons of mass destruction

Had to go to the doctor with mastitis. Feeling appalling. My breasts look like armed and dangerous weapons. Worst thing is you have to feed through it. The baby's mouth opens and you think: 'Here it comes. Here it comes.' Agony and only slowly relief. Then it all starts again.

## Saturday, 24 December 2005

### 'Here it is, Merry Christmas'

At the school Christmas play, my four-year-old gleamed in his tinsel halo and gold netted wings with white cotton surplice. His angel marvel shocked me, truth be told. He watched his teacher and pressed his hands together with all the other small-est angels for the night. The piano struck up; I blinked the tears away. Sweet warbles sounded as he lifted his right hand and grabbed a handful of air to catch a most particular and falling star, slid the shiny handful into a non-existent pocket to save it, and rainy-day-danced his fingers down from the sky. He kept his star from fading; I melted all at once, singing 'Gloria'.

Apart from the school play and the fact breastfeeding is finally getting easier, I am bloody hating bloody Christmas. This is ghastly. What am I doing? In London, I love Christmas time. We see a show. I go to a schmaltzy Christmas movie on my own. We have supper with London Diva and the God-father, spend an evening with the Perfect Mother and her Hectic Husband. Have drinks with my Islington Beauty. We do the stuff you do. Talk about people we know. Bitch about work. Laugh at our children's latest outrages. Hang out. I miss them. On Christmas Eve, I make one last dash to the shops on New Bond Street and Oxford Street and snatch bargains from rails for sales that officially begin on Boxing Day. I like my last trawl through the streets of London on Christmas Eve. Usually it is quiet. Everyone is happy at the prospect of going home. My husband and I go to midnight mass at one of London's most beautiful Catholic churches. There are glittering candles watched over by wooden martyrs, pictures stain the glass and a wise man in brocade vestments walks behind a cross with a nailed-on saviour, then speaks of peace and goodwill to all men. I miss that too. Tomorrow, the children would open their presents till I think we have tipped from festive into obscene; I would clap my hands and say: 'Enough.' We would walk in St James's Park and wonder if the passing tourists are happy to be in London on this day. You cannot tell as they walk by you. If you say 'Merry Christmas' and smile, some-times they look at you blankly; sometimes they lob an accented greeting back. Now I know how they feel inside. They are not feeling any Christmas cheer; they are as displaced and lost as I am. I have never felt so lacking in goodwill. Someone should buy me some for Christmas and wrap it in stars.

Here, my parents are with us again: aside from them we have not seen anyone close to our hearts or wished peace to all men or, indeed, to anyone. Shopping in the local market town is not the same as Selfridges and Fenwick. We have not even been to church. I am without my rituals. I hate it all. I am in mourning for my life.

## Monday, 26 December 2005

### Fire, fire

My parents bought the boys a fire engine for Christmas. It has an electric motor and is big enough for them both to sit on and drive. Because we could not be sure of the weather we had to leave it for them in the sitting room. The room is small at the best of times, even smaller when it has four grown-ups, three children, a Christmas tree and a fire engine in it. Even though I told them not to start it up indoors, every now and then one of them would lean down surreptitiously, turn the plastic key in the ignition, press the accelerator and drive it two feet forwards, or slam it into reverse and drive it two feet backwards, narrowly avoiding Grandad's gammy feet. As if I was not stressed enough. At least they waited until they got it outside before filling the pump-action tank with water.

## Saturday, 31 December 2005

### 'Celebration time, come on!'

My parents have gone home. All wrapped in coats and scarves, they squeezed into their small car. My father in a flat cap, my mother with dark glasses and a white stick – a Mafioso Cossack in a towering fake-fur hat. Their car is so small and their outfits so large that sometimes I wonder they fit at all. As she hugged

39

me and then pulled reluctantly away, my mother said: 'That was the best Christmas ever.' She always says that. Then she cries. She was so weak this Christmas time, she could not even hold the baby in her arms unless I stuffed cushions underneath her elbows and laid the baby on a pillow across her knees. That or leaned her at an angle into the sofa and pinned the baby to her breast like an oversized brooch. The baby sleeps and my mother sits happy and useful – more happy that she is again useful – till the baby wakes. She adores the baby; I see her remind herself not to hate me when I lift off the child to bring her a cup of tea.

I know my daughter is stirring up memories for her. My father is technically my stepfather; he married my mother when I was nearly six. My mother's first husband, my natural father, died when I was not yet nine months old. She had been married for a year and a half. At thirty-six, left with a new baby and her own elderly mother to care for in a small box of a home, she could never cry in the house. If she cried, a chorus of rocking, keening widow sounds would break out in the front room – her own mother, my dead father's mother and then her elder sister would begin to cry, together loud enough to strip the walls of papered blooms. Instead, she would tuck me up tight and woollen in a silver-trimmed and large-wheeled rocking pram, and push me across to church and up the marbled aisle to cry among the plastered saints. When I had a therapist in my glory London days, he would listen to me earnestly whinge about my life and lot and say that he thought my mother must have been depressed when I was a baby. I would think: 'No kidding, mate.'

My parents are not keen on New Year's Eve. They stayed long enough to wish my youngest boy a happy birthday, then went. Today marks my two-year-old's hop and bounce into a madly passionate three. This term he will start three mornings a week in the Early Years unit in school. I am hoping it will help him settle – he pines for what he knew in London almost as much as I do, and loves me as utterly and profoundly as I love him. My older boy is more settled here than his brother or his mother, more cautious in his display of loving. I scoop and hug and hold tight my older boy. I lock him in my arms and convince him of my mother love, my pride in all his boy perfection. I drink in his smell and he says: 'Your hair tickles.' Caress his cheek and he says: 'Your breath is stinky.' Sometimes he lets me. Sometimes he wriggles from my grasping clasp to ask: 'Can I watch TV now?' It does not deter me, I wait and pounce another day.

## Sunday, 1 January 2006

### Friends reunited

When I announced we were moving, my Islington Beauty said to me over dinner: 'Tell people you are coming back to London in a year or two. Otherwise' – she shook her blonde head in regret – 'no one will bother with you while you are up there.' I thought: 'Will you bother with me while I'm up there?' She has; friends are bothering. The Godfather loves it here: cold winds, beaches, beer. London Diva arrived and immediately muffled herself up in thermals and fleeces – to sit inside. It is like looking in the mirror. Blank misery stares back at me. 'Look how much I love you,' she said with every ounce of her being. 'I hate it here; I'm here because you are.' This must be what it is like for my husband to live with me. I drone and moan and groan – the weather, too cold to bear; distant strangers you have no inclination to be closer to; isolation, geographical and any other which way; endless muddy driving to get anywhere you want to be. She said: 'Remind me. Why do you live here?' I no longer have any credibility as a twenty-first-century woman; I have ratcheted back to the 1940s and deserve to live there. She has a career, a Georgian house in North London and air miles. I have no job, a cottage nowhere I want to be and a family railcard.

Despite the freezing temperatures, we had dinner outside by a spitting brazier: holes punched in a dustbin, small windows to hell; sparks flying up into the black north air and lighting up the jollied, flamed faces of our neighbours along the road who were also up for the New Year. I felt a self-indulgent, sleepy melancholy, an ill-behoving humour. I shall make a resolution to quit this melancholy before it becomes a habit. Diva's twenty-four-hour flying visit flew by. Zoom. They left and I collapsed, not so much from melancholy as misery. The baby was in her Moses basket, asleep; I was draped across the arm of the sofa, weeping hysterically that my friend had gone, when the front door opened again. She had forgotten something. I stopped crying and started sniffing back the tears. London Diva gave me a brief hug, said: 'We will see you very soon. OK?' and walked back out again. She did not pick up the scarf she had left behind; she did not bid my body-snatcher husband a tender second adieu. I do not think she likes him any more.

## Monday, 2 January 2006

### Inside out

This is my London Diva girl. Beautiful, of course, as divas always are, and glamorous. Glamour, too, is the diva's way of going on. But I call her 'Diva' not because of narrow, selfish ways, buffed nails or rhinestone-studded shoes; rather, because she claims her life while others – I include myself – watch their own pass by. She stands centre stage, not to own the spotlight, which is hers by right, but to anchor the performance, give depth and meaning to the words of those who surround her star. Her fellow troubadours seem small from the stalls. She will turn her head an inch to whisper: 'Stand tall. Move up to your mark.' When they miss their cue and lose their place in fright at life, she will say: 'Here, try these words for size.' I blame her for setting such a high tidemark in friendship, leaving seaweed and stripped and silvered driftwood in its wake so that I cannot forget where she has been. For never failing me when darkness came around and sadness washed right through and over me. For being there when it would have been simpler and far cleaner to give me 'space and time' and all those things that mean: 'I don't know what to say.' For sitting and listening, feeding me and all of mine, and pouring red communion wine into my crystal glass. I hold her thoroughly responsible for all her wisdom, gentle comfort, the ringing supper laughter and the kitchen bar-stool smiles. I love her children as I love my own; if terrible things happened – and terrible things do happen – the first to come around and pick up those that had been mine would be my London Diva. Cue: applause.

## *Wednesday, 4 January 2006*

### Lily and me

My four-year-old is five today. The years scramble by in children. I thought they stood still for me. There must have been a time I did not look in mirrors. I swear I never noticed the lines come, my cheeks hang, my thighs fatten, my hair grow grey and dull. Did mirrors turn away from me when they heard my step? When I could not find them, did I think: 'I'm sure I look OK'? So lacking in vanity, or, perhaps, so profoundly vain, I slicked my lips, gilded the lily, but never looked at my face? Never questioned whether what passed for beauty was now past beauty? Never stopped to ask: 'Am I getting older, as my children are getting older?'

Or was I too consumed by my children and my work to note the ravages? Did I think: 'I don't have time to paint my face and comb my hair. Instead, did I flannel-wash a youngster's face, slip on a power suit, not notice that years were sliding by? Foolish girl. Today, I caught a mirror before it could hide. I reached out to its gilt frame and took it in my arms. I expected to love the woman I found in there. To see her beauty and gasp: 'My love. My familiar.' Instead, I found her unfamiliar and bitter, an ugly sister. No, in truth I found her crone ancient mother. As my children grow slender limbs and rosy cheeks, I decay. My lily is not gilded. I have raisin-withered on the vine.

### Saturday, 7 January 2006

### Sweet dreams

The nights have been bad lately. None of my babies ever sleeps through the night. I hate women who smile at you with their sparkling eyes and say: 'Gerald was only three weeks when he slept straight through.' It makes me want to bludgeon them about the head with Gerald's redundant baby alarm. My oldest was eighteen months before he slept through a night; my three-year-old was fourteen months. It is my own fault; I think tragedy may lurk in every night; I have to keep checking them to make sure they are still breathing. If I am unconvinced, I poke them. Quite often, they wake up with a start; look, as if to say: 'You terrifying nutter.' They scream very loudly for at least an hour after that.

## Sunday, 15 January 2006

## The loneliness of the long-distance mother

The day is grey and cold and grim. Northumberland appears to be entirely shut. What happens here in winter? What do people do? Everywhere you might want to go is closed till Easter. Where are you supposed to go when it rains? When the wind blows so hard it would carry you out to sea? When the children cry at the mention of the beach? What are you supposed to do in these dreary wintry months? Whittle? I have no knife. Scrabble? My children cannot spell. Buns? I will grow to be the size of a house. In London, I could take them to a café and pretend to be going to a museum or a gallery. They could skate on cold and marble floors, worry security guards into early retirement. In London, we could see friends. I could drink tea, my children break other children's toys.

There is the couple who arrive, hectic, on bicycles, exuding good health and Christian vigour. The Evangelical Woman and her Evangelical Man are brave, I think, to risk themselves on us. They seem to like our company. I like to hear their knock and see them come in steaming slightly from their efforts and happy from their prayers. They are different from the people we know in London; they believe in God for a start. I like different. I am flattered they think to straddle their bicycles, push off on their pilgrim journey and come so far for us. The Accountant drops round to chat. He arrives at teatime to find food fights and misrule but stands and chats a while, enough to let me know I am seen. Then he goes and chaos breaks out again. I know people here, but we do not have friends in whom I could confide, whom I could make damp with my weeping. Friendship takes time. I have scarce arrived in my northern jail; I have not served time enough for friends. Do people just go out and get wet, then? Is this why they have farms? So they can go feed the animals when it rains? Dear God. I shall have to buy a cow.

## Saturday, 21 January 2006

### Dear old London town

I have come down with the children for a brief visit to London. It is growing stranger to me, even for a weekend. My move has divided old friends. There are those like London Diva and Islington Beauty who think my husband is a Bad Man who has done a Bad Thing. They believe I am a Poor Sap and Should Know Better. The morning after the baby sleeps through for the first time, they expect me to sit up in bed, shriek loud enough to be heard in Westminster and Come To My Senses. Just like that. They expect me to kiss my husband good morning, hit him roundly about the head with a cricketing almanac and start packing. Others, like my Best Friend From School, believe I have 'Done the Right Thing'. When I was angsting before the move, they said that I should 'Give These Things A Go', as 'You Regret What You Do Not Do' and I had 'Nothing To Lose'. We saw friends in both camps this weekend. The Perfect Mother did something similar herself when her Hectic Husband's work took him to Sweden. She cracked after years of his pleading to go abroad. Pester power is not just a tool for children. Even though she hated it, she said she thought it right to go because it gave them an experience they would not otherwise have shared. We were sitting having dinner in their kitchen, both men nodding throughout this exchange. 'Mind you,' she said, topping up her glass of white wine. 'I was bloody miserable.' She reached for my glass and started to pour.

## Tuesday, 24 January 2006

### Death of hope

The big news up here has been the disappearance of a farmer's wife with a history of depression. She went missing six weeks ago. Posters with her smiling face have been all over the windows of the shops in the local market town. Her husband discovered her gone after he came in from milking the cows one morning. She was forty-six, worked in a book shop, helped out at church fetes. In a local paper, her husband described her as 'low in recent months' after her eighteen-year-old daughter went to university and her twenty-one-year-old moved away to another job. 'The house has been very quiet since they left,' he said. The day she disappeared, they found her car abandoned by an eighteen-arch viaduct which carries the East Coast Main Line over a river, and yesterday they discovered her body. You could almost hear a county sigh in sorrow. I wonder, did she think her job was done, her girls all grown? A mother who did not want to take the pills and emptied of all hope, leaving those who loved her best to search for who had been.

## Saturday, 28 January 2006

### Away, away, away

My husband is away. Again. I do not cope well when he is away. I tend to think: 'What am I doing here?' As I look at a framed and tender beach kiss between the two of us, I rub away at him sitting there content and think: 'I don't much like you at the moment.' As I look in my mirror, I think: 'You do right to look so worried; I don't like you either. What were you doing coming here?' Friends have come down from Edinburgh to admire my baby and assure me that my husband may not be with me but still loves me. They know this for a fact. They have seen it in his eyes. He has told them so. That fact I do not like him at this point will not affect his loving of me. They are sure of this. They are sure I love him back. Even if I cannot quite remember. Sure that we will be for ever after happy. They are sorry, though, to miss him. As I am. I am sorry, too, he is not here with us.

## Tuesday, 31 January 2006

### Food for thought

Yesterday I drove down to a shopping outlet outside the nearest big city, which is almost an hour away, to buy pains au chocolat. This is my life: hosting a coffee morning. By rights, I should add 'for my sins'. That is the sort of thing you say when you hold coffee mornings. I have to get to know some mothers. How else do you do it? Do you say: 'Come over, we will compare C-section scars'? I do not have any. Do you say: 'Come over, we will have lesbian sex'? I suspect they would not come.

You could tell this morning, when it emerged that the pile of pains au chocolat on the kitchen table were freshly imported, that they thought I was mad. I think in retrospect I might have been supposed to have baked something for it. What the hell? I made fresh brewed coffee in my Gaggia with hot frothed milk, and tea, Earl Grey and Tetley's. There were bagels, smoked salmon, cake, biscuits and, of course, French pastries. I do not think I looked like I was trying too hard for one second. The Oyster Farmer's Wife came with one of her two little boys. She has a lovely figure but I noticed she carried herself quite carefully. Apparently she has a back with metal pins up and down it, courtesy of sport and country dancing, and is on painkillers for the rest of her life. She seemed very phlegmatic

48

about it all. She said: 'My children know I can't carry them so they just get on with it and walk.' The athletic, bright-eyed Evangelical Woman also arrived on her bicycle, full of conviction, sincerity and goodness. The sort of woman who makes uncertain, insincere, bad women like me look, well, uncertain, insincere and bad. I also liked the easy laughter of a down-to-earth Yorkshire mother. She is short and smiley, with dark curly hair flecked with grey, and was the only woman at the school gate to introduce herself to me before I managed to introduce myself to her.

## Wednesday, 1 February 2006
### Work and other four-letter words

If you have children in London, you can find things to do to divert attention from the fact you no longer have any control over your life. If you have children in windswept, muddy Northumberland, there seems no dodging the issue. I feel like I am in a runaway wagon skedaddling along the rails in a poorly lit coal mine. I am screaming and any minute now I am going to run out of track.

I come from Leeds – I have 'done' the North, and you know what, I like dear old London town just fine. I feel like I am a character in one of those epic sagas of a northern lass who gets hersen down to London and suffers vicissitudes along the way. But does she let them get her down? She does not. She's got grit has our heroine, and she makes a reet success of her life in London and she gets a posh job and brass and nice frocks and a fella, and then bugger me if the fates don't decide to blow our scrappy heroine back up North to the mud she thought she had escaped so long ago. It is not just the mud and the loneliness. Three small children hang off our heroine at every available opportunity, and they should know that really their mam is not just their mam, she is a career girl. Well, maybe she is a little past her sell-by for the term 'girl', but there was a time when she definitely wanted to conquer the world. I mean, in what chapter did it all start to go so horribly wrong? Was it that fateful moment, clutching a tear-stained photo of her little ones, she handed in her resignation at t'Big Office where she had t'Big Salary? Now, her glory days behind her, she works at home, and when I say 'works at home', that covers a multitude of sins.

Today I took on a job to visit a North-East school, have a look round, see some teaching, do some interviews. Fine, in theory. The only problem was I had to take the baby in her sling, who cried when the mathematics lesson started. In fact, she cried every time anyone started to say anything of interest. I never judge another woman's choices. If I do not work, I get lonely and depressed. If I work too much, I hate myself. Like many mothers, I have chopped and changed, compromised my work, felt guilty about my mothering. 'Career' is something I associate with too much booze and office romances. Not where I am right now. Not where I have been for a long time. Like thousands of other women with children, I work because I have to if I want to pay my bills and keep sane. I work from home and part-time so that I can see my children more than I might do otherwise.

My lack of status offends me. I am in a state of 'becoming'. I was a working woman, a professional; I had respect. I worked for it, earned it, kept it when I married. Suddenly I am my children's mother, my husband's wife. The school seems confused that I have a different surname from my children. My husband strikes these strangers who surround us as glamorous, sliding up and down the railway lines between Northumberland and London. They ask him what he does. They are anxious for his opinions. I want to tell them: 'I have opinions. I have things to say. Stop talking to my husband. Please talk to me. He would tell you himself that I'm much better company.' They do not ask what I do. I impress no one. If, bizarrely, they ask, I say I freelance. In their minds, they think: 'Ah, a sad-case woman pretending she still works.' They may be right.

## Sunday, 5 February 2006

### Keeping holy the Sabbath

Husband still away. Thought: 'Fuck, I'm desperate. I will take them to church.'

Somehow you get on a list. We have had invitations – by name – for a Sunday school before a family service at a local church. The Church of England knows we are here. That means God knows we are here. We arrived late, missing the games and snacks. The boys were not impressed. They kept turning to accuse me: 'You said there would be snacks.' I kept saying: 'Shhh! You're fine. Concentrate on colouring in your leper.'

## Thursday, 9 February 2006

### Running on empty

I feel as if my dignity is being stripped from me inch by inch by my ineptitude at coping without my husband. I woke up and it was snowing. My first thought: 'How am I going to get them to school?'

I strapped the children in and we drove really slowly through the blizzarding snow. If you had walked the five miles, you would have got there quicker. It is a twisty-turny sort of country route with hills and curves and a level crossing. I was particularly worried about a steep hill which I just about got up; then I said a prayer and just about got down, sliding part of the

51

way. I was trying desperately to remember all my husband's advice about driving in the snow. Did he say 'brake' or 'don't brake'? Did he say 'go into the skid' or 'fight it'? I decided he said 'don't brake', wait for the wheels to grip in the skid, then try to get control back. About half a mile from school, I look down and away from the snowy road. The arrow on the petrol tank is in the red. I am on a slight downward slope, so I coast into the school car park and then rest my head on the wheel. My five-year-old says: 'That was fun.' I stop shaking long enough to press the button which tells me exactly to the mile how much petrol I have in the car. It reads a nice fat zero. I think: 'Bugger.' Then again: 'Bugger.' I heft the baby on to my hip, take the boys in to school and go back to the car. I am thinking: 'Is there a chance I could make it six miles to the nearest garage?' After I clip the baby back into her car seat, I check the gauge again. I did not misread it. 'That would be a no, then,' I think.

Another mother comes out to her car; unlike mine, it is undoubtedly full of petrol. Two things come to mind: her husband is a sheep farmer and I forgot to invite her to my coffee morning. I wonder if she bears a grudge. I wave as if she is my long-lost sister. It is still snowing. I say: 'You couldn't do me a favour and take the baby and me down to a garage, could you? I appear to have run out of petrol.' I giggle as if it is not a big deal to have run out of petrol in a blizzard with a new baby in the car.

Wives up here say things like: 'I'll ring my husband.' I am thinking: 'When I ring my husband, the air is going to be blue. He was supposed to fill the sodding car with sodding petrol.' But farmers' wives have farmer husbands who can get you out of a hole rather than into one. Hers appears in a muddy Land Rover with a sheepskin hat, a large and well-prepared boy scout. He has a metal canister of petrol with him, an empty plastic bottle and a knife. He saws off the end of the plastic bottle and shoves the cap end into the petrol tank to use it as a funnel. I am so grateful I would have had sex with him if it were not snowing, we were not in the school car park and his wife were not standing next to us. I am so grateful I would have had sex with her too if she were not a woman. Talk about conforming to the stereotype of a city girl adrift in the country. I think: 'Thank God I am not wearing high heels.' I check to make sure I am not wearing high heels. The snow has got worse. The Sheep Farmer says: 'Do you want me to follow you home?' I think: 'He believes I am an idiot and shouldn't be out on the roads.' I shake my head and say: 'No. Golly. You've done enough. I'll be fine.' The Sheep Farmer's Wife drives off in her car, grinning, and he follows. He gives me a friendly wave. It is difficult to tell, but I think he is shaking his head from side to side as he pulls away.

I get back in the car and start up. I make it up the slight hill and round the sharp bend. Along the track, through a very narrow bridge and up a very steep incline, then round another sharp bend and along a narrow twisty-turny road. Luckily no one else is about. I take the hill down to the level crossing excruciatingly slowly and drive across it looking both ways in case a train is going to complete the morning by killing me. It is slow and slippy. I have narrowly avoided a couple of hedges and a cold-looking chicken but have not yet crashed. I pull out on to the hill about a mile and a half from home. I slip into second gear, then take it down to first and start driving up it. I take it back to second and I am almost at the top when the car loses its grip and starts sliding; it hits a patch of ice and I find myself jackknifing in reverse, the car twirling round and careering back down. By the time I reach the bottom of the hill, I am even less happy than I was when I ran out of petrol.

I am critically aware I have a three-month-old baby in the back. I know this because I can hear her screaming. She is hungry and I am late feeding her with my unfeasibly large nipples. I try the hill again and make it no more than halfway this time. The same again. My hands are damp and trembling on the steering wheel. I press the accelerator to find the wheels have no purchase on the road at all. I am stranded. There are no cars on this road. It is still snowing. I reach for my mobile phone and ring my husband. Unusually, there is a signal. This is good news for me, bad news for my husband. I shout at him. Then I cry. I say things like: 'You moved us here. You bugger off. You let the car run out of petrol. I have a baby. We are stuck in a blizzard and you are a bastard.' I may have got louder as the conversation wore on. Mid rant, I notice a car pull up ahead of us and a concerned-looking man starts walking towards us. I stop shouting at my husband. I want the nice man to feel sorry for me rather than frightened of me. He puts me and the baby in his car, which has pink fun-fur seats. He cannot get my car up the hill either but does manage to tuck it into the side of the road so it is less of a hazard. He takes me home.

## Monday, 20 February 2006

### Kicking away the chair

Half-term. The Dairy Farmer's Wife is on holiday, my husband is in London and both boys are sick. First one, then the other. They stop watching television only long enough to retch into a bucket. I mop it out. The other one retches. This one into a bowl. The baby cries. I start to feed her. One boy retches. The other retches. I have to put the baby down. She cries again. My husband rings. He says: 'How are things?' I say: 'The children are sick and I hate you.' He says: 'OK. Bad time. I'll call back.' A child retches. I say: 'Don't bother.'

I was holding the bowl for the three-year-old while trying to quieten the screams of a hungry baby when I decided I was in a post-natal dip. If that is what you call wanting to kill yourself.

I am trying hard not to want to kill myself. I first saw the health visitor not long after I came back up with the baby. She would turn up on my doorstep. I would tell her I was fine. Then she would come back. I couldn't work out if she thought I was at risk, or enjoyed my company. For some reason, I never knew she was coming. Apparently she would ring, or write a letter, but I never seemed to get her messages. She is patently an extremely kind and capable woman and I know she has a job to do, but that does not mean to say that I did not resent her visits in a very British way. I would say: 'Tea?' I did *not* say: 'I do not want to tell you, exactly, in so many words, out loud at least, to fuck off. That would be rude. But could you please take the hint and fuck off anyway.'

I have had enough babies to know I do not like health visitors. If I were to write a dictionary for mothers based on experience accumulated over the years, my definition of a 'health visitor' would read:

Someone who arrives uninvited on your doorstep soon after you have returned from an overcrowded maternity ward with your new baby who screams like a banshee if put down for a blink. You are so frightened by the noise that you decide you are a believer in kangaroo care and that you do not want to put the baby down even for a cup of tea. This is the first of many lies you tell yourself as a mother. You neither know, nor care, where your husband is. You do not like him any more. You are, of course, holding the baby when there is a ring on the doorbell. You are wearing a grubby cotton waffle dressing gown. It is tied with a worn pair of black nylon maternity tights and you sport a muslin square on your shoulder. You and the muslin square do not smell nice.

'Hello,' says the woman on the doorstep on Anywhere Street, Anyplace Town. 'I am your health visitor. This is Mary Jane' – and she points to a large girl with a bob standing next to her. 'She is training to be a health visitor. I hope it's all right if she sits in.'

Black-eyed with exhaustion and grim-faced from the agony of learning how to breastfeed, you nod at Mary Jane, who nods back.

'Right,' says the health visitor, settling herself into the only arm-chair without laundry on it. Mary Jane perches her ample posterior on the sofa. The health visitor gets out a clipboard and a Biro. 'We haven't met before, have we? How are you getting on? Is that the baby? Sweet.' She asks a few questions, ticks a few boxes. She leans in a little, pen poised. '"In the last seven days, the thought of harming myself has occurred to me . . .?"' She looks straight at you. '"Quite often, sometimes, hardly ever, never?"' She waits. Mary Jane waits.

The noose is knotted and swinging expectantly from the plastic flex going into a dusty cream lampshade on the landing. In the sitting room, you widen your eyes slightly. 'No. Gosh. Suicide? Golly. Never. I'm fine, thank you.'

She ticks a box.

I do know I cry too much these days. I had dropped the children at school and was shovelling the baby back into her seat. I was snuffling out my new mother's grief as I strapped her in. Fat hot tears ran down my face. Suddenly there was a voice of another mother next to me wanting to see the baby. She looked slightly taken aback when she realized my sorry state. I said: 'I'm fine. Baby blues. Really. I'm fine,' sounding all the time like the depressive I am but have been so careful to keep hidden in a box. She put an arm round me, said all the right things about 'having been there' and 'must be difficult'. It made me realize I had better do something.

I went to the Doctor. She is a friend of the Oyster Farmer's Wife, who said the other day I ought to meet her. She meant socially, maybe for a coffee and a cheese scone rather than for pills. She has pictures of her three children on the door of the surgery. The Doctor did not ask me whether I thought about killing myself; instead, as I walked up and down her surgery, jiggling the baby, she leaned back in her swivel chair and pushed it slightly away from her computer. She said: 'Do you ever think about going away?' I spend a great deal of time thinking about going away somewhere and how to manage it and still leave the children safe and cared for. Is it an accepted euphemism for killing yourself, I wonder? Is it my euphemism? My world has tilted; I am unbalanced, clinging on as life spins by. I must fetch myself back before I lose my grip. It will come right again. My world has tipped before. I just need a moment.

## Tuesday, 7 March 2006

### Books and groups

I was invited to join a book group by the Oyster Farmer's Wife, who set it up and promptly announced she was leaving it. She is already a member of another book group and decided she could not manage two. How on earth am I going to get to know her any better than I do already? I walk into a stranger's sitting room. There is a fire roaring in the grate and tea and cake on the table. The Doctor is already in the room; she has also been invited to join. I am thinking: 'This gets worse. This is what it is to have an affair.' I know that she knows that I feel suicidal. But does everybody else in the room know that she knows that I feel that way? The Doctor smiles and says: 'Hi. How are you?' I wonder how she wants me to answer. Do I say: 'Fine,' and wink? Say: 'Not so good,' and cry? Country life! I had two brilliant and very kind female doctors in London who could easily have been my mates. The thing was I already had mates and once someone has seen your perineum it is difficult to eat carrot cake with them.

## Tuesday, 14 March 2006

### Friendship

My Best Friend From School came up. She always makes
me feel better about everything. Never judges me. Not true:
she says I live in chaos. Aside from the ill-founded chaos
accusation, she never judges me. Low: she listens. Make a joke:
she laughs. Some man I once loved said: 'Kiss me'; she did not.
Sometimes, to embarrass her, I say: 'I love you.' She hates that.
She does not do emotion. Does 'doing things' and 'getting
on'. I named my daughter for her; she plants spring bulbs for
me to get me through the winter. Says: 'Throw that out. You
do not need it.' I say: 'I can't. I might.' She never needs me.
One day she might; but I think it unlikely. Too practical for
that. Too capable for need. When we are both old and our
menfolk dead, when my children find me dull and burden-
some, I will hunker down with her in widow black. We will
drink gin, keep lap cats and grow cacklesome together.

## Friday, 17 March 2006

### Running on empty 2

I cannot believe that after the blizzard my husband would let
it happen again, but he did. I ran out of petrol. Again. I was
driving into the village to go to the shops with all three kids
when shudder, shudder, stop. I must have looked desperate
because another car stopped and a young girl with a child seat
in the back of her car got out and offered to go to a garage for
a can of petrol for me. I gave her £20 and when she arrived
back, it was with an enormous battered metal petrol can which
looked like it had been used to fill tanks up during the Second
World War. At some point during the intervening sixty years it

would come and get her at the end of the week and find her somewhere else to live. I wondered how long it would be before she forgot the niece's promise. When she went back home, I rang the niece again, said what I could not say in front of the old lady: that her aunt was confused and in a state of considerable distress, that she could not be left on her own any longer than she had to be. The niece told me that she had already invited her aunt to live with her but her aunt thought her house too far away from the hotel where she worked. She assured me her aunt would be picked up within a few days and looked after. She thought it time for her to return to Thailand, where she could live with her family and be looked after by them.

It saddened me, the idea of an old lady ironing out her days, slipping into confusion in a plasterboarded room and listening to the banter and noise of young people she barely knew, while fretting to find a place to sleep at night. She knocked on my door and I was in. What if she had knocked and I had been out? Or in Northumberland? What if she had not had a niece who loved her? Would she have folded her clothes and packed them in large gingham plastic bags, let herself out of the house which was no longer her home, left her front-door key hanging on a hook in the hallway and launched herself on to the streets? Would she have found a little room?

### Saturday, 25 March 2006

### Party animals

Had a lot of work on this month, which has been good but hectic. At least it will help pay some bills. Writing about how rich people make their money for a Sunday newspaper supplement which ranks the wealthiest people in the country – something that always makes me want to go out and spend furiously. We actually went to a party last night. A father at school had a fiftieth party in a village hall. We talked to quite a few people, but I find the men quite different from the men I am used to down south. I suspect that some of them who farm or work outdoors are not naturally at ease with women. I have no work in common to talk to them about. They tend to eye me warily – I imagine in much the same way as they eye live-stock which they have brought on to the farm and whose parentage is unknown to them. To fill out their side of the conversational bargain, I find myself chatting inanely with them like some feathered flapper who has quaffed one pink gin too many.

At the party, I asked the Oyster Farmer to dance. I stood in front of him, waiting. The farmer is a man who thinks carefully before spending a word he may need later in life. My husband watched. It was a long wait. The Oyster Farmer thought about my question and the consequences. To move out of the darkness, to dance in the coloured light, to talk to a stranger. His silence spread to the circle of farmer friends where he was standing. After several days and nights of waiting, courtesy won out over caution; he slowly put down his pint on the table behind him. His wife's jaw dropped as she saw me haul him away to the gallows. 'He doesn't dance. He never dances,' she called out to me. 'You never dance with me.' She laughed out loud at the sight. As we jigged away, he shouted out his youth into my bass-battered ear; he used to come as a twelve-year-old boy to discos in this very village hall. I could see him, standing in the shadows with his young and spotty friends, drinking warm shandy from plastic cups and hoping the mad girl who never stopped jabbering would not ask him to dance . . .

## Friday, 31 March 2006

### The only black man in the village

Friends came up for a weekend with their little boy, who is my five-year-old's best friend in London. My son was desperately pleased to see him and show him his new world: the bedroom he shares with his brother, the garden jungle, the beach. Despite the months apart, they picked up as if it were just a moment. My three-year-old still hankers for London – maybe he senses that I do. The five-year-old adjusted very rapidly to living here, but seeing him and his friend hurtling round together makes me realize he has also paid a price for the move even if he does not know it himself.

The mother is beautiful, Spanish and works in the fashion industry, while the tall and handsome father is an actor-cum-model. And black. The only black man in the village. I have hardly ever seen a black or Asian face here – apart from the occasional holidaymaker. There is a Chinese takeaway, but other than that, redoubtably white. There are Polish people – everyone tells you that. In the East End, my children never saw colour, never saw a difference. How it should be. At least half my son's nursery class was something other than indigenous Cockney Brit. In the nearest city, when we went to a restaurant recently, the five-year-old whispered when our waiter arrived: 'That man is a different colour.' In London, on our latest weekend visit, he said: 'That lady is wearing lots of material' as a woman drifted by in her burka. The nearest thing to an ethnic minority in my son's school now are the redheads.

## Friday, 28 April 2006

## The affair

Discovering your husband is having an affair is not easy, as any number of sore-hearted women will tell you. I should have recognized the signs – a certain distance in his suddenly steely eyes, money missing inexplicably from the joint account and a mysterious answerphone message I picked up on his office phone yesterday morning about a meeting I did not know he was having.

When he rang me later that day and, indeed, when he came home that evening, he never mentioned the meeting; I sat tight, waiting for the inevitable. Eventually, he confessed. He had fallen in love with a topless sixteen-year-old Swede with 'fantastic bodywork' and wanted to bring her home. What? He had also spent £3,600 of our money on her. What? She just needed the odd tweak and a little bit of tarting up. I'm sorry? I was only marginally appeased when I realized he was talking about a car, a Saab 900 classic convertible, in a colour my husband describes as cherry red, which is actually closer to rusty brown. He bought a car without telling me. I woke up last night, saying the words out loud. 'He bought a car without telling me.' If I keep saying it, I might eventually believe it.

In London, we lived in a partnership of trust and equality. My husband did not do anything without telling me – trim the hedge, have his hair cut, buy rigatoni instead of penne pasta. All of a sudden, he hits his forties and decides he is going to buy a car. Without telling me. Without my realizing, he has fallen into the arms of a mid-life cliché: he is a forty-something man heading for the border in a soft-top. I am supposed to take comfort in the fact it is 'just a summer romance' and that she will be sold by the end of the year. Yeah, right. He is a man of habit, keeping his cars till they go mouldy. Literally. Our last car went entirely white inside because the sunroof let in water and even then he made us all sit on black bin bags and wipe the mould off the seat belts for two months before he sold it. He has no intention of a brief encounter with this mechanical floozy whose bodywork, in my opinion, leaves a lot to be desired. She is for keeps and I am going to have to live with her. There is only room in it for four. 'So, the baby then?' I asked. 'There's no room for the baby?' 'No,' he smiled blissfully. 'But she's very shiny.'

## Saturday, 29 April 2006

## Pulling the plug?

My mother and father are up again. Courtesy of steroids and anti-arthritis drugs, my mother seems to be over her health crisis for the moment. Well enough for me and my one true love to leave the sleeping children with the two of them and go out for a 'chat'. If I am honest, it is long overdue. Sitting side by side at a bar table in a local hotel, my husband told me he needed the 'consolation' of the convertible. I looked to see if it was possible he could be drunk already. He did not look drunk and did not slur his words. 'I bought the car to make myself feel better,' he said. 'I presume we are pulling the plug on Northumberland. You seem so unhappy.' Full marks for observation, then. He went on: 'We said we'd give it a go, but I don't want you being unhappy.' He stared down at his pint of beer. 'We'll go back to London.' By now, I was wondering whether this was a very clever device to turn the tables. He is the offender, the one who bought a car without telling me. He should be the one in the wrong. Instead, I am the one in the wrong for being miserable and wanting to leave for London. In the car he had to buy because I made him so unhappy.

The conversation moved on from car to 'Life', quicker than

a blink. I said: 'Actually, I have been miserable. But lately I have just been getting on with it.' I could have added: 'Because I didn't think I had a choice. Do I really have a choice? Looking at your face, unless I am ready to leave you, I don't think I do.' I picked up my glass and my glass picked up the bar mat for a bit of company on the way up. 'I am not anything in particular,' I lied. I picked the bar mat off the wet foot of the glass and put it down on the glossy wooden table. 'I am too busy trying to hold everything together for all of us. Too busy living life to think that much about it.' I cannot say I am happy still to be here, but I do not want to crawl home defeated. The experiment in northern living is not over. It goes on. Life in Northumberland is back on. Oh, and the car? Staying.

## Monday, 1 May 2006
### King-sized bed, queen-sized smile

I was lying in my king-sized bed in a wallow of cotton sheets and tumbled duvet, gazing at my rompered baby, when she looked up from her bean-filled, pink velour bear to smile into my heart. A smile so dawn-breaking in its loveliness that I thought: 'Kerboom. Crash. Bang and Wallop. I am mended.' I thought: 'Life can't be so bad when you have this plump-cheeked and queenly baby to smile at you like that.' She is all glory hallelujah. A beauteous and a smileful child, enough to make your heart sing out its joy and her majesty.

## Saturday, 13 May 2006
### Running on empty 3

My husband was at least with me this time when we ran out of petrol on the way to the village. He said: 'I'll run to the garage;

it isn't far.' He tucked his inhaler into his back pocket and set off. My five-year-old leaned into the front of the car and watched his father disappear down the road. 'Why do you keep running out of petrol?' he asked. 'That's a very good question,' I said; 'let's ask Daddy when he gets back.'


## Monday, 22 May 2006

### Mr Bump

The five-year-old has been accidentally hit with a wooden bat as he passed behind a boy playing rounders in the playground. He is remarkably proud of the large egg in the middle of his forehead.


## Monday, 29 May 2006

### Batman

The planners are driving us bonkers. The architect handed us over to an architect colleague who came up with a plan to knock the two cottages together which no one likes but us. The council warned us they would turn us down because of something to do with sewerage. We resolved that one; now, they have turned us down because of bats. Any excuse, it strikes me. Apparently, bats are protected. I ask you, why protect bats? Did they ask for our protection? They may be libertarian in their batty inclinations, feel patronized and cope well enough on their own. We could well get dragged into something and find it difficult to retreat. We may lose men out there.

To keep English Nature happy, we had to get the local Batman out. The boys got very excited, but were unimpressed when a nice chap in a Barbour arrived rather than a guy with psychosexual issues, a black rubber face mask and swirly cape.

He listened on his receiver for the screams of the common pipistrelle. If there was screaming by this point, it was mine rather than any bat's.

Luckily, we did not have bats in the arches we want to convert into a sitting room, bedroom and shower-room for my parents when they stay. The prospect of bats circling overhead as my aged parents slept, the bats scuffling as they roosted with their leathery tinies and pooing furiously, was appalling to an urbanite like me. My mother would have been even less impressed. Country people like bats. Say 'bat' to someone living up here and they say: 'Yes, I like bats. Our only flying mammal. We have some our way.' Say 'bat' to a city type like me: I hear 'flying rat', think 'blood, gore and fangs'. Batman, naturally, was a big fan. We did not want to make him cross with all our London prejudices, so we did a lot of fascinated mmm-ing, took his leaflets and tried not to look too relieved when he said we did not have them. We may even have said: 'Shame!' He did manage to find a nesting wood pigeon which we must not not disturb until after September. I mean – a pigeon. I admit my sympathetic nature-loving smile slipped slightly at that one. I compromised on leaving it in peace but gave it a very hard stare as we walked away.

## Saturday, 10 June 2006

### The other woman

The red convertible otherwise known as 'that old banger' arrived. Saab apparently believed she would be driven by idiots judging by the sign inside: 'Do not attempt to drive car until top has been fully latched or lowered.' You don't say. The boys have immediately fallen in love with her. Like any self-respecting mother I am brainwashing my children not to want to smoke cigarettes (dirty, smelly, they kill you), climb mountains (high, cold, they kill you) or ever get on the back of a motorbike (far too fast, far too dangerous and – did I mention? – they kill you). Their father, on the other hand, has now introduced them to the concept of speed as a god to be worshipped.

This morning, I watched him drive away with my three darlings, their chubby little arms reaching over the crunched-up roof to wave, the baby's pink flowered hat just visible, my husband all Ray-Bans and beaming smile in his side mirror. I make my children wear bicycle helmets if they so much as look at their bikes, and the stabilizers are coming off around about puberty. Suddenly, however, I am expected to shout a cheery 'Ta-ra, then' as Daddy takes them for a spin in his convertible. It hasn't got a roof, for God's sake.

London Diva comforted me as I explained my shock at the discovery of my husband's infidelity and his new infatuation. 'It was either going to be a car or a woman. Just be glad he went for the car.'


## Monday, 3 July 2006

### Haunted by the past

One of the mothers wants to get something published in the local paper where I trained as a journalist twenty years ago. I like her and said I would try to help. She is, as many women are, married to a farmer. She has a picture-book six-year-old girl with dimples and black wavy hair, beautiful and autistic. A little girl who struggles to survive in a world she cannot understand and that does not understand her, who screams if you pull the plug out of the bath, flush the toilet for her or switch off the television. You learn to leave her to her habits. She cries real tears and runs away if she hears the vacuum cleaner, hides if an unexpected visitor calls, covers her ears when there is music at school assembly. When the frustration becomes unbearable, she hits out and kicks her mother; over-whelmed with anger, she can attack other children. As her mother was telling me this, I thought: 'How desperate.' I thought: 'You must be very patient.' You would weep tears of blood for such a child. The Patient Mother will not risk another baby, fears the next child too would be autistic. In any case, she said, the needs of her autistic daughter come first. 'To me, she's everything,' she smiled. 'The world.'

## Saturday, 15 July 2006

### Beach babe

I am not immune to the summer glory of Northumberland: the magnificence of the castles and the beaches, endless skies, sand-blasted, freckled children. We went to the beach today. I pummelled the boys into their wetsuits. This is not easy. Occasionally, you lift up the wetsuit by the neck with your child in it, let his legs dangle, then shake it vigorously up and down to free the suction. The only thing harder than getting a child into a wetsuit is getting him out of it again.

I am entirely supportive of bodyboarding. In theory. I want my children growing into blond and sandy teenagers clutching surfboards and equally sandy friends. In theory. It is just the practicalities that drive me to distraction and back in a beach buggy. It is hard enough getting on to the beach. I staggered from the car, down the slope, on to the beach and across the sands with the buggy and the baby. The boards across the top, bags and buckets dangling from the buggy's handles, the two boys dropping spades and reluctantly dragging towels behind them through the sand.

You get wet when you pull the children along through the surf on the board. As I rammed the boys into their suits to muffled screaming, I jealously watched two small swimsuited tots playing nicely in the water while their mothers stood, dry-foot and chatting. I thought: 'Why can't I do that? Why am I expected to drag screaming banshees through the waves?' Today, I had a plan. I am fed up with getting wet and cold while pandering to my own salt fantasies of a perfect childhood. I unrolled the wetsuit I bought in the Aladdin's cave of a gift shop in the village. I looked at it. I thought: 'Who designs a wetsuit for a middle-aged woman with large white stripes down the side, hips and thighs?' I squeezed my less-than-svelte figure into the stretchy, synthetic rubber, gazing in awe at the bulges of natural flab which suddenly emerged. The white stripes pointed inwards to the flesh on my inner thighs. Do I need arrows pointing to my cellulite? This is not a good look for me. With the help of careful upholstering, I can manage 'respectable', if the light is kind, the alcohol flowing and I wear something that drapes. Sober, in wet and chilly daylight, my shortcomings are evident. I began to hope my nipples would poke through the rubber and act as a distraction. I thought: 'At least I can hide in the sea.'

The boys decided they did not want to play in the sea, they wanted to play in the little stream that spills out from God knows where, just down from the car park. Holidaymakers ambling down to the beach with their dogs and windbreaks paused. I would like to think they were admiring the sight of mother and boys playing lightheartedly together in the water while the baby slept close by. I do not, for one moment, think they were saying to themselves: 'What does she think she looks like?' and 'Someone should tell that poor woman about her arse.' OK, I wore my new wetsuit and I am not wearing it again unless I am drunk or in the dark and my husband asks. Repeatedly. He too would have to be drunk. If he was drunk enough, I could say: 'Why don't you wear it, darling?'

## Monday, 17 July 2006

### Is there anybody there?

I went for tea at the Patient Mother's stone-built, hill-top farm, surrounded by green slopes and sheep. Her husband is twenty years older than her; she also has an elderly father-in-law sat by the old range, smoking hand-rolled cigarettes. He cannot leave the tenanted farm, for lack of funds. The Patient Mother cannot be patient with everyone. She says he expects her to wait on him hand and foot, but that she is wife to a different man and a different generation. She showed me a room full of ruin: broken furniture, eggs in cardboard trays and old newspapers. The father-in-law, she says, will not allow them to renovate and turn it over to anything useful. It stays as it is, a monument to his awkwardness. Occasionally, she says, the husband and his father stop speaking to one another over one thing or another and weeks can pass before they speak again. To top it all, she thinks the house is haunted: she smells steak-and-kidney pie and her long-dead mother-in-law's perfume on the stairs, heavy wooden doors swing open then close again, rocking horses move in the night. She said: 'I like the spirits to visit me. This is how you let them know they are welcome,' and rang a crystal bell. I swallowed down hot tea and thought: 'I hope they didn't hear that.'

## Friday, 21 July 2006

### Missing keys

We live in a state of permanent chaos. Why is that? I couldn't find the car keys when I went to bed last night. That is never a good sign. It tends to mean that I won't find them first thing in the morning either. My husband only got back from London after I had gone to bed, and we both looked for them this morning. Nothing. I took my eldest to school and kept searching. It was important we found them because we are due to set off on holiday tomorrow – five days in Wales with family, the weekend in London with friends and four days in Disneyland, Paris.

Suddenly, I hear the whirr of a bicycle. That whirring noise precedes the arrival of the Evangelicals, rather as the sound of wings precedes the heavenly host. They are natural enthusiasts and hideously fit, but I like them despite that. They watch the God Channel. I have never known anyone who watches the God Channel. When one of them first said: 'We were watching the God Channel the other night,' I thought: 'Is there a God Channel?' Then I thought: 'Does God watch the God Channel or does he prefer the BBC?' The Evangelical Man is an artist. Recently, I asked him what he planned to paint. He told me he was considering the four horsemen of the apocalypse riding along the beach. I said: 'Really? How interesting.' He said: 'I believe the world will end, the four horsemen of the apocalypse will come among us, death and destruction, the whole package, you know. I would only say this to another believer.' I shifted uncomfortably in my seat and thought: 'How can I tell you that I am not? Not 'a believer'. Not like you.' 'Evolution?' I enquired. Evolution he dismissed as 'a theory'. 'Homosexuality, then?' Homosexuality an 'abomination' – it says so in the Bible. I said: 'Slavery's in the Bible.' But slavery too went through on the nod, providing it met the biblical caveat of justice within it. I said: 'You can't have justice within slavery, can you?' He knows now I do not share his views; there is a chance my new friend thinks me damned, but I have not liked to ask.

The Evangelical Woman was clambering off her bike when I called down to her from the bedroom: 'We have lost the car keys. Say a prayer we find them.' I could have added: 'Or I won't let you in.' I didn't. I think it went without saying. What is the point of having religious zealots as friends unless they are of some use to you? No one remotely divine was listening to me and I wanted my car keys back. Right now. She raised her right arm, closed her eyes. 'Lord,' she said. (She does do this. Even without asking.) 'Please help us to find the car keys. Our friends need them and we need your help in finding them. Thank you, Lord.'

I thundered downstairs to put the kettle on. 'We're supposed to be going on holiday tomorrow,' I said, panting in my anxiety, as they came into the kitchen. 'Have the children got them?' she asked calmly. 'No.' I shook my head. 'I asked the boys and they say they don't have them. They've been helping me look for them. They know we really need them.' 'Have you looked outside?' she said, even more reasonably. Christians are very reasonable people. Reason had long ago deserted me for blasphemous fury. I marched out to the garden and crawled through the undergrowth to the boys' den. I looked around their sanctuary: a shiny Roman shield, three foam rubber swords, a broken Thunderbird 1 rocket and underneath a pile of leaves among the roots of a fuchsia bush, the jutting end of a key. Praise the Lord, pour the tea and saddle up my horse.

## Saturday, 22 July 2006

### Summer holidays

Tactical mistake – we are holidaying in the country. I pointed out to my husband we are living in the country. Why would we want to spend more time than we have to in it? I want time off for good behaviour: dirt, smog and traffic jams. I want binge-shopping. I certainly do not want rural Wales.

It takes eight hours to get from Northumberland to West Wales. No one in their right minds would want to make the 300-mile cross-country journey – either way. My husband said:

'We won't book into a hotel. We will start driving and stop when we get to about Chester.' His ideas are rubbish – I am surprised a siren does not go off when I hear them. The problem is he is so eminently plausible when he explains them. You find yourself saying: 'OK,' and admiring the blue-green of his eyes. This time, my husband had not bargained on the Golf Open.

North-west England was full of golf fans, and the Welsh borders were no better. I never realized that golf had groupies. As the three children slept in their seats, we traipsed round hotels much as Mary and Joseph did on Christmas Eve (but with more children and less of a result). No one offered us so much as a bunker for the night. Driving round a street brawl in Wrexham, trying to avoid killing the staggering and drunk (I presume they were not golf fans. I would hope golf fans do not behave that way), I said: 'Do you know, darling? I think we should have booked a hotel after all. We will have to drive through the night.' We had set off at 9.20 p.m.; we arrived in my brother-in-law's farmyard at 5.10 a.m. I am so pleased to be able to enjoy a grey dawn in the Welsh countryside, such a nice change from Northumberland.

## Monday, 24 July 2006

### Hell is . . .

We had to go to the Royal Welsh Show organized by the Royal Welsh Agricultural Society. Why? I am not royal. I am not Welsh and have no interest in tractors. It was also far too hot and I hate crowds. Did I want to go to an agricultural show? I did not. Unfortunately, my brother-in-law and his Welsh wife did.

Someone tried to blag money from us as we parked the car in a field, halfway up a mountain. Moonies? Communists? Someone with a clipboard and a tofu smile. He was certainly a risk-taker asking a woman with three children and a thunderous black cloud over her head for money. I had already seen him inveigle another mother with a small boy, as she tried to lock up her car. I snarled on my behalf and hers as he walked up the grassy slope towards us: 'I don't think so. Do you?' He looked mildly outraged that someone, at the start of such a nice Welsh family day out, would refuse him money. I rejoiced. I wanted to offend him. I wanted to bite his leg. After I had seen off the panhandler, I had to pee in the field. I always know it is not going to be a good day if I have to pee in a field.

Heatwaves are rare in Wales but we hit one. We baked in large, hot crowds of large, hot Welsh people speaking Welsh and looking at combine harvesters. I rather liked the Welsh goats, but the highlight was the Welsh sheep shearing. Aside from the sheep shearing another personal favourite was the pole climbing, which is much as it sounds. We sat on the grass, watching the pole climbers clambering up enormously tall poles. I doubt I was the only person in the crowd hoping one of them would fall. The children were picking up tips on dangerous activities they could try when we got home and I was musing: 'Would I hate living in Wales more or less than living in Northumberland?' when the woman who was our nearest neighbour suddenly let out a yelp. She started frantically tossing her hair from side to side and wriggling her shoulders. She had been sitting down, leaning against a wooden shed while she ate her ice cream. Never lean against a wooden shed at an agricultural show: it is likely to contain a sizeable animal which will piss down the wall and all over your ice cream. If you are lucky, you will notice what is happening before you finish it. I decided I would hate living in Wales more.

## Friday, 18 August 2006

### Pegging out

I do things in Northumberland that I would never do other-wise. I hang out washing. I enjoy the weight of a wet shirt in my hand, the reach of my arm and the tidy clip of the plastic peg. Sunshine in my eyes, I squint-string the clothes along the line which runs across the common grass between the sea-fringed fields and the cottages. Then, I catch and heave and hoist them up to the clouds; a length of skinny, metal piping, standing guard, the line caught in its wooden, snake-tongued mouth. They flap and flurry in the northern breezes, lift, noisy and excited in the whippy gusts straight blown from the world's other side to here. It relaxes me to do it, see it, hear it. Mind you, I do not like to iron it. No other sort of house-work relaxes me. I will avoid housework of any other kind. I make an exception for laundry. Washing and drying I like to do. You can keep the rest.

## Tuesday, 22 August 2006

### Silence is golden

I have worked quite hard this month writing features for a student guide to universities. The problem when I work is that my life shrinks to this row of cottages. Sometimes when I look up and see the sea on the horizon, I think: 'That must be the edge of the world. Will I drop off it today?' Thought we all deserved a break, so I invited over the Sheep Farmer's Wife and another mother, who happens to be a shepherd's wife, for a playdate. I keep having these moments where I say something and there is a long pause while the person I am talking to thinks about what I have said. During that pause, I start wishing I had not said it at all. I did it recently with the Evangelical Man when he biked over for tea and buns. I said: 'Do you ever think when you are reading a book and the children sit down next to you and you can't move your arms that it's like being in a limo with two Mafia hitmen?' There was silence. The man, who is a devoted father to his three children, shook his head, took a mouthful of tea and said: 'I can't say I have.' I wrote a mental Post-it note to myself and stuck it on a synapse. 'Shut up!' Then I did the same thing today. The children were all playing nicely together. The Sheep Farmer's little girl and the Shepherd's two boys were running in and out of the shrubbery with my two. The Sheep Farmer's younger boy played at his mother's feet as we sat outside drinking tea and my baby sucked on her fist. I said: 'My five-year-old was deciding between giving me a plastic teddy bear filled with rainbow-coloured sand or a dinosaur and he gave me the dinosaur. He said he thought I was more like the dinosaur.' Silence. Pause. The Sheep Farmer's Wife said: 'Really?' The Shepherd's Wife said: 'Weren't you upset?' I am thinking: 'A) They now know my child thinks I'm a monster; and B) that I quite like it.'

### Friday, 8 September 2006

#### The farmer wants a wife

It is true to say that if I was not a wife, I would not be here, but as I get to know these women, I watch how the clock on the kitchen wall of the farmhouse runs slower than other clocks. Times may be a-changing but they change more slowly for farmers' wives than for many, I think. A farmer may choose a wife because of her shapely calves; it helps, of course, if she comes from farming stock and knows the drill, although he may be willing to bring in fresh blood to improve the line. She marries not just a man but his family and his farm. She must be more generous than many women. Chances are, the farmer has not just a wife but an aproned mother and a tweed-capped father who may still be partners on the farm. These in-laws may still have an interest in the farming of the land, financial and otherwise. They may still live in the big farmhouse, the home where she wants to live. They may have an opinion on how she runs her own house and her own life and how she looks after her family. She may bite her tongue more than many women. They may take money out of the farm when they retire, and even when she gets into the big house it may never feel like her house. There may be no money to take and they may have to sit on by her range. If the farm is a tenanted farm, she is but borrowing the house. She may be more nervous of the future than many women. She may have stuck to her traditional role, cooked a breakfast, cooked a lunch, provided afternoon tea, then cooked a dinner to mop up any emptiness. Her hands may be redder and her feet more sore than many women. She may feel, when the children go to college, that she should stretch her wings; that may be harder to do than she thought. She may get a little job, open a farm shop, a café, run a B&B or run round cleaning holiday cottages on Saturdays. She may get up earlier and go to bed later than many women. She may watch her own children grow, and wonder if they will be farmers and whether they will earn enough to keep the farm in the family. She may worry more than other women.

## Tuesday, 12 September 2006

### The neighbourhood

At dusk, when the children tip into sleep, I step outside and walk along the access road a little way, stopping to look across the pasture, waiting for the lighthouse to blink, for the bats to notice me, swoop down and then away. I walk past the empty, ranked, blank windows of the row. I think: 'This is their cottage home from home. This one theirs. And this one here is theirs.' I nudge a wooden bench tighter against a wall, lift up and right a terracota pot, wonder: 'Will she come this weekend or next? ... How soon will they be up again? Half-term perhaps?' I think what I might say, what he or she might say to me. I hope we make good neighbours; at least, I like to think we do.

## Thursday, 14 September 2006

### Hedgerow

Brambles hang heavy, sweet with berry temptation on their hedge branches. You drive by; they shout after you: 'Pluck me!' You stop, glance back, reverse, stop again and wind down the window. 'Fill up your mouth with my round sweetness,' they call and pout. 'Roll me over in your warm, wet darkness before you bite and swallow me. Eat me up till your lips blacken and your tongue shrinks from my taste. Wrest me from this thorny green and let me die happy in a shortcrust pie.' You nod. You say: 'How much?' They say: 'Your lucky day. Today, all day, I'm free.'

## Saturday, 16 September 2006

### Nit happy

I have been asked by a newspaper to ring round Labour MPs to see how they are feeling about Blair. I have known some of them the best part of twenty years. That makes me feel old. You can get a surprising amount by phone but I miss being there at the heart of it. Blair is not the only one with problems.

The Dairy Farmer's Wife decided her own husband needs her more than we do, and leaves at the end of the month. I decided I would get a full-time Girl Friday to help with the children and the house and to give me more flexibility with work. All I have to do now is bring in some work so that I can pay her. The King of the Castle said he knew the perfect girl for the job – his farm manager's daughter, who works as a carer in an old people's home. She showed me a note from one of the relatives. It said: 'God bless you for all that you have done to make Mum's life as good as it has been during this dreadful disease. I shall always consider you to have been one of the "Angels" who blessed our lives and made the "unbearable" so much more bearable . . . You have always brought such joyous smiles to Mum's face. I am well aware that you mean so much more to her now than even we do.' I thought: 'That's good enough for me.' So far, so good. Then my five-year-old catches nits. The hairdresser found them. Yuk. Even worse, this being Northumberland, the hairdresser is my new nanny's sister. The shame of it.

I looked 'nits' up on the Internet and immediately wanted to shave my son's head and burn his bed. Instead, I go to the chemist to buy a nit comb. It would have been less shameful to buy flavoured condoms with tickly bits at the end. I whispered: 'Do you have a nit comb?' The overalled assistant said: 'Pardon?' They should not employ deaf girls behind the counter of a pharmacy.

My head is crawling and hot even thinking about it. Do I have nits? If I have nits, I will borrow a gun and shoot myself. School sent round a note after I told them, telling parents: 'There are nits. Treat your child's hair.' But every mother I mentioned it to has resolutely not treated their child's hair. Some of them claimed they had not even seen the note. You do not spontaneously combust with nits. One of their children passed them on and the problem will not go away. They will come back. *Nits: The Revenge*. I think I may have made a policy mistake. I mentioned the nits to one mother. She said: 'You are very brave to admit your child has nits.' You should never do anything other people label 'brave'. 'Brave' is just another word for stupid. My poor baby came home from school. Some little beast had called him: 'Nit head. Nit head.' What that mother meant was: 'You have just told me your child has nits. I am going home to tell my child. He will tell another child, who will brand your child a nit head.'

## *Wednesday, 20 September 2006*

### Ladies who lunch

I took the Yorkshire Mother out to lunch. It was a strange sort of occasion. She has four sons – sprawling, brawling sorts of boys, much like my own – and an older daughter. She should have five sons, not four. Her eldest would have been twenty-one today, but no key of the door for him. Dead before his time, seven years ago. Last week, waiting for our boys to come out of school, she said: 'Wednesday would have been his birthday. I'll be going to his grave instead.' My heart took on the colour of her sadness. I said: 'Would it be weird to have lunch with me before you go?' A mother does not forget a son's birthday, however far from home he is. We chinked our glasses, drank up the champagne fizz, wiped out the bubbles with our fingers, then filled the empty glasses with our tears.

## *Tuesday, 26 September 2006*

### Good night, sleep tight

My three-year-old and I play this game. At night, after we have read our books, I lean over him the better to admire the curtain lashes and the deep blue of his eyes. I pause in wonder at the boy. I kiss his nose and say: 'You're great.' He lies pressed flat beneath the tiny duvet dinosaurs. He says: 'You're great.' I say: 'You're magnificent.' He says: 'You're magnificent.' I say: 'You're wonderful.' He agrees that I am too, and on and on we go until I catch and giggle at how marvellous this echo thinks me. I do believe that he will tire of me before I should ever tire of playing such a game.

We had to take him in to hospital for a biopsy because every six weeks he throws up for about thirty-six hours. He has always been tender and mirthful to the core; now he complains of stomach ache and joint pains and is grumpier even than me. Whatever is askew in his body leaves him with large black circles that look as if they have been carved into his face. He was pale and so very good as we walked together from his bed on the children's ward into the operating theatre. He hung back slightly and hard-gripped my hand. When he lay down and they put him under, his eyes closed, his head went back and he was gone. Seeing his sudden slide into oblivion was terrible. My husband and I waited outside in the sunshine, drank black coffee, thought black thoughts and fielded 'How is he, do you think?' phone calls from my mother. We went in again just after he woke up. They were looking to see if he might have coeliac disease, but could not find any evidence for it. The grey-bearded consultant came to see us as we sat by his bed, my black-and-white boy against his pillows, watching technicolour cartoons. The doctor, who is a gastrointestinal specialist, told us he believes he has what he called stomach migraine and that it will keep coming back. We now have two very large bottles of medicine. You need nerves of steel to be a parent.

## Saturday, 30 September 2006

### Old school ties

It is not just my children who have gone back to school. My Best Friend From School made me do something I did not want to do. I do not mean smoke and drink a cocktail of gin and canned tomatoes (she made me do that too). Something I promised I would never do and I will never do again. Go to a school reunion.

You have to be old and sad to go to a school reunion. It was a reunion of girls who had gone to what used to be a boys' independent school in York. When I was a pupil, there were around twenty girls in the sixth form; now the school is co-educational throughout. They were the children of businessmen and farmers. My father sold cheese and sliced bacon in a city-centre shop; my mother worked part-time as a bank clerk and looked after my grandmother. When I got myself to that school on two scholarships, I wanted to be Prime Minister; now I just want to get through the day without crying. Mind you, that is probably how the Prime Minister feels.

Standing in the old assembly hall, drinking warm Buck's Fizz with our names emblazoned on our breasts, I elbowed my best friend in the stomach. The self-made millionaire has a personal trainer. She is wearing expensive clothes she picked up in 'some airport' in Europe which cling to her taut, sculpted figure. A figure which is better than it was when we were at school. 'You so owe me,' I said. 'I'm going to this reunion when I'm fat, I don't have a job and I don't even live in London any more. At least it would sound glamorous if I lived in London.' 'No, it wouldn't,' she said. I carried on: 'I'm a washed-up hack who had her children too late and who is living in the wastelands. I'm telling everyone I'm a teacher.'

She poured the remains of her warm Buck's Fizz into mine. 'There you are' – she pointed at an old school photo of me, all bangs and flounces. 'You were fatter then.'

There were six of us from our year and others I knew from the year above. You found yourself looking for the girl in the mumsy figure in front of you. I suspected a few had eaten the girl they used to be. You would peer at the woman to see through to the sixteen-year-old you knew was in there. In her turn, she would peer back at you. You thought: 'Who were you? Who was I? Who are we now?' Looking around, I thought: 'This is who buys those strange clothes you see hanging on the rails in certain department stores, the rails you walk by and wonder: "Who the hell wears those?"' We do.

I had no memory at all of one girl, not a shred. I recognized neither her nor her name. Am I so forgetful? Or was she so unmemorable? Did she remember me or was I equally unremarkable? One of my contemporaries had to leave straight after lunch to get home to make a birthday cake for her son. I thought: 'This is the first time you have seen these women in twenty-four years. Buy a cake for him. As if he will care.' Perhaps I am wrong, perhaps he does care and she is a better mother than me in the same way she got better A-levels and went to a better university. This is what going to a school reunion reduces you to. How do I compare to this overblown summer rose? Do I look better? Or fatter? Have I done better? Am I married? How many times have I been married? Have I more children? By how many fathers? Does my husband love me more than her husband loves her? Do I make my children's birthday cakes or do I buy them from a shop? I buy them from a shop.

## Monday, October 9 2006

### Running on empty 4

I rang my husband from the pub car park I had juddered into off the A1. I was slewed across the asphalt where the car had crawled with its last breath of petrol and died. He picked up. I said: 'The mobile is about to die. I have two seconds to tell you where I am,' which I did. I said: 'And I probably just have time to tell you, you are a . . .' when the battery died on me too.

## Thursday, 19 October 2006

### Buncase

Girl Friday seems lovely. Naturally she has great hair, blonde and highlighted, since her sister is a hairdresser. When she started, she told me she couldn't cook. I said that was fine – anything we needed her to cook for the children would be very straightforward. Unfortunately it turns out she is naturally a great cook. She appears to be on a permanent diet – unlike me; everything she bakes, I eat. Occasionally I throw a bun at a child, but basically the baked stuff is mine. It is a catastrophe.

## Friday, 20 October 2006

### Knock knock. Who's there?

One of my acute frustrations living up here is the lack of space. Outside it's all glorious green rolling acres everywhere while the beaches are empty stretches of washed sand. Inside this rural dream of country life, it is hell. Five of us squished together in what is effectively a two-bedroomed, toy-strewn hovel. Six, counting Girl Friday when she is here. But the house is like something from eighteenth-century pre-Industrial Revolution England – all cottage industry and screaming children with a little less smallpox.

We were supposed to buy and then knock through into next door to create a perfect domestic environment – full of living spaces rather than rooms, and positively bursting with Agas, en-suite bathrooms and under-floor heating. Today, we finally got planning permission to knock the cottages together. It has taken nearly nine months. I could have had another baby in the time it took.

I have decided I hate planners and builders. Irony. We finally have planning permission; we cannot afford any of the builders who have tendered for it. 'Tender' is just builder speak for 'extort'. They are extortionists in hard hats. I hate builders. Why do I want to hand over good money I have not got, to build a house somewhere I do not want to live? I am going to have to think about that one. Of course, I cannot find anywhere quiet enough to sit down and think this all through, which could be where I am going wrong.

## Sunday, 22 October 2006

### Blackberry man

Half-term. The Perfect Mother rang, said: 'We'll come up.' 'He won't be here,' I said. 'We'll come see you then,' she said; 'we're leaving the children with my parents – it will just be us.'

Her Hectic Husband took my sons on an all-boy expedition while I went for a walk with his wife and my baby. The beach was glorious, endlessly flat with horsetails whipped up by the cold winds whisking across the sands. A washed-out golden sunlight persuading walkers that winter had not yet come to it. As we walked along the beach, I confessed: 'I'm angry with him. At being here.' She told me: 'I'm angry too.' She was silent for a moment. 'The hours he works, the endless business trips, the Blackberry. He's better than he used to be – even so, I've had to tell him if he doesn't engage with them as children, they'll be strangers to him when they're adults. I've felt as if I'm doing it on my own too often. I love him, but there was a time I thought about leaving him. Then I thought: "Why put the children through all that? I'm a single parent anyway, I may as well stay. At least we're more comfortable financially."'

I believe there is an army of angry women. Each rage different but a common theme – the high-earning husband, clever, ambitious and obsessed with work. This obsession drives the man to work through nights and weekends, year after year. Unregarded, his wife will wait to be a widow, while his children can lengthen, blossom, hurt, smile and leave home, all unknown. Throughout this time, his resenting wife will do that thing commonly described as 'picking up the slack'. This generally translates to 'looking after the children'. Morning, she will get up with the children to allow her husband to have an extra hour lie-abed to make up for how late he stayed at the office. 'This job is killing me,' he will tell her, his eyes closed. His staggering wife, already clocked on for her all-day/all-night shift. Her weekends she spends as thoroughly alone, albeit with the children, as she would be if he were dead, while he 'tidies up some loose ends' then swims through the Sunday papers.

We walked on, ploughing the sand with the buggy. 'I hope he's getting on OK with the boys,' I said. 'He'll be fine,' she replied; 'it'll do him good.' When we got back to the house, her Hectic Husband was looking dazed. He said: 'I forgot I had a conference call with India and London and I didn't know how to press mute' – he gestured to the Blackberry – 'so I started the call standing outside the car while the boys bounced around inside like monkeys. The call dragged on and it was getting dark so I had to drive back, and when I got back in, they'd emptied out their wellies and buckets and turned it into a beach. They were so noisy one of the bankers said: "Half-term, is it?" and I told him: "They're not even mine."' His wife started to laugh.

## Monday, 30 October 2006

### On my knees

Maybe it is my friends leaving, but if someone said to me: 'Describe yourself in one word,' I would say: 'Mother.' If they said: 'Make it two,' I would say: 'Lonely mother.' My husband is away for three weeks, including the half-term week which has just gone, and I do not feel there is anyone here I can turn to in a crisis. I do not know them well enough to impose. The baby is teething, and after four sleepless nights on the trot I am desperate. I hate my absent husband, myself and my children in about that order. I spent the Saturday on my knees. When yesterday dawned, I crawled to the phone to confess to my husband that I simply did not know how I would cope, what to do with myself or what to do with the children. 'I know,' he said. 'Why don't you go to Alnwick garden, gather autumnal leaves and make a collage?' 'I know,' I replied. 'Why don't you just come home and you can make the fucking collage?'

I could have called in Girl Friday. The Evangelicals or one or two of the school-gate mothers would have welcomed me if I had 'fessed up to a crisis, but I did not feel I could say the words: 'Please. Can you help me?' It was, truth be told, not so much a crisis as another day. How do you tell someone you hardly know that you cannot cope? That you are desperate? I was too low; my children too ghastly to inflict them on anyone. In London, I would have had no scruples. I would have thrown everyone in the car and expected those I love to welcome me into their homes even if my mood was black and my children monstrous.

I am struggling. Without work and colleagues, my main route into friendships is through school. The village church school is tiny; the potential pool of bosom mates is small. In any event, one of the perks of rural living is a free bus for the kids, which cuts down the number of mothers you see. I was gutted this term when the Oyster Farmer's Wife started using the county bus service to take her son to school and bring him home. Unlike me, she did not consider the forty-minute round schlep, twice a day, worth a few minutes of chirpy banter, and who can blame her? Unless, my 'chirpy banter' was why she stopped driving him and switched to the bus. Oh God, do these women think I am stalking them?

## Friday, 3 November 2006

### Like mother, like daughter

My dandelion-haired babe is one of rounded cheeks and skylighting smiles. Glorious. The only problem occurs whenever she crunches up her perfect face to scowl out her frustration; in those moments, when she looks perturbed or volcanic angry, my husband will say: 'Look. Look at the baby. She looks just like you. That's uncanny.' I will glance across at the small Tasmanian devil child and say to him: 'I don't look like that.' He says: 'You do. You look just like that. It's uncanny. She's got your face.'

He missed the baby's first birthday. We had a small party with the Oyster Farmer's Wife and her boys and the Evangelicals. We ate chocolate cake in the shape of a caterpillar then the children played out in the dark. I held the baby to the phone for Daddy to wish her a 'Happy Birthday, darling'.

Forlorn, he said: 'I'm not there.' 'No,' I said, 'you're not. You'll be here tomorrow. I'll save you a piece of cake.'

### Wednesday, 8 November 2006

## The palm of your hand

All those times, as a mother, you lay your palm against the curve of your child's cheek in admiration or in comforting. Tonight as I was lying with the baby tucked next to me feeding, she reached out her little hand and laid it soft on my withering cheek. She left it there for half a minute, enough to let me know she cared, and in that brief touch, I thought: 'All right, I will try again tomorrow then. Tomorrow I will get it right.'

### Thursday, 9 November 2006

## Cyber-scream girl

I have decided to start talking to myself and anyone else who will listen. Write an online diary. Blog it. Has to be cheaper than therapy. An MP I know blogs about politics. Now I have actually signed up and done it, I am slightly astonished to see what I am thinking out there in the blogosphere in black and white. It is all anonymous. I have called it 'Wife in the North'. I do not think anyone would guess it was me – not unless they read it, and they would have to find it first. Even if they did, I get the impression that in Northumberland everyone knows your business anyway. There seem to be convoluted networks of distant kinship and long-standing amity in the county which means that even if they have never met you, they already know more about you than you would think possible.

## Tuesday, 14 November 2006

### Awake in the dark

Autumn, all stripped branches and dark damp, no getting away from it. November, a month for remembering the dead. In London, this is how we mark the day. We go to mass in the church where we married and watch the sun's diamond rays slice through the stained glass to fall on empty oak and beeswaxed pews. We buy parrot tulips wrapped in brown paper. 'Thank you, we won't bother with the ribbon bow.' We drive to a grave in an Essex churchyard, walk through wet grass and fallen down leaves, unplug a tin vase from a headstone and fill it with water, spring flowers and could-have-beens. Pray for resurrection day, get cold and wet; go to a hotel and sit in armchairs at a small round table drinking tea. Occasionally, our hands touch and our wedding bands click one against the other. If we are to stay in Northumberland, will my bones lie not in this yard but in a northern grave? My husband has already said he wants to be buried in the North. Will I rest easy if I lie with him? Or will I toss and turn in my damp silk cell and silent-call, my mouth stopped with strange soil: 'Take me back to dear old London town'?

## Saturday, 2 December 2006

### A poke in the eye

We left the three-year-old and the baby with Girl Friday and took the five-year-old to hospital for a stitch courtesy of a broom being accidentally poked in his eye when the children were tidying up the classroom. He has a small cut above his eye and a facility for standing in the wrong place. He took my hand, looked up at me and said: 'Do you think I'm brave?'

I stood still and Solomon nodded up and down and up again: 'Very, very, very. I'd just rather you were careful.'

## Tuesday, 12 December 2006

### You do. Voodoo

If I practised voodoo, I would be completely out of wax and pins by now. Last November, we were told the knock-through would cost us around £75,000, according to an estimate from our cheery chartered surveyor. By February this year, that had gone up to around £100,000, according to the architect. Unfortunately, no one told the builders, and when it went out to tender, the estimated cost had climbed to £240,000 – including VAT (that's all right then). I am currently waiting for a man and his mate, who are coming to have a look, go to the pub, get totally drunk, write down the biggest figure they can think of and attach a pound sign to it before they pass out.

## Thursday, 14 December 2006

### Karaoke in Soho

My husband has wafted back to London for his office Christmas party. I no longer have an office so I am saved a trip to a smoke-filled Soho den, the cringe-making karaoke and annual haka 'God, we were good this year. Really, really good. Be proud of yourself. Really, really proud, because God, we were good.' The amount of time he spends in London he might as well live there (oh yes, that's right, we used to. Until he decided to stick a pin in a map and move us all to the back of beyond) and his complaints while he is there frankly only serve to irritate. 'I've had such a bad day,' he tells me from a friend's house where he enjoys his child-free shaved-truffle supper.

'I don't want to be here, you know,' he moans from my favourite Covent Garden patisserie. Really? Neither do I.

I open the front door to my world: silence and the wind, darkness flooding the fields around, filling the sky and pressing down on the cottage. I shut the door, turn back to the TV and the camera pans along a London skyline. I feel homesick – quite desperate. London Diva told me my situation made her weep for me and that I have become a 'victim'. Oh dear. Am I indeed a victim? Maybe I have been too gloomy about my life up North. I drew up a Pollyanna list of everything that is good about living up here: empty beaches and glorious skies, school and the opportunity to make new friends (who says you should put up a 'No Vacancies' sign just because you are forty-something?). There is also the 'community' – to my surprise there really is one – and then there is the garden, which is bigger than anything we could have in London. Not to mention a happy husband – at least he had better be.

## Tuesday, 19 December 2006

### Maybe it's because I'm a Londoner

I am slightly daunted by Christmas. Last year, it was so very bad. This year, I escaped to London for a couple of days with a toothbrush and a certain amount of guilt. But it was worth the guilt – seeing friends, an exhibition, a movie, a haircut, a bit of shopping. Amazing what you can fit in – and how much money you can spend for that matter – when you are on a tight schedule.

As I walked out of the National Gallery, my heart pinged, I heard it; caught firm in London's manicured grasp as dusk stole over Trafalgar Square with its Christmas tree and carollers. It was as true and lovely as any painting I had seen the hours before. An authentic masterpiece. I am heartsore. It is the feeling you have when someone you love leaves you, although I know I did the leaving. I am ashamed of myself for the teenage angst of it all. So I moved. Big deal. I should shrug in a sophisticated way, inhale hard from a cigarette held in a costume-jewelled hand and slowly blow a smoke ring into the already cloudy air. I do not live here any more and yet I carry it with me. Where is my home now? There is just one year left to go of this experiment and I cannot read the runes, do not know whether we will stay in Northumberland or come back? Whether we *should* stay or come back. If we did return, could I cope with the crowds, the squalor glimpsed out of the corner of your eye, the 'body on the line in North London' which delayed my travel back to King's Cross station?

I am missing not just the dirty magnificence of city streets, I am missing 'me'. The 'me' who used to be, before children came and ate up her trim figure and all her time. What a foolish thing to miss. A memory of seventy-hour weeks and lie-abed Sundays. There are days motherhood, in all its worn, ill-tempered glory, grinds my bones to dust. Rage, repetition, losing the will to live as you try to herd your cats out of the house. Then there is that sweeping, yearning love that floods you as you kiss and kiss and kiss again your baby's cheek, and her too young as yet to run from you. And talking to the Islington Beauty and London Diva made me realize that maybe I should open up and let some people up here in. Get them one of those red enamelled badges prefects used to wear when I was young. Instead of House Captain, it could read in gilt lettering 'New Mate'. Maybe I will call some people.

## Tuesday, 26 December 2006

### Merry Christmas. Everybody's having fun.

Well, that's that then. Am I the only one who thinks 'Thank God, it's over'?

I was quite keen at the start, but frankly I am just relieved that is it for another year. I try my best. I really do. But by God, it's an effort. I think I hide my occasional desperation quite well, but as we left the eleven o'clock Christmas morning mass with the five-year-old, three-year-old, babe in arms, elderly father and blind mother, even the priest whispered in my ear: 'May God give you the strength to get through this day.' Amen to that. I go into it with the best intentions. This year, I say to myself, this year I will make my own cranberry sauce, remember what it was exactly the children asked Santa for in their letters (mental note: don't forget the camera next year), and establish those traditions which my children will remember when they too are adults with children of their own. Those very special moments that in forty years time my daughter will remember and ask herself: 'Why did my mother do that?'

It all started to go wrong on Christmas Eve when I spent twenty minutes storming round the house looking for the literary classic *The Night Before Christmas*. I eventually found it under my five-year-old son's bed, but I do wonder whether my fury outweighed the cosy few minutes of festive domesticity under the duvet reading the damn thing. I can just imagine: 'Yeah, my brother and I had this bet each Christmas. We would hide this old book she was desperate to read to us and we'd see how long would it take her to say the 'F' word when she couldn't find it. Dear old Mum. Of course she is in a home now for the criminally insane. She did love her Christmas, though.'

## Monday, 1 January 2007

### A Happy and a Gay New Year to all

I have had social exchanges with more than thirty people today. Neighbours, up for a couple of days' festivities in their holiday cottages, pop in and out of the kitchen like we are all in an episode of *The Archers* without the tum-ti-tum-ti-tum-ti-tum tum-ti-tum-ti-tumty. I am always pleased to see them, particularly the Consultant, whom I find to be so steadfast in her kindness, but neighbours can come as a bit of a shock when it is usually just us chickens.

My Gay Best Boyfriend is visiting with his partner. They have taught the boys that if they pull their mattresses off their beds and slide them down the narrow staircase, it is possible to sit on a sleeping bag at the top of it and hurl yourself down it repeatedly until blood is spilled. In between the mattress mayhem, I hosted a children's birthday party complete with chocolate fountain and *Happy Feet* cake for my now four-year-old, who has excellent timing for a birthday.

Once the children were in bed, there was a dinner party for my two London honeys and the Oyster Farmer and his wife. We ate, drank and scored the year we were leaving behind: four out of ten in my case. My husband looked horrified. He then scored his year six and a half. I said: 'Six and a half? Six and a half? What the hell does it take for you to give it a ten? You are living where you want to, you have two beautiful sons, a new baby daughter, and you bought yourself a car, you miserable sod. Six and a half?' 'OK,' he said. 'Seven.'

The conversation moved on to what we all wanted out of 2007. I wanted some idea of where we should live long term and more patience with the children. But by far the best moment was the audible gasp I thought I caught from the very straight Northumberland farmer as the bongs tolled for midnight, London's fireworks began, and my beloved boys wished each other a 'Happy New Year, darling', plunging into a lip-smacking, luscious smackeroonie. I swear that must have been the first and probably the last time my farmer friend will ever witness a gay kiss. Marvellous. I asked my Gay Best Boyfriend: 'Will you be here next year?' He said: 'If you remember, we are with my in-laws next year.' 'But I want you every year,' I said. He took my hand and held it between both of his. 'It's not like that any more. Remember. We're all grown-up now. Turn and turn about.' Sometimes I hate being grown-up.

## Friday, January 5, 2007

### Sex and chocolate cake

Have revised the way the blog looks. That is to say, I have changed the colour of the background from white to pink, changed the font I am writing in and am dropping in pictures, a process which makes my head melt. I figure I will work out the technical stuff as I go. It is done; it is out there. I consider this my launch. Look, Wifey is waving.

My five-year-old turned six yesterday (unsurprisingly, he will henceforth be known as 'the six-year-old'). He and his brother (previously known as 'the three-year-old', henceforward, etc., etc.) had a hideously noisy party yesterday afternoon. God, I hate children's parties. Does that make me a bad mother? No, I don't think so. It's all the other things I do that make me a bad mother – start drinking at 4.30 p.m. while I make their tea, shout so loudly I scare myself, object on religious principles to sewing their name tapes into their school uniforms.

Anyway, my six-year-old takes far too much for granted. Enormous wooden play castle meant for the garden, which his father constructed during the early hours in our teeny, tiny sitting room and I then gift-wrapped: he came down, tore off the paper, stooped his head to get through the arched doorway, came out again and said: 'Thanks. Can I watch *101 Dalmatians* now?' The boys had a party for twenty-eight children later that day in a soft play centre: 'Yeah, it was good. Are there any more presents to open?' By rights, he should have drifted off to bed utterly blissed out and dreamt of balloons and ice-cream mountains. He remained studiously phlegmatic throughout and had a nightmare his brother's head fell off. On the upside, there is a large amount of uneaten chocolate cake which I am steadily ploughing my way through. I figure if my husband is going to continue to make me live in the North-East, I will get fat in silent protest.

## Tuesday, January 9 2007

### Playhouse

To say we have dithered about what to do with the house is putting it mildly. Let's spend nearly nine months waiting for planning permission to knock two houses together and go through a very painful tendering process. Yes, let's do that. Then let's take some advice from estate agents and our accountant and decide we can't knock them together after all because we won't get back a big chunk of the building costs (latest estimate: £120,000) when we come to sell one big house rather than the two little ones. OK, then let's decide to go house-hunting. (This involves vast and incomprehensible arrays of numbers on bits of paper and calls to a variety of building societies – some of whom laugh at us.)

I know what! On the same day (today) as having a meeting with another prospective builder, let's see a house we could buy for the laughable sum of £615,000, which we could just about afford if I sell the children's kidneys. Luckily for them, I didn't like it; my husband did. If, however, he thinks I am letting him decide which house we live in up here, he has another think coming. By four o'clock in the afternoon, we are so fed up with not knowing what to do, we decide we will go back to London. That's straight then. By seven that evening, I decide that is a bad idea because we will feel we have been beaten by the system and if we go back to London I want it to be for positive reasons and not because we can't make up our mind between scrambled or fried eggs on a morning.

There was a time when I used to be quite good at making decisions. Those days are gone. The latest decision is to knock the two houses together (what do estate agents and accountants know anyway?) and stay. I reserve the right to change my mind tomorrow. Over breakfast when I shall be having cornflakes. Or porridge.

## Friday, 12 January 2007

### Mama? Mama?

I was thrown out of the house last night – well, maybe not so much thrown as eased out gently with a flashlight and a duvet and told to sleep next door in Number 1. My husband is spending more time with us and has had enough of the baby's nocturnal breastfeeding. Since we are pushed for space and there is nowhere else for her to go, the baby's cot is in our room. Unlike my husband, the baby rather likes her nightly routine and, in that halfway state between sleep and wakefulness, I have been unable to resist her plaintive bleatings of 'Mama? Mama?' in the cold darkness. She starts up and I stumble out of bed, pluck her from the cot and sink back into the bedding with my little victorious suckling. As she sees it, I'm lying there and it's not like I'm doing anything else. But my husband was right: it has gone on long enough. She's nearly fifteen months old and God knows, I could do with a night's sleep. It might help me regain my reason. I will feed her in the morning and before she goes to sleep, but I am giving up the night-time feeding on demand. Apparently, while I slept, the baby was weeping uncontrollably and went to look for me under my pillow. 'You'd have caved,' my husband boasted manfully this morning. 'She was utterly pathetic.' He sobs in imitation of her over the breakfast table and she gazes at him from my arms as if she hates him.

## Monday, 15 January 2007

### Babes in Gotham City

I may be struggling socially but the boys went to yet another birthday party yesterday, this one, a fancy-dress discotheque. I seem to spend an awful lot of time handing round greasy pizza slices to their classmates, but at least I am doing better than my parents, who seem locked into a hectic round of interments and funeral teas.

The problem with children's birthday parties is other people's children. This time was no different. When two four-year-old boys squared up for a fight, I was faced with the eternal dilemma of whether you attempt to parent someone else's children or shrug, turn away and think: 'Thank God, you're not mine.' Initially I tried to ignore them, but the pushing and shoving went on. I looked round the church hall, desperately trying to spot a mother who might be willing to claim ownership of one of them, but nada. The boys were rapidly taking on that Friday night look of 'Did you spill my lemonade?' Reluctantly, baby on hip, I went over. 'Look, this is a party,' I reasoned as I knelt beside them. (I have seen those *How To Be a Good Parent – At Least When the Camera is On* programmes.) 'No fighting.' One of them promptly shoved the other.

'Hey, hey, hey' – my voice grew slightly less liberal. 'Where is your mummy?' The half-pint Batman looked at me. 'I don't have a mummy.' I hoped he meant 'here' – 'I don't have a mummy *here*.' On the off-chance I had found the room's only orphan, I decided to pick on the other one before the orphan started crying loudly. I turned to the cowboy. 'Where is your mummy then?' I cannot say his mummy looked as grateful as she might have done when I interrupted her cup of tea to explain why I had brought her little hard man back to her.

What are you supposed to do? We had already let some ghastly brat hold on to and then unwrap the pass-the-parcel present when he really should have passed it on to the child next to him. I only just stopped myself pulling it out of his jammy fingers and slapping him around the head with it.

## Tuesday, 16 January 2007
### Dollies and disability

We had to go into school this morning for a daddies' reading day, which entailed my husband reading a book called *Vesuvius Poovius* – all about poo and how to get rid of it. Not quite sure if that is what they had in mind when they asked my husband in to read, but the children seemed to like it. I am, however, disowning responsibility if any of the other mothers start telling me little Johnny is stashing his number twos under the front-room rug. They probably would not care: everything my husband does seems to go down well at school. I am merely a mother; my husband has been elected a school governor. They asked whether 'one of us' would be interested in standing. They would have settled for me, but I suspect they wanted my husband. While I was there, the baby crawled across the classroom to the doll's house. As she pulled out the dollies, each was revealed as more unfortunate than the next. Among the inhabitants was an old lady clutching a Zimmer frame – fair enough, grannies do get that way. Granny had a lot going on, living there as she did with her middle-aged son on crutches and a blind daughter who could not move anywhere without her white stick. Talk about the Curse of the House of Usher. If there had been a cat, it would have had three legs. Apparently, local education authorities require schools to buy Afro-Caribbean and Asian dolls at the same time as Caucasian. Quite right too – the children up here never see a black face. But all things in moderation and it was more of a care home than a doll's house. I picked up a small girl in an overly large wheel-chair and a deaf black teenager and held them out enquiringly to Guitar Girl. 'What are you like?' she said. I thought: 'Am I not supposed to notice?' She giggled, said patiently: 'It's all about diversity and inclusion.' Really? What about escapism and imagination?

## Thursday, 18 January 2007

### Define 'special'

I spent the morning being a 'special person' at school and was awarded a certificate with red felt-tipped hearts, a daffodil (a whole one – all to myself) and a chocolate Rice Krispie cake by my sons. The boys were very keen for me to come in and pick up my awards. They had a vested interest, which worried me. If I came in to pick up my award (along with a cup of tea), my boys also received a chocolate Rice Krispie cake. Sometimes, though, it is best not to look too closely at the quid pro quo.

My own recipe for chocolate Rice Krispie cake:

* Buy Rice Krispies. Tell the boys to put back the cheesy Quavers, blackcurrant Fruit Shoot and seventeen comics

complete with seventeen unnecessary toys Sellotaped to the front cover. Ignore wails of 'But I really wanted one of those.' Stand in queue at supermarket. Think up fifty-three retorts to the grim-faced shop assistant, who seems to have taken a personal dislike to my children. Pay with a £20 note just to irritate her. Leave the shop. Return.

* Buy organic and very expensive chocolate. Hope not to get grim-faced assistant. Fail to recall any one of the fifty-three retorts when she looms up behind the till and snarls at the four-year-old for standing on the conveyor belt with a shopping basket on his head.

* Return home. Realize six-year-old has technically shoplifted the Quavers. Turn on TV for the children. Make cup of tea. Eat large amount of chocolate and bag of cheesy Quavers. Feel slightly sick.

* Break hypnotic spell of *Scooby Doo* to drag children into kitchen for mummy time. This, after all, is why I quit the day job. Explain empty Quavers packet away to small and accusatory inch-high private eyes.

* Melt chocolate.

* Allow four-year-old to pour in box of Rice Krispies.

* Realize this was a mistake.

* Clean up half a box of Rice Krispies from floor, kitchen surface, top of the oven and room upstairs that we never go in.

* Allow both boys to stir concoction with wooden spoon.

* Tell boys that hitting each other with a wooden spoon is a bad thing to do.

* Realize there are no bun cases in the house.

* Drive to supermarket for bun cases. Hope not to get same woman. Give her £50 note. Smile sweetly.

* Return home. Scoop gungy spoonfuls of crisping chocolate gore into bun cases.

* Carry over to fridge with immense pride.

* Wash baby thoroughly.

## Saturday, 20 January 2007

### Lost boys

We had not managed to snatch breakfast before we left the house in a bid to catch a 7.30 a.m. train for a brief weekend in London. My husband had driven too fast down a dark and dangerous road and I had been worried throughout that we would miss it. Once we parked the car, we figured that if we ran, there was seven minutes left to buy food before we crossed the bridge over the tracks on to the platform. Standing with the pushchair, I queued for five croissants, coffees and warm milk at the coffee stand on the concourse. The pressure mounted as I glanced at the large wrought-iron clock which hangs over the heads of passengers, warning them not to be tardy. The boys, muffled in their red wool hats and overly long scarves, were dragging at me and it was the sort of cold that makes you pull your shoulders close to your ears and wish you were anywhere else. One of those old men you find only in railway stations shuffled over. He asked me how old the boys and the baby were and stooped down to caress her small silky head. 'A boy?' he asked. I did that up-down rapid calculation you do to decide whether the stranger spells danger and decided he was safe, sad and lonely. 'I had a boy but he died at seven,' he told me. This is the moment at which the coffee seller decided to ask me what I wanted. I ignored her. 'That's terrible,' I said. 'You don't forget, do you? What happened?' He told me the boy had a hole in the heart.

'In four years, I lost six people,' he said. 'How dreadful,' I said, as you do. Anxious as I was to get us all some breakfast, there was a moment I turned away from him to order the milk and pastries for my own little family and I never asked him his son's name. I should have – I have wondered about it ever since.

Then again, who says God does not have a sense of humour? We spent six and a half hours getting to the centre of the world for another children's birthday party – at a city farm with my six-year-old's best friend. I said to my husband: 'If you love the country so much, you could get a job here, mucking out.' He pretended not to hear me. The city farm is yet more evidence that nobody really has to live outside London. The boys and the baby saw animals and got lots of fresh air in between the balloon fights and butter-creamed cake. The city even 'does' the country better. At the city farm, there was a café with proper coffee. One Northumberland café I go to boasts 'instant cappuccinos' on its menu, and they are talking not about the wait but about the 'tear along this corner' perforated packets. The London farm also offered classes in upholstery, stone sculpture and bike maintenance, with particular attention given to 'wheel truing'; I have always wanted a true wheel. Best of all, there were helpful signs attached to the animal paddocks. I never knew, for instance, that sheep have very good memories and 'can remember a face up to two years after a first meeting'. That is better than me. I picked up a magazine while I was there (as you do at the farm). It was full of suggestions of what you could do and where you could go if you had young children in London. In it was an advertisement offering 'life coaching for children'. I nudged my husband's arm and pointed to it. 'Look. If we lived in London, the children could have life coaching,' I said. He looked at me. 'Alternatively, we could let them grow up,' he said.

## Thursday, 25 January 2007

### Beauty and the Beast

Motherhood takes so many things away from you. Or should I blame age? Various things happen when a woman reaches a certain age. There is a moment in her youth when she unzips her make-up bag, wipes a sponge around a peachy cream in a silver compact, loads a sable brush with beige powder and looks into the mirror ready to start her work. She scrutinizes the face in the glass and pauses. She thinks: 'What is there to do?' She uses her thumb to flick the powder from the brush and the cosmetic dust explodes into the sunny morning light flooding the bathroom. She lets the water run warm from the tap and holds the sponge beneath it, the foundation running in rivulets down the white porcelain and into the drain. She zips up the flowered make-up bag, which came free in a glossy magazine she never read. Fresh-faced and perfect, she goes out into her day. There is another moment in a woman's journey when she unzips a larger and altogether more expensive make-up bag. Rubbing at tired eyes, she fingers the duelling scar slashed across her cheek by the Egyptian linen sheets. She gazes at her face and thinks: 'Where do I start?' and then: 'How long is this going to take?'

I am at, indeed past, that 'Where do I start?' moment at the vanity table. As the fine laughter lines begin to tell around my eyes and jaw, I start to see my mother in my face. But as I do, the real McCoy slips from me. I look at her carefully coiffed and greying hair, her hesitant walk and white stick and I think: 'My mother is getting old. I really do not want my mother getting old. She never told me she would get so old. When exactly did that happen?' Now, instead of baking sultana cakes and folding vests, she wears elastic stockings on her legs, an electric whirligig seat climbing the staircase instead of her.

Last night she rang to say: 'Daddy and I have had a little accident.' It was late and I was lying, melancholy, on the sofa contemplating sleep. 'We wrote off the car,' I heard her say, the wind knocking at the sash window. 'We're fine. I broke a rib, that's all, and your father is a bit bruised.' They had been crossing a carriageway, given the nod by the driver of the car in the lane nearest to them but unseen by the driver of the car in the other lane. A classic accident. As she speaks, I play it out in my head. My father, reassured by the kindness of the other driver, slowly, oh so slowly, old-man slowly, pulls out and across the road and whoomph. Slammed into by the other car, spun round and round in squealing, metal-shrieking fear. Twenty minutes on the side of the road waiting for the paramedics; panic attacks under a yellow airtex sheet in a metal-framed bed in the Accident and Emergency cubicle. 'It could have been worse,' she said, cheerily. 'Because I'm blind, I was relaxed when the car went into us, and everyone was very nice.' I should have been there. I should have draped them in foil blankets and given them sweet tea, held their soft papery hands and told them they were OK. I do not want them to go out any more. I want them to live in my wardrobe, safe from the mishaps of old age. I will bring them food in plastic trays, a torch and a wind-up radio. I will keep them safe from harm.

## Friday, 26 January 2007

### The thin blue line

As my mother lay ill in bed, bones aching and eyes tightly shut, a shiny silver-buttoned policeman knocked on the door. 'I've come about the accident,' he told my father. 'Who is it?' my mother feebly called. They climbed soft-carpeted stairs to her bedroom, the policeman and the stooped offender; a gilt-framed Sacred Heart watching from the Anaglypta wall, a rosary-wrapped St Anthony bearing witness from the dresser, as the policeman cautioned my aged father. 'Now, I don't want you getting upset but I have to caution you,' he told him, this aged threat to the public good. 'It's like what happens on TV,' he reassured them, getting out his notebook and a black-inked pen. The plaster saints looked away in shame. 'You do not have to say anything. But it may harm your defence . . .' the officer chanted on. My mother, crash-bruised and still in shock, began the ages old lament of the criminal's wife. 'My husband,' she spoke out from the soft pillows, in between her tears, 'did nothing wrong. It was an accident.'

Later, steel-tempered by her encounter with the law, this fan of TV's Morse and Frost rings. 'I told him straight,' she says. 'Coppers don't frighten me.'

## Saturday, 27 January 2007

### Tally ho

Now for something I thought no one would ever hear me say: 'Boys! Put your boots on, right this minute. We are going to be late for the hunt.' They probably shoot you if you are late for the hunt. 'I say. Do you know what time it is? You're ten minutes late. Stay where you are while I pour the powder into my pistol and load the shot, dammit.' I did not want to miss a moment. It must be – gosh, how long is it since I went hunting in London? Oh yes, that is right – never. I have decided to roll with those moments which make me think 'Who am I again?'

It was one of Northumberland's apple-crisp, beautiful mornings. The winter-blue sky looked like a child had smeared white paint across it with his fist. There we were, cold, with mud on our rubber boots, on a faraway farm, the snow-capped Cheviot hills brooding in the distance and surrounded by nice giletted women thrusting haggis balls at us – well, it works for me. It is ten o'clock in the morning and suddenly something called a Percy Special seems like a good idea – a half-measure of whisky mixed with a half-measure of cherry liqueur. In the city, this would be called an alcohol problem; in the country, it is a tipple. I could not decide whether it made it more or less likely the riders would fall off. It would certainly make it less likely they would notice if they did.

The Sheep Farmer and his wife have a lot on – their farming business, two children, she keeps the books and they are involved in an application for planning permission to get a wind farm on their land, eighteen turbines at 125 metres high, and not everybody likes the idea. In fact there are posters up saying 'No' alongside a picture of a wind turbine, which must give you a nice warm feeling as you drive by. Despite being so busy, she has decided I should get out more. She invited us along since the hunt was meeting at her farm. Out of respect to her, I worked very hard not to think city thoughts like: 'Didn't Tony Blair outlaw this?' I also decided against talking the pros and cons of hunting through with the children before the outing. The risk of 'Mummy says animals have rights too, don't you, Mummy?' over the coffee and shortbread was just too high. I must reprogramme them tomorrow before they think what we did today was entirely normal.

Clutching warm sausage baps, we stood in the farmyard

watching the clipped horses grandly pirouetting amidst stiff-tailed hounds. I fought not to morph into a Japanese tourist, politely insistent that strangers in flat caps and down jackets take digital photographs of me to display to the folks back home. I failed. I explained to one farmer: 'This is just so different from what we are used to.' 'No offence,' he said. I braced myself for the inevitable left hook. 'But I am constantly amazed how naive townsfolk are about country ways.' He walked away, leaving me standing there with my Percy Special and camera.

I have occasionally wondered what happens on a hunt. Riders come along in muddy Land Rovers pulling horseboxes; they do not just leap out of the nineteenth-century print a favourite uncle hung in the hallway in the shadow of the grandfather clock. I am not knocking hunting. The outfits are great. Before today, the nearest I had ever been to a hunt was a Jilly Cooper novel in which I am sure jodhpurs were eased down over taut thighs. It is certainly true that everyone looks sexier on a horse, jodhpurs tight over taut, etc. They played it all wrong when they fought and failed to keep their hunting rights; they should have campaigned on the slogan: 'We look sexy – leave us alone.'

They set off, hounds legally following the trail of a bunch of rags tied to a quad bike, rather than a fox. Fox, what fox? The Sheep Farmer's Wife and I gave them a head start and then followed on with my husband and the five children piled into the back of a Land Rover. The slightly strange thing about hunting is that the hunters too are hunted by quad bikes and 4×4s, some of whom follow the riders into the fields and some of whom wait at vantage points with binoculars as if they are on safari. 'Is that an elephant over there? No, no, it's just Edgar on Tinkerbell. Tally ho, Edgar.'

## Sunday, 28 January 2007

### Of mice and mess

We eventually found a couple of builders on the recommend-
ation of the Evangelical Man, and in just under two weeks'
time we are due to move into an unfurnished, rented house in
the village to allow them to start work on knocking through
the cottages to create that dream home I was promised. I suspect our stone-built rented house is cold. I am so cold, so much
of the time, I am contemplating sewing myself into my thermal
underwear like someone from the Depression.

We have to clear out next door, which we have used as an
enormous cupboard since we took possession. 'Hello, I come
from London. I like to live in one house and buy the house next
door to keep my clart in.' I cannot think why there is a rural
housing crisis, or for that matter why second-home owners are
despised by locals up and down the country. The only good
thing about moving is that we will escape the mice, who are
overrunning us at the moment. They chewed the baby's romper
the other day – even worse, I put her in it. The move means
packing up this house in all its Playmobil glory. Who invented
Playmobil? Who had the bright idea to invent a children's toy
that comes in one zillion bits? I figure if we leave enough
Playmobil behind, when we move back in five months' time
the mice might have built the Viking longboat.

Because we have decided that we do not have time to sort
out next door, we are renting an enormous metal container
to put in the barn at the back of the cottage and shunt our
mess into. We really need that container. There are TV programmes which feature busybody women with sharp noses
who declutter your house; I do not watch them. I am incapable
of decluttering anything. I have not even started packing. I am
hoping Walt Disney will appear in the kitchen one day and

start drawing arms and legs on my pots, pans and general detritrus which could then pack themselves while they whistle an Elton John hit.

A friend dropped by for a cup of tea. 'I so admire you,' she said, gazing at me as I moved a dirty saucepan to get to the kettle. I looked round my kitchen at the enormous Gilbert and George-style painting of the children we all did together, the wilted yellow roses on the table, their heads just visible above the breakfast cereal packets. I picked the baby up from the wooden floor where she was eating her brother's buttered toast crusts. 'Do you?' I said, touched. 'When I was a young mother,' she carried on, reaching out to take the grubby baby from my arms, 'I was always cross with the kids for making a mess, I was always picking up after them, cleaning and keeping house. You just don't bother. I do admire that.'

## Monday, 29 January 2007

### Cherry scones

The Yorkshire Mother invited me for coffee this morning. As we arrived, she was still rubbing her fingers free of doughy gloves and the smell of baking cherry scones hung about her busy kitchen, spilling fragrant through the open door into a wintered garden. 'Drop by for coffee, I'll make scones' – I say it out loud to see how it sounds. Unconvincing, in my case. She, on the other hand, knocks out a warm batch of home-baked treats with the same nonchalance as I swill a crystal glass of cool and gooseberry-tanged Chablis.

Some friendships you keep for a life. Others for only a train ride. Some friends you lose and never know why, and when you are old you think: 'Whatever happened to?' or 'What did I do?' Some friends you mourn; some walk away and you do not notice. This friendship is spring green and sweetly brief, lasting weeks. Now my new friend is about to move somewhere bouncing hot and sandy to feed oily egg and cigarette-thin chips to fat Englishmen who would prefer to eat their egg and chips at home. I want to say to her: 'Don't go out of my life. You have only just arrived there.' But in her head, she has already quit this place for a different tomorrow.

As I drink the coffee and graze on blossom-coloured cake, I gaze at the bonfire of trucks and old jeans piled up on her dining-room carpet, salvaged from the rooms upstairs. Each of her four boys is allowed one black plastic bag of toys to carry with him into his new and sunnier life. The missing boy-child slipped through her floury fingers in one of those 'Dear God' disasters that make you catch your breath. Mowing early summer grass and daisies, he cut the lead. Zap. I have seen his face smiling out of a sharp school photograph, and in his mother's eyes you can see him yet. They are packing for the sun and a fresh start. I admire her determination that the four remaining boys will run from school bench straight into a warm and salty sea, nylon homework bags spray-wet and abandoned on the beach. But I will miss her. She is a new friend and no one else will make me pastries and froth my coffee. While she was packing, she found bed treasures her missing boy once slept with, his teddy bear and a keepsake velvet cushion. In a suitcase at the top of a wardrobe, she found his summer coat, its pocket packet rustling, the crisps long gone. Prawn cocktail. She slipped the packet back into the coat and the coat into a bag to carry with her.

## Thursday, 1 February 2007

### Ferreting around

As soon as I had the baby, I tried to blend in by abandoning the black, the stripy tights and the embossed leather baseball boots

to 'dress country'. I think it important to look the p...
you do not know your lines. This required the pur...
corduroy skirts in autumnal colours with contrasting aut...
tops, and flat brown boots. I looked dreadful. I have far ...
large an arse for corduroy. Anyway, when I looked at them, the
women around me were not wearing the country camouflage
I had adopted but mish-mashed clothes of every hue bought
on-line or from country ladies' fashion shops I never knew
existed. I may try another way – animals.

Women up here have strange pets: chickens, pedigree sheep,
ferrets. Those who have chickens or sheep seem to spend their
entire lives gifting eggs or trying to do something useful with
the fleeces. I do not think a ferret produces anything apart from
ferret poo. Perhaps you could make jewellery? I am strangely
tempted to get one ferret or even two; you keep them in
pairs. This is something, rather like the hunt, I would never
have previously considered in my metropolitan life. 'Oops
there goes my ferret,' would not get you any award as
Passenger of the Year on the Underground. You handle them
from when they are a 'kit' and they get used to you and play
with you. We do not have a multiplex up here, so needs must
on the entertainment front.

Two points make me hesitate. The first: I seem to think they
are very smelly. My contact in the ferret world denied this.
'They just smell of ferret,' she said. I do not necessarily think
that is a good thing, particularly if you decide to hang it around
your neck and make it part of your ensemble. That and the
fact I do not know how the ferret would feel if we went back
to London. She might mooch round all day, missing her little
ferrety friends and moaning about the quality of the coffee
and the lack of a decent hairdresser. I am not sure I could do
that to her.

## Sunday, 4 February 2007

## A Catholic superstition

I visit my parents in Yorkshire. Cloud: it turns out my mother
has five or possibly six broken ribs. Silver lining: the police
have accepted it was an accident. There is no case against my
father, so the miscarriage of justice campaign is cancelled.

There is a window halfway up the staircase of my parents'
house. There, the glass swirls around itself in a thick and crazy
dance. You cannot see out and you cannot see in, but as a
young child when I climbed the stairs, a plaster Sacred Heart
reached out wide to me from that windowsill, his heart aflame,
ready to embrace. So familiar was he, burning for us all, that I
forgot him quite; but one day when I was total grown, I glanced
across and noticed that his heart still flared but the plastered
crimson of his cloak and the chestnut of his hair had faded
back to white. Undeterred by age, he reached out still for the
souls that climbed the stairs. Then horror, my sightless mother,
dusting, knocked him off his perch. His arm fell off, his holy
head rolled far and snap – his body broke in two. A second
suffering for this ersatz Christ. Guilty Catholic woman, tear-
streaked at the demise of her companion through fifty and more
years, gently placed his body in a box and bag-wrapped it. An
Asda shroud. Accomplice father dug a garden hole, said a quiet
prayer and buried quick her shame.

Now a new Sacred Heart stands sentry on the sill and blesses
those who slide by on their aged way up and down the staircase
rails. I do not like this newcomer to the family home. I think
his cloak too bright, his head too big; his heart too tame a flame
contains. While underneath the clay soil where tortuous rose
roots grow, the broken saviour burns on and waits for resurrection day. My mother confesses to me later: 'I think there
may be someone by the bushes too. I can't remember who.'

## Monday, 5 February 2007

### Just one of those days

I have had one of those days where you go with the flow or you go under. After a weekend with my achy-breaky mother ('Mummy, you have been away a hundred days,' my four-year-old told me when I got back), I hared off to London for meetings about work. The builders started today, but I decided that since he was home, my husband could take care of them. First warning that all would not be well was the fact that I discovered on the train that my mobile was dead; I decided that was all right because I did not have to ring anyone. Until the train shuddered to a grinding halt and it emerged that someone had stolen the overhead power lines on the track. Who would do that? What do you do with second-hand power lines? Start your own train company? Do you sidle up to a likely lad in your local boozer and go: 'Psst. Wanna buy a lot of electric cable — I mean, a lot? Like train-track lot?'

I get to my first meeting an hour late courtesy of the copper thieves. It is an important meeting. I have not met the person before. I am already at something of a disadvantage because I am late. I am at even more of a disadvantage when I realize I have been waiting in her glass-walled office, examining the books on the shelves as you do, my back to the open-plan seating area outside, with my skirt firmly tucked into my knickers. You are not telling me nobody saw that. You are not telling me people weren't emailing each other about the mad woman with her skirt in her knickers and deciding whether anyone was going to tell her or let her leave that way. I thought that happened in bad sitcoms. Well, it happens in real life too. It happened to me. How I laughed.

Because I was running so late for the next meeting, I missed my train home. That should have been it. But no. I rang my husband. The builders have discovered rotten roof joists in the arches. They may all have to be replaced (the joists rather than the builders). The builders had been on the job an hour before they made their discovery. One hour.

## Tuesday, 6 February 2007

### Love letters

When I was young and peachy, men wrote poetry for me – all of it bad. A little older, and earnest suitors would quote Dante and Marvell, at length and in letter form. I have had my share of those who missed me and wrote to tell me of their sighs. Indeed, I have done my own share of letter-sighing. But there came a time I put away the ribboned, heart-felt bundles of my youth and wed a letter writer. Married, there is little need to write your passion down. Instead you write: 'Darling, please remember to buy milk.' Who else then is there to write to me of love?

This afternoon, when I got home, fatigued and city-worn, a torn cream corner of my heaviest paper was propped against a wild dog and a soft furred cheetah which both sat on a plastic stool. 'Welchm homw mummey,' the letters tumbled across the page, hasty to escape. Later, my eldest, urgent boy hurtling in from school, threw himself at me. 'Did you like my note?' he demanded. 'They were my spellings. I might,' he pulled away slightly, 'have got one of them wrong.' 'No,' I shook my head and hugged him mother-tight, 'it was entirely perfect.'

## Wednesday, 7 February 2007

### At the window

The nights are dark here, darker yet when my husband is away. A short necklace of orange pinpricks breaks the darkness at the edge of the village across the fields, and occasionally a car's headlights will sweep down the lane, their hurrying beam broken by wintry hedges. If I crane my neck out of the study window, I can sometimes see a light from the Accountant's house along that lane. I like to see that homely light and think: 'My friend lives there.' But the brightest light around is that of the lighthouse; its white-gold beam sweeps around and out to the shushing black sea and then around again. When I have yawned enough at my desk to know that it is time for bed, I will check one last time on my sleeping and oblivious sons, pulling up feather-filled covers and kissing dangling feet. Then, shucking off the day and its clothes on the landing, I will carefully lift the iron latch to my bedroom's wooden door, catch it with my finger, then drop it quietly back in place. I pause and listen with intent to see if the baby's sweet breath has caught in protest at my breaking and entering into her night. If she slumbers on, I edge barefoot around her cot to wheedle my way through cold silk curtains, one naked shoulder and then the other. I lean my forearms on the horizontal bar of the sash window, then rest my warm head against my forearms and watch the beam slide round to me. I am wondering what I will do when we move into the village, where I will have no lighthouse to bid goodnight. I am wondering whether its beam will miss me or slide by oblivious to my absence at the window. Miss me, I think.

## Thursday, 8 February 2007

## Moving on

We are supposed to move tomorrow. My husband, however, has adopted a policy position on the move and decided we do not need to pack anything. Cardboard boxes, tea chests and plastic crates are just so last year that we have refused to use any of them. What he is going to do is drive a white transit van up to the back door and throw things in it. This does not necessarily strike me as the best idea, but my husband says it will work. I cannot face doing it on my own having gone through the upheaval of moving when we came up from London; instead, I have decided to give him the benefit of the doubt and do it his way. The plan then, for want of another word, is to manhandle the contents of the cottage out into the van on a room-by-room basis, drive it two miles down the lane to the house in the village and then unpack the contents and install them on a room-by room basis in the rented house, recreating our life exactly as it was before. Perhaps he was a museum curator in a different incarnation? In fact, he could probably submit it for the Turner Prize. He could call it something like: 'Our Life – A Mess in Two Places'. If I videoed it while he was doing it, he would probably win. An Emmy, too.

I blame myself. I think I am coming to the conclusion that what I have always regarded as a certain easy-going quality is, in reality, a deep passivity. Part of me thinks: 'You have to be joking' and wants to stand and giggle while it all goes on. But the other half of me increasingly wants to jump up and down in rage and shout: 'We move tomorrow! Move! Do you know what that means? We need to be sorting things out, putting them in piles, throwing them away. Good grief.' That is the point at which I take a deep breath. I honestly do not mind the chaos and relentlessness of it all most of the time. Just occasionally I wonder what it would be like to live a Von Trapp sort of life, before Maria arrived. I bet he could always find his car keys, for instance. I am partly feeling this way because I was told off by my London Diva the other day for being so meekly acquiescent to the chaos of our life. 'Doesn't everyone live in chaos?' I pleaded with my sister-in-every-way-but-DNA. 'No,' she told me as she bundled me efficiently along a North London canal path from her high-powered office to a pastel-coloured haven that looked like a toy shop but actually sold coffee and iced cupcakes. 'I don't live that way. Most people don't. You shouldn't.' I know she is right. I just don't know what to do about it. I do know that all my closest friends keep telling me to get a grip on my life. I can refuse to eat the cupcakes they put in front of me, I can put my fingers in my ears and hum while they talk, but deep down I know they cannot all be wrong.

### Friday, 9 February 2007

### Mothers and daughters

My husband had to start the move alone because the permanent amber alert we are on with my mother switched to red. Because of the pea-brained way we had decided to move house, the builders had to stop building and heft furniture and our belongings out of the cottage and into the van. My husband thought they were being nice; I think they decided that getting rid of us was a day well-spent. Meanwhile, I went back down to Yorkshire to see what I could do. A ghastly day cleaning up old lady poo and watching my mother being brave.

My mother is a fastidious, ever-busy little body, neatly suited and booted with hair like the Queen. She smells of Chanel

No. 5 and floral perfumes that carry jasmine notes. Not yesterday though. When I arrived, her hair was spread across the pillow in an iron-grey frizz and she was lying still and sad. Loudly, I said: 'Mum, Mum, it's me,' and I placed my hand against her cheek as I do with my own children and I bent to kiss her. 'Is it you?' she asked. She grasped my wrist and pulled me closer into her and hung from me like an eight-year-old daughter would, and cried into my neck, sobbing at the latest pain to strike. Sickness is a heartless robber, preying on the old. It carries a rubber cosh and a cold-barrelled gun that it holds smack against an old lady's wrinkles while it shouts into her face: 'I want your dignity, right now. Hand it over, you old bat.' The *Daily Mail* should run a campaign.

She told me the nurse was going to give her an anemone. I thought this unlikely. The bustling Scottish nurse arrived, not with flowers but with rubber gloves. Mother mine, teeth biting into the cotton pillow and tears falling on to my hand shrieked in silence as the nurse got on with it. Old age smells of shit and shame, not Chanel. Do not go there. Find another route into the hereafter. Old age is not the way to go. People are not nice to you. They do not bring you flowers. Instead they carry rubber gloves and make you cry and bite the pillow.

My mother is the best reason I know for living a life of decadence and debauchery. No cigarillo smoke, gin slings or mistakes between the sheets for her. Instead, a life of heroic virtue, good deeds and care – her own aged and bone-tiny mother, an early husband who coughed blood and died, arthritic sister, small pupil-children taught to bake, cancer patients, the list drones on; and me, of course. The parish council, the school governing body, the Catholic Education Board. Her reward for all that goodness? An invitation to a garden party with the Queen – too sick to attend, sorry – and an old age of broken health. Well, poo and phooey! Her goodness did not keep her well. She still got old and sick, and I will learn by her mistakes. I will inhale smoke from pink cigarettes, drink absinthe and have unrepentant sex with strangers in dark places.


## Saturday, 10 February 2007

### Marriage and mayhem

OK, the move. I am at risk of spontaneous combustion. I am at risk of the children coming to find me and discovering instead a flaming office chair and a pair of charred sheepskin slippers smelling of burnt wool and cheesy feet. What was I thinking? What was I doing agreeing to move house in such a cack-handed way? I hold myself responsible. I believed my husband when he said it would be OK. It was not OK. It is still not OK. The idea of a white transit van pulling up to the front door and loading the house into it did not work. Hah! Who said it would? Who thought it would? Ever? In a month of Sundays? I feel like I have one of those creatures inside me that gave Sigourney Weaver such hissy fits. An alien locked brooding behind my ribcage, all teeth and slaver. One that does not like my husband one teeny-tiny bit.

Apart from the blizzards of last year, today's was the worst weather I have come across since we arrived almost eighteen months ago: three degrees, with driving wind and rain that wanted to hurt you. At least my husband was here for it. At least he got wet. The only other good thing to be said in the day's favour were the three friends who came to our rescue. They included the Oyster Farmer, who arrived with a horse-box because that is how you move things in the country; the Evangelical Man, who arrived with God on his side; and the Accountant, who shook his head a lot. He said things like: 'Tell me. Why didn't you get a removal company?' I was so grateful to them I wanted to cry.

At one point, I ended up driving behind my husband, who was in the hire van. I flashed him eight times and beeped the horn continually to get him to stop because we were about to go through a flooded section of the road. He drove on – oblivious. I know you should not say these things with children in the car, you should at all times present a united front, but I might have said: 'Your father is a bloody, bloody idiot' as he sped his way through the flood, abandoning me, the three children and the low-slung car in the black as pitch darkness on the other side of the water. We were lucky: we made it through in first gear by keeping to the centre of the road. When we got home, my traitorous six-year-old ran in. 'Why didn't you stop the van, Daddy?' My son looked back at me with china-blue eyes. 'Mummy says you're a bloody, bloody idiot.' I tried to look like he made the last bit up, but I do not think my husband was convinced. Over dinner, he said: 'I think I have done really well. My arms are tired.' Usually, I am more than prepared to play the 'Yes, I think you are marvellous too, darling' card in the game of marriage. Instead, I stood up and filled the kettle.

When you get married and you stand there in an ivory satin dress with its slightly grubby train caught up in a loop that weighs down your wrist, at some point in the evening an apple-cheeked couple will totter arm-in-arm across to you. Your great-aunt, or someone who looks like she could be, will take your French-manicured hand into her little bony one. She will look up at you and say: 'We have been married 138 years, haven't we, Arthur?' Arthur, who is leaning precariously on his stick, will say: 'Coal-tar soap.' She will put her hand on his arm and she will shout into his good ear: 'A hundred and thirty-eight years, haven't we, Arthur?' and Arthur will nod emphatically and say: 'Fish-sticks.' 'My advice to you,' and she will draw you so close that you smell Parma violets on her breath, 'is never go to bed on an argument.' You look across their munchkin heads and you think: 'How wise.' When you are a wife and not a bride, you remember your great-aunt's violet-scented advice of that night and you realize she must have been senile by then.

## Monday, 12 February 2007
### Missing keys 2

I drive my six-year-old to school. I drive back to the wrong house because I had, understandably in my opinion, momentarily forgotten where I lived. I curse. I drive back to the rented house where I am now living to find my husband running up and down the street. As I open the door of the Saab, he tells me I drove off to school with the keys to the Volvo and to the hire van on top of the roof. He put them there. He has miraculously found the keys to the Volvo a mile down the road at the roundabout. He cannot find the keys to the hire van. He says he wants to cry and that he is going to have an asthma attack. We drive very slowly down the road with my head out of the passenger window looking for the electronic fob. As we crawl along the road, a friend's car passes us and we wave cheerily to the driver. I am not feeling remotely cheery, but I am mindful of my husband's reputation locally. Once, when my husband locked us out of the cottage, the driver who just passed us had to scale a ladder and vault through our bedroom window to let us in again. He must be sixty if he is a day. I am pretty sure he told people. We drive on into the village and I start going into shops to see if anyone has handed the keys in. What I really want to say is: 'My husband is an idiot. Have you seen his car keys?' What I actually say is: 'You haven't seen any car keys around, have you?' Eventually, the lady who works in the butcher's directs me to a woman down the road, who has handed them to another woman, who has handed them into the local school. I find them and say thank you.

## Tuesday, 13 February 2007

### Trolley-dolly bye-bye

The rented house looks like a shipwreck. Clothes, books, toys and bedding are strewn across each and every room while in the hallway plastic bin bags breed like something from a low-budget sci-fi movie. I keep thinking: 'Socks for school tomorrow' and realize I have no idea where they are. Then I think: 'Knife, I need a knife for the bread.' No idea either. I may send the boys to school today wearing saucepans on their feet.

Everything got much worse because my husband left to catch the train for London last night. He is away for three weeks on a work deadline. Just before he left, the children wanted a hug so he went upstairs to kiss them goodbye. This gave me the chance to pour and swallow the remains of a bottle of Chablis in the kitchen and burst into tears. I was just getting my act together when he came down again to tell me he had screwed the tops of the children's wardrobes on so they would not come down and kill them but I had to ring the TV repair man tomorrow because the TV is not working. I stopped crying at the thought of three weeks with three children and no TV. But by the time we said goodbye, I was already snuffling away again. As he headed into the night with his smart trolley-dolly suitcase on wheels, I closed the heavy wooden door behind him and went back to the kitchen to pour another glass of whatever I could find. Cooking oil, probably. I was just about holding it together when I heard the siren wail of my six-year-old from the top of the stairs. Two minutes later and my husband cracked open the door to slide in a stray children's car seat; he glanced up the staircase to find a sobbing six-year-old dressed in a robot sleepsuit with his legs wrapped round his crying mother. 'We'll be fine. Go and get your train. Hurry up or you'll miss it.' I waved him away. As the door closed heavily behind him again, my four-year-old came out of the bedroom. He knelt down and kissed me. 'I love you, Mummy,' he said, and lay next to us on his tummy as I patted his brother's back and rocked him gently back and forth. 'Shush now,' I whispered. 'Shush. We'll be fine.'

## Wednesday, February 14 2007

### This is an intergalactic emergency

I have a headache. It is hardly surprising I have a headache, because I just fell down the stairs, six of them at least. Why did I fall down the stairs? Because they were carpeted with slick, shiny wool, I was running and they were there. I was answering the door to the Yorkshire Mother and her husband, who are storing things with us before they leave for sunnier climes. I fell because it is that sort of day.

I spent all of yesterday driving around with a silver spaceman toy in the footwell of the passenger seat. Just when I thought I was safe from his cultural imperialist tendencies, he would blurt out: 'This is an intergalactic emergency' and 'I am Buzz Lightyear. I come in peace.' Between the children and their paraphernalia, it is surprising I ever feel lonely. I think the noise pollution put out by toys is worse than the acute feeling of paranoia they can engender. It is not just Buzz. Yesterday morning, I was struggling to find my way to school because I now live in a different house which means I have to drive along different roads. The problem is you drive by different fields which all look the same as the fields you used to drive by. I was running late because that is what I do, and looking for a turn-off which could have been anywhere, when my six-year-old decided to 'start up' his orange plastic steering wheel. This engine noise is the sound another car would make if it joined you on the back seat and it distracted me long enough to miss the turn-off. I have to admit I did not say: 'Oh dear, Mummy missed the turn-off.' It was definitely one up from the 'bloody, bloody' of the weekend. My six-year-old, with the infinite for-bearance of a child for his mother, turned off his wheel while I manoeuvred my way back to the turning. Thinking about it, his teacher recently told me how advanced he was verbally. I wonder how advanced he really is. I must remember to teach him that discretion is an underrated virtue.

I still haven't finished cleaning out the kitchen before the builders gut it, we still don't have a working TV in the rented house, apparently the dishwasher is faulty and last night the lights downstairs fused about twenty minutes before my newly installed Internet connection gave up the ghost. Worst of all, I forgot to buy my husband a Valentine's Day card. Actually, that was not the worst thing: I forgot to buy one and he remembered.

Did I mention my head hurts?

## Friday, 16 February 2007

### Ding dong

There are some days so bad that the only thing which could redeem them is a proposal of marriage. Today was one of them. As I hunkered down by my pyjama-clad four-year-old to start cleaning his teeth, he gazed intensely into my eyes. 'When I'm big, I want to marry you.' He paused. 'If you're still alive.'

## A ponytale

The Yorkshire Mother has packed up her house, her children, her husband, a people carrier and a white van and gone. Phut. *Disparu.* I went to say ta-ra. I sat on an old black couch in an empty room. She sat opposite me on a beaten-up armchair. She looked tired. A plastic bin bag in the corner; bits and pieces of a family life littering the floor. I kissed her cheek, hugged her goodbye and tried not to cry.

She is brave, I think, to search for happiness. A casual, civilian bravery; not that of the uniformed and heroic soldier, a gun in either hand, carrying between gleaming teeth a wounded comrade from the bloody, muddy battle-scene. I like that courage, too – who does not like a saviour? But I have particular regard for the everyday, matter-of-fact bravery of the civilian caught in accidental crossfire; the bereaved, the lonely, the mothers of the sick. My cousin has a daughter, elfin-faced with a silken ponytail which slides down her slim back. She is seven and has one missing tooth. I know it is missing because today I saw the gap and looked; the tooth was definitely not there. On a half-term too-quick visit, my Beloved Cousin flicked open her laptop and clicked the mouse to show me pictures of her daughter at three and kidney-sick. 'Look, no hair,' she said, and pointed to the JPEGed child. I remember.

I took her daughter to a village shop. Instead of a ponytail and pink feathered clip, her head was tufted bald and round, the soft hair harvested not by fairies but by chemicals. There is nothing like sporting a child with cancer in your trolley to bump you, spit-spot, to the top of the queue in a supermarket. Other shoppers smile at you and pass you tinned goods so that you do not have to lean too far, and the woman in front says:

'I'm not in a hurry. You go first,' as if you might have particular need of that extra minute or two with your trolley child. Your shopping, too, is not mother-wise but a mix of slurpy yoghurts, cheese strings and chocolate bars. The shop a child might do if you said: 'Buy what you like, darling.' I had no intention of making a child with cancer scream out loud in a supermarket aisle by saying no to Pringles. Now, my cousin's lovely daughter is out the other side of pain. For two days, she bounced around my house in screaming fun games with my sons and babe. I held her by the ponytail and thought: 'Little one, I like your hair this way.'

## Monday, 19 February 2007

### My morning so far

I am asleep in a large wooden bed, unusually a husband slumbering by my side on a 24-hour stopover. I do not see enough of this bed. I like it. I enjoy its company but somehow we have drifted apart. I have been asleep for nearly two hours. The hands of the Mickey Mouse ticking clock march on and reach their destination. It is 2.40 a.m. The silence lets out its breath and the door opens to reveal my six-year-old caught in the landing light. 'Mummy, I feel like I'm going to be . . . *bleaurgh.*'

Our rented house has carpets. I sweep the wretched boy into the bathroom, trailing sickness after us, and my husband wrenches himself from the warmth of the bed to fetch a bucket with soapy water for the carpet. My son refuses to go back to any bed but the one in my office, so he and I curl up together with an empty Tupperware box close by in case of emergencies. Best to say 'No, thank you' to biscuits when the biscuit tin is full in my house, although I am always very careful to wash it afterwards.

My poor white-faced, black-eyed child is sick at 3.15 a.m. and again at 4.20 a.m. At 5.45 a.m., his sister wakes up to be fed and I bring her into bed. She is far from happy when she has to stop at 5.55 a.m. when her brother needs the biscuit tin again. I tuck the poorly one up and take the baby downstairs for a cock's crow breakfast with my husband. At 6.55 a.m., he leaves for London. 'Bye, sweetheart,' I say, baby on my hip, waving to him cheerily as he drives away.

When my four-year-old comes down for breakfast, I pour him a china bowl of strange puffed rice shapes, add semi-skimmed milk and lie on the kitchen floor with a soft woollen jumper for a pillow. The baby comes over to sit down on my head, then crawls away again. As I lie there, slightly chilly, I debate whether curling up on the kitchen floor is a symptom of mental illness and decide no one can see me so who cares. I have to get up when the doorbell rings. A mechanic stands waiting to fix the Volvo, which has stopped working. As ever, I cannot find the keys. I say: 'Give me a minute,' and close the door. I clench my fists and beat my head with them to see if that will help me find them. It does – hanging on a hook, where I left them.

Surprisingly, I had found the china bowl without self-harming. My Beloved Cousin has organized my kitchen with startling ferocity. She talked me through her reasons for putting pots, pans and raspberry jams away. They have been placed around my borrowed cupboards and shelves with the same gimlet-eyed efficiency Wellington would use to deploy his troops in battle. Since I am the sort of general who would be hopping up and down with one foot in his shiny leather boot looking for the other one when the trumpet sounded, I have not got a clue where anything is. Last night, I ate my dinner with a spatula.

## Tuesday, 20 February 2007

### Picking up the pieces

I broke my six-year-old's favourite egg cup. This was not good. I was trying really hard at breakfast. I had scrambled some eggs for one of them, boiled an egg for another, made porridge on request, fed the baby, spread three jams (pear and raspberry, raspberry, and strawberry) in stripes on one piece of bread. I had not laid down silent on the crumb-strewn floor and gazed blankly at the ceiling and its beams. I remained upright and mobile at all times. Then I broke the egg cup. Technically, the baby broke it, but really it was me because I said to my eldest: 'She'll be fine with it, don't be silly' when she grabbed it and he wanted to take it back from her. She looked straight into my eyes to thank me for my trust in her, slowly opened her porridgy fingers and dropped it. The cup, last year's gift from the Easter Bunny, smashed leaving a yellow spotted cheetah holding nothing but disappointment. My six-year-old gulped, folded his arms together, laid them on the table and buried his head in them. I think his despair was half because of the egg cup and half because of me. I noticed for the first time how closely bitten the fingernails on his hands were. I thought: 'When did he start to bite his nails?' My four-year-old came over. He laid a consoling little hand on his brother's heaving back. 'Never mind,' he said, 'you can share my lion.'

## Thursday, 22 February 2007

### That cabaret life

Why won't children let their mothers sing? I like to sing. Admittedly, I can only remember the first line of any song.

Still, I like to sing that line and do it tunefully. But children like to keep their songbirds caged and dark. 'Don't sing,' my youngest son dictates from the table where he plays with plastic soldiers, guns moulded and ready. 'I mean it. Don't sing.' He fires a cannon and five men die in friendly fire. 'Why not?' I ask, my painted smile slipping as I stand in the spotlit darkness of my kitchen cabaret. 'Why can't Mummy sing?' I lob my question into the blackness and hear my six-year-old's voice: 'We like it quiet.' This from boys who moments before, arms spread wide and mouths a-roar, were jet-screaming round the table. The super trouper flickers and turns off.

## Friday, 23 February 2007

### Bed rest

Getting up was so difficult today I almost did not bother. If I had been given a choice or my children had shown a degree of compassion, I would be in bed yet. I finessed my sons into the sofa in front of a video in the hope of another couple of precious pillow minutes. The baby, however, is made of sterner stuff. She was awake. I had to be awake. I had brought her in to feed, but after that she was a lot keener to get on with the day than I was. I steadfastly refused to move; eventually, she clambered out of the large carved bed, clinging on to the sheet and lowering herself carefully on to the floor, where she discovered my handbag. I did a mental review of whether she might find an ecstasy tablet, prompting horrified headlines and a visit from my health visitor. I decided it was unlikely since I have never bought an ecstasy tablet. Reluctantly, I opened one eye to check she was still there and had not crawled off to fling herself down the stairs. She was standing by the bed, watching me. Next to me was a pile of money lying on the mattress – every note and coin I had loose in my bag.

I felt cheap. I do not think a fifteen-month-old baby should feel she has to bribe her mother to get out of bed.

I got lost again today. I think that getting lost is becoming a metaphor. It is happening so often, part of me must want to get lost. Maybe if I got lost enough, I would one day find myself on the fringes of London. Then I could ring and say: 'You'll never guess what. I got lost. Guess where I am. I don't think I can find my way back.' What made it worse was that my children noticed. I hate it when they notice I am lost. I suspect it diminishes their respect for me, which is probably low enough already now they pay me to get up. My six-year-old said loudly: 'Mummy, you are going the wrong way.' I denied this. 'I really think you have gone wrong, Mummy.' Of course, he was quite right. As I slewed the car round, narrowly missing a horsebox, he said: 'I was going to say something, but I won't.' I pulled back on to the hedged and narrow road. 'What were you going to say, darling?' I looked back at him through the rear-view mirror. 'I was going to say "I told you so",' he said. I could see the tiniest smile as he glanced down at his bitten nails. 'But I decided not to.'

## Saturday, 24 February 2007

### Beach boys

There are days I feel quite proud of myself for giving this a go and trying to carve out a new life for all of us. Today was not one of them. I just thought: 'God, this is such an effort' when I woke up, opened the painted wooden shutters and gazed out on to the foggy village street of stone-built houses. I hate weekends up here when I am on my own. The week is bad enough, but then at least I have help with the children from Girl Friday, who is a godsend, and there is school to give the day some structure. The weekend completely tips me over the edge of darkness; I roll down the scree, leaving pieces of myself along the way.

I decided it would be better not to be alone – when I say alone, that equals me plus three children – and I turned to my phone book. I list the mothers up here all together. There's a slightly grey trail down the page of names; the trace you would get if you regularly ran a finger down it slowly, name by name, looking for someone to call. One woman was out; one woman's husband is only at home at weekends; I rang another woman once before when I felt this teary panic and she sounded so surprised at the call I would rather not repeat the experience; two others have their own domestic difficulties; another I had seen too recently for it to be respectable to call again so soon. I called the Shepherd's Wife, although I only know her slightly. She invited me round for lunch tomorrow. I think I may have sounded desperate. I still had to get through today.

In the classic tradition of the unhappy female, I gathered the children up and went out to shop. I hate with a vengeance the supermarket in the nearest market town. My husband goes shopping there with the three children and tells me the shop assistants cannot do enough for him. They do nothing for me. They might occasionally say: 'Do you want help packing?' but I do not believe they mean it. They might say: 'Do you want cashback?' but I believe they want to ask me: 'Why did you have three children? You can't control them.'

Instead, when I am left to live alone, I prefer to make my own rounds of the butcher, the baker, the grocer, the news-agent, the chemist and the electric shop. When they know you live here and you are not a tourist, small shopkeepers do not seem to mind if you shout at your children. That can come in handy. The rented house is in a village which used to have grocer's and draper's shops, inns, a church and two chapels. The church is still there, but the shops have long since been pulled into the fishing village next to it. The main trade here used to be curing herrings, which would then be sent to market by railway, and the export of lime for agricultural fertilizer. It has a timeless feel, making its money from tourists who prefer to take a boat out to the Farne Islands than to fly to the Canaries. It has a main street with a fancy goods and hardware shop and another that sells kettles and TVs, a small supermarket, a magic shop which sells kites to tourists and one of those shops that sells everything and anything to anyone who can find it. It feels 'complete' with its second-hand book shop, undertakers, a parlour for beauty and another for ice cream. Visitors come once then come again – they walk the sands and dip in and out of shops to buy memories. They take paper-wrapped fish and chips and eat them on raked benches overlooking the pretty harbour's lobster pots and bobbing boats. As seagulls wheel and screech, they lick vinegar from their fingers and think: 'This is like the holidays I had as a child – the sort of place I'd like to live.'

After the shopping, I took the children to the beach. This is why we live here – one of the reasons anyway. 'Right,' I said, 'we're going to the beach.' My six-year-old jutted out his jaw. 'I hate the beach,' he said. I was not in the best of moods. 'I don't want to live here,' I replied, perhaps over-hastily and not what the children need to hear, but the words pushed them-selves out regardless. 'We live here so you can go to the beach. We are going to the beach. Whether you like it or not.' My son shook his head. 'I'm not going. I'm staying in the car. You go.' Forced to choose between the beach or straight home to bed without tea, he caved and chose the beach, where the fog was so dense it obscured even the castle. The boys played in the misted-out dunes, doing what they call 'adventuring', and I ploughed the sand with the buggy and a chilled baby. 'There, you see,' I told them, the wind so cold it felt like it was tearing strips from my head to hang from its beaded belt, 'isn't this nice?

## Sunday, 25 February 2007

### Let's do lunch

Today's expedition for lunch with the Shepherd, the Shepherd's Wife and their two boys – having inveigled myself some company so transparently yesterday – also involved passing a sign saying 'Horse-drawn vehicles and animals' at the second cattle grid on the track. We had already passed the 'Beware the bull' sign, which always makes me feel acutely nervous in case he is waiting round the corner with a mask and a pistol. I could see the Cheviot hills stretched out along the horizon, the beasted fields slipping away from their gorse borders. 'Where are we, Mummy?' asked my six-year-old. 'About 1956,' I told him. The three of us talked sheep and books and the Shepherd's Wife turned out to be one of these fabulous cooks who can make a Sunday lunch into a miracle on a plate. As I piled muddy children back into the muddy car parked in the muddy farmyard, meal eaten, playdate played out, she said: 'Do you know, you're the only people we've ever had to lunch who weren't our parents or my brother and his wife.' I said: 'You're kidding me?' She shook her head. As I pulled out of the farmyard and headed down the track, I thought: 'I must have sounded really desperate.'


## Tuesday, 27 February 2007

### A note to the wise

I admit I am mad at my husband for ripping me up from my city streets. I do not think I have ever been madder. I suspect London Diva and my Islington Beauty think I intend to scrawl a note, written in Cif and blood: 'Darling, I am leaving you and this place. I am taking the small children, the large notes and as many houses as I can fit into my Louis Vuitton bag. Your dinner is in the hard drive of your computer.' I know they would not blame me if I did. But all things considered – living here, the move and what-not – I rather like my husband. I think I'll keep him till we grow old and then dead together.

I remain unconvinced I am ever going to fit in, but I have decided to stop sitting around wittering about what I am missing in London and try out some Northumberland activities. Maybe it will help me understand where I am and what it is all about.

## Wednesday, 28 February 2007

### Bells on my toes

The King of the Castle introduced me to his equally tall and very beautiful partner. I liked her immediately, despite the fact she is younger, blonder and infinitely leggier than I am. She rides and has said she will take me out with her. I said: 'I don't want to fall off.' My Riding Pal replied: 'You won't fall off.' 'Have you ever fallen off?' I asked. 'All the time,' she said. People up here like their animals, usually in bulk. They tend not to have one dog, they will have two: an old one that limps and a young one that does not. They would never have one chicken, they have to have a yardful. Occasionally they will have a horse, but they are happier if they have two. Unusually, she just has one horse, but she borrowed another especially for me.

I arrived at their farm all panting expectation; it might have looked like cold-palmed terror, but it was merely the way we city types anticipate a close encounter with something that has bigger teeth than us. My hopes of a rapid mount were soon dashed. Despite the fact I estimate that my Riding Pal is twice as tall as I am, my head was too big for all four of her hats. She said to the King of the Castle in wonder: 'She doesn't fit any of the hats.' He looked at my head. I thought: 'He might be thinking my head is stuffed with brains, but I suspect he is thinking I have a really fat head on a really short body.' My Riding Pal phoned a friend. No joy – apparently, we city girls do indeed have bigger heads than country gals. Much bigger. But we don't just sit around in the country, we take action. We jumped into her 4×4 and drove to the local market town, snacking en route on the horse's Polo mints. I only had one or two in case the horse could smell them on my breath later.

I like country shops. They are much more interesting than city shops. You know what you are going to get in a city shop – it is going to be expensive, beautiful and a little predictable. They don't do predictable in the shops up here. The shop sold handbags and tops. As we climbed the stairs, I said to my Riding Pal: 'I like those big wide leather belts.' She snorted. 'They're girths,' she said. Still no idea what a girth is, but I laughed along with her and went: 'Oh right, girths.' There were also saddles. I had never been in a shop that sold saddles before, along with bridles, bits and crops. I could go on. It was also some sort of mecca for equine grooming products. A bizarre 'Hair Today' shop for the horse in your life. There was plaiting gel 'for a truly professional finish' and dark horse shampoo for the 'dark horse in your stable'. It went on like this for shelves. I kept expecting to see a horse sitting in front of a mirror getting a blow-dry while it caught up on *Grazia*.

Luckily it also sold fat-head hats, and away we sped again back to the farm. My hat was black velvet with a peak, a large padded button on the top and a cute taffeta bow on the back. Despite the fact it was padded, it gave me an excruciating headache after half an hour and, disconcertingly, it had not one but three pictures inside of a horse attempting to buck a rider. It also had a complex strapping arrangement around the back of your head and under the chin which felt like small hands were wrapped around your windpipe. I often feel like that. I am not sure I needed to buy a hat for it. The hat weighed slightly more than a plant pot, but would, I was assured, offer more protection.

My horse was short (twelve hands), but then I am short so that was fine with me. She was an Exmoor pony, a breed I was told is rarer than the Giant Panda. I have never ridden a Giant Panda so I am not sure which of them would have the advantage in a Darwinian head-to-head. I was in the saddle by the time the word 'wild' was used. 'She can be a bit nippy,' I was told. 'Great,' I thought. 'My feet are far too close to her teeth.' Once I was strapped in, instructions started flying about – sit upright, press down with your heels, the balls of your feet in the stirrups, your elbows in, the reins held 'like coffee cups' in your hands. (Latte or espresso, I wanted to know. You would hold them differently, wouldn't you? What if you are thinking 'latte' and the horse is thinking 'espresso'?) The only thing that stops the horse are the reins. There was no brake pedal. I checked.

My Riding Pal ambled on with her immaculate seat and immense Irish horse of seventeen hands – I couldn't see them, but apparently they were there somewhere. The shaggy pony and I came to a working joggle; an arrangement whereby she agreed to carry me without throwing me to the hard ground and stamping on my velvet-hatted head and I agreed to go to mass every week for the next year. I even managed to look up long enough at one point to admire the wrap-around blue-grey sea, the Farne Islands, the lighthouses and the magnificence of their castle as we trotted round the green fields. My Riding Pal is very chatty. Halfway round, she starts telling me how my shaggy pony bolted across the same field with its rider the last time she had been out. I am looking at her, thinking: 'Why are you telling me this story?' Luckily, she saved her tales of a broken arm, a broken foot, her teeth through her lip, her black eyes and various other injuries sustained from horses until we made it back to the kitchen for tea and Aga-toasted bagels. Before we got to bagels, I had to dismount.

You would think that if you had managed to get on a horse and then sit on a horse, you would be able to get off it. I think there is a fault in the design, because there appears to be nothing to hold on to while you take your feet out of the stirrups and swing one leg over to join the other. Neither do I know how you swing your leg over when you have lost the use of both knees. Only the incentive of getting off the horse persuaded me to attempt the manoeuvre. I used my hat to take away half a dozen eggs from my Riding Pal's chickens. I am not sure what else I can use it for. I am wearing it as I type. Maybe I could just wear it around and about. It might help me to blend in.

## Friday, 2 March 2007
### Smile for the camera

The album which holds my baby photographs is worn and grimy with the years – a bit like me. It is a pale and padded plastic blue with white buttons, held whole with tape that has begun to curl and a sorry silk tassel whose burlesque days are through. When you open it, joints creak and it sighs a little. The inside cover, once virgin cream, is now a rusting and unpleasant brown, as if one day I snatched it from a hearth where it was smouldering.

Many of its flattened subjects hold me tight in there and once loved me. Some still do. But others I could not keep by me: a father, two grandmothers, godmother, godfather, a curly-haired aunt and her cross-legged son. The lost blood list goes on. Then, they were mine and I clutched their fingers. Now, they are mine only in memories and an album – for as long as they smile 'Cheese' and the page is open.

I think the album sad, though it showcases a content and lace-dressed child. Perhaps the thought that these days have come and gone arrives too soon for me. On the very first page, a suited man relaxes, leaning against the rails on the windy prom at Blackpool, a cigarette between his fingers. You can only lean so long. Look again, he is sitting down on a wooden bench, my mother's leather handbag and a parcel beside him. The snaps are of my father, who should perhaps have tossed the cigarette into the cold black-and-white sea behind him. My mother tells me I was six weeks old when she left with him for three or four days in Blackpool. My brand-new father had not confessed to coughing blood, but pleaded for a seaside break. 'I didn't want to leave you,' she tells me, 'but I knew he wasn't well and so we went.'

One year and eight snap-filled pages later, the cigarette has quite gone out, the coughing stopped and there is no more suited man. Instead, another trip this time to Ireland; the camera shutter closes on a young matron in a tilted, black straw hat with her solemn fat-faced babe. My widow-weeded mother holds me for ever in her arms in front of roses, river, bridge and church. He may be gone but I am her victory over death, a triumph in pantaloons and bonnet. I think she may be sad. I'm sure she is, as she carries me around with her, a memory of him, until, in the way of things, she meets another kindly father man, marries him and smiles again.

Here is the confusion. I opened the album up because twice lately I have had the sensation as I looked at my own daughter that I was looking at myself. I never felt that with the boys. My sons are my lions, terrorsome and grand. See how they go; march and strut and shout. But the other day, as I gazed at my baby standing proud in the grass, deciding should she walk or not, I felt: 'That's me. I'm looking at myself.' Again today,

I held her in my arms at the bathroom sink, glanced up at the mirror and thought again: 'That baby in my arms. That's me.' So I dug out this relic of the past to see if my baby-self had escaped her black sugar-paper prison. But no, she was still there, safe in her mother's arms.


## Saturday, 3 March 2007

### Conjugals

So you wake up and you stretch out an arm and find a man in your bed. Your first thought as you wrap yourself around his warmth: 'Fabulous, there's a man in my bed.' His hand slides down your smooth and naked thigh and he murmurs something you cannot quite make out. Your second thought, and it follows light-speed quick, bearing in mind the room is black dark and you have only just made it to the surface of the day: 'I can have a lie-in.' You remove his fond hand as the baby starts to mew along the corridor. 'Darling,' you tenderly whisper into his ear, 'you're on.'


## Monday, 5 March 2007

### 'Is it . . . umm?'

I have noticed a real difference having full-time help, but the problem is that any free time is immediately mopped up by the builders. Maybe I should give up on work, look after my own children and get a nanny for the builders. Site meeting with the architect and one of the builders today. There is suspiciously less house than there was. I was reconciled to the loss of the kitchen wall, but there are walls missing all over now. It is as if someone is rubbing out bits of my life. The meeting went quite well, apart from the fact Number 1 needs to be entirely replastered because of the state of the existing plasterwork. 'Is it in the spec?' I asked hopefully. No, it's not in the spec, so that is an add-on cost. At least we did not have to get the roof joists replaced, only patched and sprayed. I spotted some cracks in the plasterwork upstairs. It looked as if the wall was thinking about leaning backwards to get a better view of the sea. The builder slapped a hard-skinned, dusty hand against its fragile plaster skin. 'We'll get a rubber mallet and we'll make sure the wall's quite sound before we do the replastering.' He slapped it again – brutish and professional. I did not find that as reassuring as he expected; I could tell the wall felt the same way.

It is the unpredictability of it all that I find mildly disconcerting, as if you had arrived at the ticket office of a railway station and said: 'A single to . . . well, wherever.' The downstairs concrete floor is uneven and I would like it to be warmer. There is a solution: polystyrene, chipboard and oak flooring. 'Is it in the spec?' Funny you should ask – no. We were presented with a bill for the first four weeks of work. It could have been worse. I still like my builders and the envelope could have had my name on it rather than my husband's. Why would they put his name on and not mine, I wondered. The architect handed it to me; I looked at it and thought: 'What the hell, it's not addressed to me.' I smiled cheerfully at my husband and passed it along.

## Thursday, 8 March 2007

### Daddy dearest

When my worn-down husband comes back from the city's fray, I think we struggle to adjust – all five of us. Men come home from war and business breakfasts and think their aproned, lipsticked wives should ticker-tape their return, break out the brass-band vinyl records and shout: 'Huzzah! Huzzah! The hero has returned. Huzzah for him!' Last time my husband came back, my four-year-old pointed out: 'The baby is looking at Daddy like he's just some old bloke.' This time, at the railway station, as he hoisted her into his arms, she looked as if to say: 'I know the face. I just can't place the name.'

Today, he took my chair at the dining table and I said: 'You're in my chair' and he said: 'No, I sit here.' 'No,' I replied, annoyed, saying it slowly so he could understand, 'you have not been here. Remember. I sit there. If I sit somewhere else, I can't feed the baby.' He moved, but he still hogs the phone for work and I have to wait to make a call, eats herrings in the study, assumes he will drive and I will sit beside him. When I do go out alone, the car keys are not where I left them, the jangling keys fewer and quieter than they were. 'Where are the other keys?' I ask. 'I took them off. The bunch is too big for my pocket.' Now, when I should cheer, I growl at his shadow. Family is a subtle, complex thing, petalled with strong emotions, hopes and history. I hear my six-year-old rage on the stairs when checked by his papa: 'I don't want him here,' and sympathize. Yet that same night, I see his father kiss a torn finger to better mend the tender spot and think: 'He's home. That's good.'

### Friday, 9 March 2007

#### A table monarch

'When I'm king,' said my four-year-old tonight, fork in hand, pasta sauce on face, 'everyone will wear pants on their head. Apart from Granny. I love Granny.'

## Sunday, 11 March 2007

### Unrepentant sex

I am a strong believer in any number of things: dark chocolate cannot make you fat; if you can make someone feel better about themselves, you should; it is a bad idea to teach children to think for themselves; and you should be somebody's 'gate-bitch' at least once in your life. That's what I was yesterday – a 'gate-bitch'. At least, that is how my driver described me when I joined him as a pillion passenger on his quad bike. My job, should I choose to accept it: open and shut gates while following the hunt.

I had thought about going hunting on a horse. Difficult since I do not ride, but I do love the outfits – so very Westwood. I thought about buying the outfit, going along and pretending I had forgotten my horse. I could still do some preening, meet new people and then go: 'Damn. You'll never guess what I've done. I've only left the horse behind. Never mind – you chaps go on without me.' I thought, however, there was an outside chance someone might see through me.

Instead, my Riding Pal suggested I followed the hunt on a quad bike with a friend of hers. I met her for coffee in a hotel by the castle. She warned me it would be cold on the back of a bike. She said: 'Put on as many layers as you can. Then put on another one.' 'Should I wear my riding hat?' I asked. 'Only if you want people to laugh at you,' she said. My outfit was rubbish – I wore one pair of silk thermals (long johns and vest), one woollen pair (similar), one extra thermal vest, one woollen jumper, one woollen shirt, one pair of woolly tights, one pair of corduroy trousers, one cream jerkin, one waterproof coat, one thermal hat with earmuffs, two pairs of gloves, two pairs of socks and an enormous pair of walking boots for my sock-blown feet. I also had in my pocket, in the event of an

Arctic winter sweeping in, a black balaclava. I was reluctant to wear the balaclava in case the hunt thought I was a 'sab' and mowed me down 'accidentally'. I also thought I might look like I had got lost on my way to rob a rural post office. But I hate being cold, so I took it along.

Sometimes the quad bikes are up among the horse riders; more often they hold back and watch from a distance. Quad-biking is basically as close as you are ever going to get to having sex with someone without taking your clothes off. I did not know my driver before clambering on to his machine. I then spent six hours slapped against his back yelping 'Ooh' every time we went over a bump. We went over a lot of bumps. I said to him as we set off: 'Do I hold on to you?' He never really replied. He could have said: 'Only if you want to stay on.'

The bikes are tremendously fat and wide with enormous tyres. Half 500cc Honda motorbike and half armchair. Farmers buy them and tell their accountants they need them to check on the sheep. They need them to get from one drink to the next. Who would not want to go quad-biking? It is like *Mad Max* in tweeds. You are totally off-road, driving at between ten and forty miles per hour through a blissful northern hillscape, ripping past yellowing gorse bushes and cutting through wooded bridleways behind beautiful women astride muddy-legged horses. Daffodils are green-budding in the lee of the jagged hawthorn hedge, and, scenting the hounds, a deer streaks out of a coppice and across the field. Better than any of this, another cherry brandy and whisky is just minutes away.

You obviously do not want to drink too much cherry brandy and whisky when you are on the quad bike. Sometimes you have cointreau and whisky instead. Sometimes you say: 'What the hell. I'm worth it,' and have cherry brandy, whisky and cointreau. This is a good thing, because if you drink enough you cannot focus on the mud-splattered instructions fixed to the bike that say: 'Never ride after drinking alcohol or using drugs.' That instruction is part of a long list. It comes under: 'Never carry a passenger since it will affect balance and steering and may cause you to lose control' and ahead of: 'Always wear a helmet, eye-protection and protective gear'. You are too drunk on cherry brandy to care by the time you make out the words: 'Loss of control can result in severe injury or death.'

## Tuesday, 13 March 2007

### Holiday blues

I have gone away and left everyone behind. It is just me for a week, and I am guilt-wracked and tense about the whole idea of a holiday on my own. Not so guilty that I did not get on the plane to Los Angeles. It has been such a long time since it was just me that I do not know if I can do it any more. What if I am really bad company?

I left my husband a note:

Be patient with the children.

Be more patient than I am with the children.

Remember the six-year-old likes peas, hates beans.

Remember the four-year-old hates peas, likes beans.

Both eat raw carrots but hate boiled carrots.

Don't try to make them eat boiled carrots.

Remember the six-year-old needs a Comic Relief red nose for school on Friday.

If the six-year-old has a red nose, the four-year-old will want one.

Best get the baby one so she doesn't feel left out.

Remember to ring my mother at least once while I am away.

Remember to hear the baby if she cries at night.

Remember the binmen come on Thursdays.

Remember you love me.

Back soon.

## Wednesday, 21 March 2007

### 'Welcome home, Mummy'

Well, I'm back. Mummy's home and did I mention the six-year-old is getting bullied at school? 'Crisis? What crisis?' I want to gnash my teeth in rage and push someone smaller than me over. I was thousands of miles away and my husband revealed the six-year-old had told him he likes school, he loves his teacher but that 'sometimes the other children aren't nice to me.' He is heartbreakingly reasonable about it: 'Some people aren't nice to other people. That's just how it is.' Cor blimey. Maybe the world is like that but you do not want your six-year-old aware of that fact.

I had already remarked on the number of accidents he had been involved in at school. The head teacher wondered if he had something wrong with his ears, or maybe his eyesight. He does not fall over at home; apparently he is like a young Norman Wisdom at school. During his time there, he has fallen over playing horse (a massive lump on his forehead), been hit with the rounders bat, and walked into a cupboard (because, a note informed us, my son 'forgot it was there'); he has also hit his head during a tug of war. Oh, and not forgetting the broom in the eye. If these injuries had happened at home, the social workers would have us on a list by now.

Accidents are unfortunate but they happen. I am infinitely more concerned by reports of physical aggression and that my son is feeling socially isolated. Now I know why he is biting his nails. One youngster told him: 'I wish you weren't at school any more.' He tells me that at break: 'Sometimes I don't play. Sometimes I just walk around the playground and sometimes I sit on the bench.' This is your cue as a parent to drop your head on to the wooden kitchen table and groan loudly. I am trying very hard to be as reasonable as my six-year-old about it. On Thursday, he was swung round and hit his chin on a wall. (On the upside, at least he was playing with someone. Fair enough: another accident.) But on Friday, he was kicked hard enough for my boy to fall to the floor, hitting his head and prompting another trip to hospital. Monday, he had a day off for good behaviour, then on Tuesday he was pushed over in the playground. Today, he was bitten on the cheek and a door repeatedly kicked in his face as he tried to get back into school from the playground. I believe, taken together, this amounts to bullying.

We now have a little collection of notes from the school. Today's note read that one boy 'hurt' my son's cheek and 'apologized' for it. That's all right then. Friday's note bears little relation to what my son says happened. It says he 'overbalanced on his chair' and 'fell, bumping his head slightly'. He says he was standing beside a different schoolmate when he was kicked and fell to the floor. This was at 10.30 a.m. The schoolmate, along with yet another child, went on to berate my son at lunchtime for taking the last morsel of something when he was queuing for his lunch. The berating went unwitnessed by staff, but afterwards my son refused to join in normal school activities. All this in the last week.

Not that my son is blameless. Leaving aside the occasional

klutz-like walk behind a bat or hapless push-me, pull-you with a skipping rope, he has a nasty habit of intervening in the world around him. He admits he was bitten after telling the boy not to swing on a fence in case he hurt himself. He says he got pushed over trying to help a younger child get her skipping rope, which other girls were standing on, while on Friday, he told me that he was only kicked over after that boy told him his work was scribbly and my son kicked his chair. Fair dos – he would perhaps have done better to kick the chair and run away.

In his former East End primary school, classes were brim full. This is a tiny village church school with a church spire visible across grassy fields where sheep wander, and up to now we have been very happy with everything about the school. Perhaps this is my fault – I have always taught my son to take responsibility for his own actions and that he has a duty of care to his little brother and baby sister and to look out for younger children. Big mistake. His father wants him to slide into playground oblivion. Stop telling other children what to do, for a start. But I do not want the sort of boy who turns into an adult who crosses the road when a teenage gang picks on a young mother waiting with her buggy at a bus stop. I want Henry Fonda in *12 Angry Men*. I wonder if Henry Fonda got bullied at school. How to survive at school? They should give lessons in it. How to teach your child to survive at school? They should give lessons in that, too.

## Thursday, 22 March 2007

### The Jungle Book

If I cry, do I look like a victim? Probably. Do I care about looking like a victim? Probably not. I am old and, for that matter, mean enough not to care how I look. I certainly wanted to cry this morning when the Evangelical Man, who was in school last week, said he had noticed that my son was unusually quiet and anonymous in class. He described him as 'a different boy'. Even the head teacher described my son's face, normally responsive, as 'set' in the last recent while. Sheesh! This afternoon I went up to school to see for myself what was going on. I was informed that the child who had bitten him yesterday, managed today to 'accidentally' sit on my son's head. The boy apologized – as you do when you accidentally sit on someone's head.

I am assured the school is taking our concerns seriously. The committed and professional teachers seem as concerned as I am by my son's unhappiness. There have been conversations and meetings; next week we go back for an official update with the head, who is a woman in whom I have every confidence. You trust teachers with your children's lives, quite literally. I have no idea what happens when you do not trust the teaching staff. Panic horribly and home-educate? God. The thought of home schooling brings me out in shingles. My children would get bullied then, by me.

In the meantime, like nice middle-class parents, we are checking with a nice middle-class doctor in case there are 'spatial awareness' problems with our son. I am not quite sure how spatially aware you have to be to avoid having your head sat on. In any event, I have issued my son with the first few pages of his jungle survival guide: 'Do not sit next to him. Do not stand near him, talk to him, play with him, have anything to do with him. Do not pull a tiger's tail.' He looked at me, puzzlement clouding his blue eyes. 'What tiger?'

## Friday, 23 March 2007

### Blog off

The blog has been good for me, giving me a professional and personal focus. I have wondered whether anyone who knows me up here is reading it. I cannot know if it has deterred some people from getting to know me better – possibly. I imagine others may feel they know me better than they actually do. In any event, it is not a secret diary, locked up with a tiny key, click, turn, in a gilt clasp; saying what you think, out loud in cyberspace, can get you into trouble. They *are* reading it. I blogged what has gone on at school and to say the atmosphere is chilly would be putting in mildly. No one said a word to me this morning when I took my six-year-old into school. Nothing. Not a 'Good Morning' or a 'How are you?' or a smile. I can understand it and I am trying not to care but my six-year-old did not want to go in and they cannot think that is normal behaviour. He clung to me and buried his face in my hip. His teacher had to peel him off me as if he were a long boy-shaped strip of skin. It almost made me bleed.

## Saturday, 24 March 2007

### Oyster, oyster

It is not often you get to see a farmer with his oysters. Man and shellfish in perfect harmony. We drove out over grassy pastures to an isolated stretch of coast opposite Holy Island. It is a bleak and beautiful shore where the oysters grow, a strangely disorienting no man's land between the North Sea and the sandy beach. The island beyond; the sea, flat in the mid distance, and grassy dunes behind you. You have no choice but to crunch through thousands of barnacled, blue mussel shells to reach their oyster brothers. Best not to look back when you walk on what was the seabed – the post-traumatic stress could kill you. You have to time it perfectly in order to plunder land which belongs to the sea and is claimed back again so quickly. When the tide slides out, it reveals trestle tables crouched low and iron in the sand. Bags made of strong plastic mesh lie hooked to the tables so that their contents are not snatched back by grasping waves. There is a spot on the river tour of the Thames where a lip-licking guide will show you where offending unfortunates were chained to rusty iron rings to drown when the tide ran in to the capital. Somehow the oystered bags reminded me of that. Presumably they are happier about their situation than yesteryear's river victims.

These are Pacific oysters rather than natives. What crime do you have to be guilty of in a previous life to come back as a Pacific oyster living in the North Sea? When my farmer friend told me his oysters were hermaphrodites, I was not quite sure what to say. It seemed like too much information too soon. Particularly when they were right there in front of us, listening. It is a far cry from a seafood platter in a London restaurant, and a strangely timeless way to harvest food. It is believed that monks who lived on Holy Island harvested oysters as long ago as the fourteenth century. This most recent foray into oyster farming was begun in 1989 by my friend's father.

Seaweed festoons the oyster bags, which are unclipped and then spilled out into a box to be sorted and sized. Tiny green crabs dash for cover between the gnarled and calcified shells, all covered in sandy mud and smelling of the sea – of nothingness and salt. Oysters as small as a thumbnail are 'seeded' in the bags and grow for three or four years before they are big enough to be promoted to crushed ice and certain death. If they are too small for gastric tastes, they are returned to their trestle to await another Judgement Day.

When the waters began to lap around my feet, I looked up

from my work and calculated the distance across the pulling sands and crisp shells to the car. I asked myself whether I would make it and wondered what would happen if I did not. As I came back, bouncing in the open back of the 4×4 with the other oyster harvesters, we passed the patch of beach where naturists frolic. I cannot believe there are that many naturists in Northumberland. They must be a hardy lot – maybe I should try that next as part of my quest to feel more at home? Maybe not. I might meet someone. The Oyster Farmer happened upon a couple of naturists as he was driving out to his oyster beds. He knew they had to be local: the man covered his paraphenalia and the woman her face.

## Sunday, 25 March 2007

### In at the deep end

Another children's birthday party in the soft play centre. I know exactly how Scarlett O'Hara felt when Rhett dumped her on Melanie's doorstep. I am a scandal. I have made a fuss. The mothers smiled and said hello, but no one mentioned it. No one seems to know what to say to me. Do they think I am an over-protective mother, a middle-class London hysteric? I am probably both of those things, but that does not mean I can step back and leave a small boy to his tears. I cannot say I entirely understand what has shifted in the social dynamic of the school, but I know that my six-year-old has gone from loving school to daytime dread and night-time terrors. The boys rocketed off to play. I plastered a beatific smile on my face and let the toddling baby finger-walk me to where she wanted to go – the toddlers' ball pool. I climbed in to sit with her in a balled-up sea of pearly white and plastic green and blue; I was in no hurry to climb out from behind the netting on to dry land again.

## Monday, 26 March 2007

### My breasts develop a mind of their own

Bizarrely my breasts have started breastfeeding again. They seem to have decided this without me. I am wondering whether it is because I am feeling particularly protective of the six-year-old or because they know there is a war on. My breasts are entirely out of luck if they think I intend to start suckling the six-year-old again. I thought I had finished with the whole shebang, having been heartless enough to stop so that I could get on a plane on my own and leave them all behind. That was a seriously bad mother thing to do, but I figured that the baby, who was sixteen months old, had had a good innings on the breast front. The nocturnal feeding finished some time ago and I was down to just morning and bedtime anyway, I explained to her, suitcase by the door. 'You won't even know they've gone', I said. 'They'll write, OK?' Despite the fact I have not fed the baby for ten days, they have flipped back into operational mode. I am rather impressed at their determination to maintain functionality. It was really quite a Stalinist mother-of-the-nation thing for them to do. They appear to have a mind of their own. I am wondering whether they will want to take charge of the television remote control of an evening.

I am a big fan of breastfeeding. I am about as far as you can get from statuesque, and if I had not breastfed my babies, I would never have known the charm of life as a woman with big breasts – and it means you can eat more. Apparently it is quite good for the babies, too. The Yorkshire Mother told me she ended up with two differently sized breasts courtesy of breastfeeding. She used to let her babies do most of their feeding from one particular breast. She used her free arm to make tea, hoover and fry sausages. She told me this, and I laughed at her and her lopsided breasts. Since I am profoundly jet-lagged and had little else to do last night with a sleeping husband by my side, I decided to see whether breastfeeding has had a similar effect on me. I did this very carefully – firstly, because I think you should be scrupulous in matters scientific and secondly, I did not want my husband asking me what on earth I was doing, or worse, whether he could help. With the right hand, I took the appropriate handfuls and then cross-checked my findings with the left hand. I scooped and weighed thoughtfully. Do you know, I think they *are* different. How about that! You do not get told that in the glossy little breast-is-best leaflet you carry away from the maternity ward – that your breasts are going to be different sizes from here on in and may want to watch *Coronation Street* on a Monday.

## Tuesday, 27 March 2007

### Bud stop

I started learning German yesterday, as you do when you go to bed between two and three in the morning every day and are so busy you think your head might drop off. A couple of months ago, it seemed like a really good idea. One of my closest friends just moved from Edinburgh to Germany at the behest of her husband, and I thought: 'I must learn German.' Another mother from school agreed to teach me. Sitting at her kitchen table, I learned: '*Guten Tag*', the word for tour operator ('*die Reiseleiterin*') and how to say '*Mein Name ist Hannelore Herzog*' – of course my name is not Hannelore Herzog, but it might come in handy. Perhaps I will call myself Hannelore when I visit my friends. I had the lesson and walked back through brilliant morning sunshine to the house. I thought to myself: 'How I feel right this minute is probably uncomfortably close to insanity.' When I got back, my husband asked quizzically: 'Why are you learning German? You know there's no time for self-improvement.' I growled at him, in German.

Later, both my husband and I went up to school to discuss strategies. The meeting went well on a number of fronts, not least the fact that I managed not to cry during it. Close-run thing at one point, but just scraped through. I do not think a parent is ever at their strongest in a staffroom, even with a china cup of tea in their hands. Part of you is thinking: 'Should I be here?' and 'Now I'm for it.' I wonder whether teachers ever feel that way. The teachers do not want to see an isolated child stalk their corridors and haunt their playground. The head teacher is determined to stop the hurt. Among various proposals: increased support in the classroom and supervision at breaktime; playground buddies and a friendship bench were also mentioned. I love the idea of a friendship bench. An honest place where you admit a primitive need. A bench on which to sit while you wait for someone to cross the painted asphalt and take your hand with its bitten-down fingernails in their warm and grubby one. Someone who will say those magic words: 'Come play.'

## Wednesday, 28 March 2007

### Playing house

I like and trust my builders. They are conscientious and want to solve problems that come up. They are helpful, intelligent and reliable. They would be good to have as brothers-in-law. One of them built his own beautiful house even further north than we are so he looks at the issue of costs from both sides – the making-a-living side and the oh-my-God-you-have-to-be-kidding side. I asked him for a list of costs for all those jobs we want doing which are not in the spec. I do wish I hadn't. But more importantly than the costs, we are struggling to bring it all together; men are sweating out their days to brick-build our future and I can see it all slipping away. Can you have a dream house and an unhappy child living in it? I do not think so. We had another successful meeting at school this week; we figured our way through to strategies that will protect my six-year-old and get him past his feelings of isolation. The only problem is my son does not yet know that his problems are over, that happy days are here again. He did not want to go to school again today, clung to me in the corridor, burrowing into me. I had to sit down on a chair or fall over. He climbed into my lap and flung his arms round me, his face in my neck.

## Thursday, 29 March 2007

### More pants

'When I am king,' my four-year-old started up again. His brother interrupted: 'You can't be king. You have to be born into a king's family to be king.' The four-year-old looked momentarily disappointed. He thought for a moment or two. 'When I am a policeman, everyone will wear pants on their head.'

## Sunday, 1 April 2007

### Running on empty 5

I think it would be entirely unreasonable to divorce your husband because he let the car run out of petrol. I think you have more of a case the fifth time it happens. That is since we moved here.

My therapist wanted to look for the meaning behind everything. That is what they do, after all. They are probably the most optimistic people in the whole world, thinking they can find a meaning to life. I was never quite sure where he was from as you were not supposed to ask questions. Well, you could ask a question, but he wouldn't answer it. I think, perhaps, he was from the Netherlands. Consequently, whenever I find myself veering off into armchair psychology, I do it in a Dutch accent. Why does my husband persist in letting the car run out of petrol? Make that: 'Vy doss he doo eit?' Doss (etc.) he want to punish me? Rescue me? Prove how much I need him? Does he want me to stay in one place? Is he clipping my wings because he thinks I might fly away? And what am I doing by trusting him with this particular job when he has consistently failed to complete it to my satisfaction, or, indeed, the satisfaction of the car? Do I welcome the opportunity to be angry with him? Do I want to be stranded and rescued like some saddo fairytale princess? More simply, are we both idiots?

Is it that complicated to fill a car with petrol? You point the nozzle in the right place and stuff comes out the end. It is a boy's job. If he is here, I expect him to do it. If he is not here, I fill the car with petrol. I drive it up to the pump, point it, fire it and pay for it. What I do not do is run out of petrol. (Unless, that is, my husband was supposed to fill the car before he cleared off to his London office and just did not bother. Then, I do occasionally run out of petrol. But which is worse: to trust him or to give up on trusting him? Running out of petrol is rapidly becoming one of my hobbies. I wonder how you say that in German?)

Friday. Again. On the school run, the last day of term. I was on my way to pick up the six-year-old; the Dixie Chicks were on, loud, when the Saab shuddered. I could not believe it was going to happen again. I drew in closer to the hedge, managed to roll back off the narrow country road into the nearest opening and laid my head on my arms on the steering wheel. If someone were to paint me at this juncture in my life, that is how they would ask me to sit: my face hidden, my head resting heavy, seeking sanctuary in the cross of my arms. If the painting had a soundtrack and you could press a red button to listen to it, it would not be the Dixie Chicks; it would be a low, long moan.

I tried to ring him. Naturally my mobile was flat. I do not know why I carry it really. An old lady looked out of her house to see me stumbling around, kicking clods and with my hands in my hair. She let me use her phone. Girl Friday answered. I said: 'I have run out of petrol.' She said: 'Again?' While I was waiting for my husband by the side of the road, another mother on the school run drove by; she smiled and gave me a nice friendly wave. I gave her an equally friendly wave back and thought: 'What do you think I am doing by the side of the road, I wonder?' I climbed back into the car to wait, ramped up the music and closed my eyes. This is how my fellow mother found me five minutes later when she drove back, having decided as she wended her merry way onwards to school that I probably should not have been by the side of the road looking like I wanted to kill someone. It was very kind of her to return. Not everybody would have done. I think to myself that even if running out of petrol is not in itself a good thing, it does restore your faith in human nature the way people go out of their way to help you recover from your idiocy. Northumberland appears to be full of Good Samaritans. I was, however, quite keen for her to leave before my husband turned up in the other car so I could shout at him very loudly.

But that was Friday. Another day entirely. Today, I woke up and my husband said: 'Happy anniversary, darling. Nineteen years ago, we kissed for the first time.' It was 1 April then, too.

## Wednesday, 4 April 2007

### Blonde bombshell

I was reading the boys a bedtime story and my six-year-old starts combing through my hair with his fingers. It reminds me that I haven't checked for nits for a while and I really should. Check the children that is, not me. He says: 'Mummy, you have blonde bits in your hair like I do.' I think this unlikely. I am the dullest and most resolute of brunettes. He pulls my hair closer to his eyes as if he was thinking of buying it. 'A sort of grey blonde.' I know my hair is now threaded with grey. I just pretend not to.

There is an advantage in having children late in life, aside from an impressive number of City Breaks in your thirties; people presume you are younger than you are. I have a baby. That means I could be anything between a clueless thirteen and an ambitious forty-sevenish.(Older, if I was desperate or deluded.) Of course, I do not have spots and I do have grey hair, apparent even to juveniles. That rules me out as a teenage mother then.

According to a photo that my LA pal sent me this week, when I smile I also have score marks down from my eyes and stretching diagonally across my cheeks, out to my ears. I was not impressed. Who sends their friend a photo of herself looking like her granny? I had noticed the lines criss-crossing my face when I got up in the morning, but I hoped they shook themselves out after a few hours. They do not shake themselves out. I can no longer fool myself. Nobody in their right minds would think I was in my twenties. I am clinging on to the semblance of thirty-something looks and rapidly losing my grip. I said to my husband: 'You have had the best years of my life; you have eaten up my prime.' He said: 'They were the best? You're kidding me.' The last time I went to London, the only men to eye me up were in their sixties. When did that happen? When did I turn into eye-candy for grandads? I am old. My children have started to notice. That is how old I am.

## Thursday, 5 April 2007

### Missing keys 3

Do you know how I know there is a God? It is not because a dozen earnest young people with backpacks carrying a large wooden cross walked by my window this morning. I wondered if it was a sign I was about to have a bad day. I did.

The reason I know there is a God is because I have lost the car keys. Usually my husband loses the car keys. And after everything I said about him persistently letting the car run out of petrol. All I spend when that happens is time and an impressive amount of bad language. Replacing the car keys is going to cost more than £1,200. (I should actually say 'car key', because obviously we do not have a spare. Why would we have a spare? It is not like we are ever going to lose it.) It is going to cost this huge amount of money because you have to reprogram the car's 'brain' and send away for a new key. Who knew the car had a brain? I find the fact that the car has a brain almost as worrying as the fact mine is missing along with the car key. I would so love to blame the children. But I know it is my fault. I keep putting things down and completely forgetting where they are. I have now searched the house six times to no avail. I lost them yesterday morning and thought I might find them before my husband got back from London late last night. No such luck. What is worse is the fact that he is turning the house inside out and not a word of blame has escaped his lips.

## Saturday, 7 April 2007

### Small mercies

Have realized this morning that the boot of the still-locked Saab contains the baby's buggy, my wellington boots and all the CDs, which put me in a good mood. It also contains three sets of white rabbit ears attached to plastic headbands (face paints included), two bags of golden wrapped chocolate chicks, two bags of rainbow-wrapped chocolate eggs and three little furry toy rabbits. That is to say, the car has eaten Easter.

I suppose it could be worse. If I had realized any later, tomorrow morning would have been eggless and I would have been forced to tell the children the Easter Bunny had died in the night.

## Monday, 9 April 2007

### 'Tony, Tony, turn around'

Do you know how I really know there is a God? My mother found the car keys this evening. Hurray! Six days they were missing. I went through the house, garden and gutter inch by inch. We rang the police and asked in the nearest pub to see if anyone had handed them in. I ransacked my sons' drawers, wardrobes and under-bed, darksome places as if my boys were teenagers and I was looking for cannabis. We were visited by the Perfect Mother, her Hectic Husband and their three teenagers; I put a £50 bounty on the car keys and set the adolescents loose. Still nothing. I offered my own children a £5 bounty. Zip. Nada. My mother prayed to St Anthony, the Catholic saint you pray to when you lose things. I prayed to St Anthony. My eighty-two-year-old aunt living in Cheshire lit three candles on successive days to St Anthony. My mother gets put in charge of the baby and starts amusing her by going through a toy box, and bingo. The baby had presumably filched them and then staggered over to one of her crates of toys and dropped them in it with all the other good stuff. I wouldn't mind. but I had been through the boys' toys in case they had done the same thing. It turned out my boys were innocent of any car-key crime, my husband is a man of infinite patience and I still need my mother. Aside from the fact it was my blind mother who found the keys – which in itself is deeply cool – I rescued the bunny ears and face paints from the boot. That is how we had tea – with whiskers. It crossed my mind, while I was painting rabbit noses over freckles, that I could say a prayer and ask St Anthony where my London life went.

## Friday, 13 April 2007

### A kitchen-sink drama

My husband is attempting to sew me into the North-East in a number of intricate ways. One of which is the creation of a 'dream kitchen'. He has a problem. I have never dreamed of a kitchen. In fact, I am so very fed up with the whole process of designing and installing a new kitchen, I am tempted to create a house that does not have one, apparently quite a fashionable thing to do now. My husband had an eccentric colleague who moved into a flat and immediately had the kitchen taken out. He did not need a kitchen because he never cooked; he always ate out. Eventually the owners of the restaurant where he ate every day asked him for a loan. He refused. Then felt he could not go back to eat there again. I suspect they asked him for a loan knowing that would happen. You can have a good customer and you can have a stalker.

Despite the need to feed three small children, I am tempted to follow this colleague's lunatic example. Part of the problem in the creation of this fabulous kitchen is that I am mean, mean, mean. I thoroughly object to the amount of money a new kitchen costs. You could buy a house in some towns with the money some people spend on a kitchen. £30,000 is not unusual. £30,000. Since I have no intention of spending that much money, we have not gone to one of those companies with 'bespoke kitchen designers' who send you a CD–ROM with whizz-bang drawers that slide in and out of virtual reality. Instead, we had two nice men out from the local trading estates. One of whom had a clipboard.

Those glossy magazines you buy for ideas do not help. They have women in them who say things like: 'I've never had anywhere to store my trays, but now, not only do I have handmade trays to match the cabinets, but they slot into a special place in the island.' I do not have a tray. Let alone one which has its own home.

These women with their double-page-spread kitchens make me feel inadequate. They all have at least one and a half sinks, ideally two, even two and a half. One sink to wash up in and another to wash vegetables in. Is that necessary? Do they get confused when it comes to washing vegetables? If they are at a sink with a vegetable in their hand and a bottle of Fairy Liquid close by, do they forget themselves and bubble up the broccoli? I thought women had shucked off the shackles of the kitchen sink. Not so. In these post-feminist times, our shackles come in the shape of double Belfasts, a granite carved drainer and an over-priced mixer tap.

I do not want a 'knobs on' kitchen. Well, I do, but only so I can open the doors. I do not need anything fancy. I want it to work. I want it to be easy to clean. Not that I want to clean it, you understand. My husband has already bought an Aga – a cooker so expensive, it promises to do your ironing. He has begun to leaf through those fancy kitchen magazines and look unhealthily interested in the big fridges. He says things like:

'The kitchen is the heart of the home.' I say things like: 'I'm the heart of the home.' And I cost less.


## Monday, 16 April 2007

### Coffee and a slice of day

This is my day:

3.30 a.m. Six-year-old wakes up screaming with nightmares.

3.31 a.m. Go to him.

3.52 a.m. Return to own bed after getting him back to sleep.

6.15 a.m. Husband kisses me tenderly to the sound of bird-song. 'Bye then,' he whispers. I hear the door close behind him.

6.20 a.m. Boys wake up.

6.22 a.m. Baby wakes up.

6.23 a.m. Lie there wondering how much harm could come to the baby if I leave her to the tender mercies of her brothers for the next twenty mins.

6.25 a.m. Hear loud baby-wail.

6.26 a.m. Get up. Extremely reluctantly.

6.28 a.m. Go to bathroom. Remember that toilet in rented house is broken and has been broken for three days. Only flushable with large bucket of cold water. Husband away for next four days. My job to sort out.

6.31 a.m. to 6.52 a.m. Change baby. Get dressed. Look in mirror. Think: 'Bloody hell.' Go downstairs. Find Rice Krispies all over the kitchen floor after boys went exploring in new packet to find non-existent toy. Curse Kellogg's. Explain adventuring in the cereal packet is a dangerous thing to do.

6.53 a.m. Breakfast. Remember that gas cylinders for cooker ran out last night. Abandon plans for bacon. Recommend toy-free cereal and toast.

7.45 a.m. Upstairs to change baby and supervise dressing for boys.

8.05 a.m. Discover four-year-old flooding the bathroom having given his toy rhinoceros a swim. Explain flooding the bathroom is not a good idea. Indeed, dangerous.

8.35 a.m. Get into car and set off for school. Realize husband has filled it with petrol. Cheer.

8.50 a.m. First day of summer term. Arrive at school to tell them we will be late because of doctor's appointment. Find school has introduced a friendship bench. Cheer.

9.15 a.m. Leave school to take six-year-old to doctor's appointment for check-up and jab.

9.35 a.m. Chase grumpy baby round the waiting room, attempt to read book to boys, persuade four-year-old off the slide meant for babies, attempt again to read book, abandon book, bribe all three with white chocolate to keep quiet.

9.50 a.m. See doctor.

10.25 a.m. Return six-year-old to school. Ignore his plaintive pleas that he does not want to play outside at break time.

10.30 a.m. Head for the house of the Oyster Farmer's Wife with baby and four-year-old. Congratulate self for remembering to put gift for new baby and siblings in car.

10.55 a.m. Arrive for coffee and the adoration of her new baby daughter with other mums. The health visitor is there. She asks: 'How are you?' I slap an enormous grin on my face, say: 'Great, thank you.' Feel like saying: 'Still here.' Think that might worry her. Hand over gifts, wrapping paper (in a nice roll, why waste it?) and card with the ink still wet. Drink coffee. Draw in deep breath in preparation for the rest of the day.

Lost the will to live and any inclination to keep checking the time.

## Wednesday, 18 April 2007

### Seasoning

A clock has struck somewhere, unwinding spring. A buttered knife smears thick yellow rape across green fields. A silent shout and, in a beat, puritan twigged hedges break out white in blackthorn blossom. Daffodils dry and fall away to paper brown. You think; 'Shame, glory gone.' Then tulips arrive: 'Ta-da' and trees applaud with branches of budding leaves. Spring moves on. In the city, you could think seasons stood stock-still. There, I was lucky to notice one slip into the next. The time it took to walk through dirty rain between tube and office. A glance from a window at grey sky scraps. A summer lunch on a slatted wooden bench, watching lorries ride by. One year rattling on to the next. Desk diaries spelling out the passing time.

## Friday, 20 April 2007

### Baby love

A moment in the dark: my bed-ready baby placed small hands against my cheeks, moved back slightly in my arms and gazed at me. Content enough with what she found, she moved again, forward this time, to rest her lips on mine.

## Monday, 23 April 2007

### Mothers and sons

Yesterday was blissful. I only realized how blissful when I woke myself up laughing. Have no memory of why I might laugh in my dreams, but I like the idea of laughter in the dark. I fell in love with my husband for any number of reasons – one of them a habit of laughing in his sleep. I presumed, of course, that he was not laughing at me. I had not realized that I could snatch the habit and make it mine. I spent a spring yesterday with my six-year-old. Him and me. Just me and him. Innocent in gardens. We watched the sea spill down stone stairs, chased each other through avenues of pink-blushed blossom and cast coin wishes. He wants to live in a castle; told out his wish and made a listening stranger laugh. As for me, I cannot tell my wish. The day moved on; we plunged back into another Eden, took a jar and microscope and watched insects turn to monsters. Naturally, we tamed them and set them free.

## Tuesday, 24 April 2007

## Publish and be damned

I was called to the vicarage by the sea, in sight of the castle, for tea with the apple-cheeked Vicar. Tea and a 'dressing down' from the Vicar. She said she presumed I would not write about the conversation we were to have. I said: 'I reserve the right to blog what I want to blog. I'm a journalist and this is most definitely not an off-the-record conversation.' She looked shocked. Continued on regardless. Explained that she had called me in to discuss the 'impression' I am creating in my blog. Did not shout at me or rant but handed me a cup of tea and said: 'Sugar?' Sat back resolute in her armchair and told me of the upset of 'teachers, helpers and some mothers' as well as those 'outside the school', because I dared to say out loud in cyberspace that my son was bullied.

I thought: 'Does this make me the blogger the Church tried to silence?' There must be a commandment somewhere: 'Blog not' or 'Put not thy blog before thy God.' Something like that. I think she was misguided. I think it more likely that God has a blog now. More apposite these days than a couple of stone tablets.

I believe she had a plan – ply me with straight talk and tea and explain why I had got it so very wrong. For my own good. Thought, no doubt, it was her shepherd's duty to the school and that she was helping me, a stranger to these parts; that I would listen, gasp, droop, bow my head. *Mea culpa.* I was to ask for her advice. She would give it. I would take it. She would say: 'Bless you, my child.' It would be very civilized. I am not civilized. She said: 'I think you are the most difficult person I have ever had to talk to.' I said: 'You must have had a very sheltered life.' I should not have said that. That is the sort of thing a difficult person says. Obviously, I am not difficult.

Life was so much simpler when you could denounce someone from the pulpit.

As a Catholic, I am used to being told what to do – by the Pope, for instance. But who listens to the Pope? Not me. The last time I was taken to task by a religious, I must have been ten. There were slimy butter beans on the waxed, blocked wood floor beneath the Formica table in the dining hall of my Catholic prep school. Despite the poor, starving children in Africa and strictures to clear our plate, an ingrate had finessed the beans on to the floor. When they were spotted, the head teacher, a 'take-no-prisoners' nun, made us all stand in a line of shame along the corridor outside the classrooms in a bid to identify the culprit. I had eaten my beans. I did not enjoy standing there. I felt it unjust. I am old enough now to refuse to stand in any line of shame. Particularly if it is a line of one.

It is always difficult when someone is nice and very clearly a good person. You do not want to upset them by telling them to mind their own business. That is the way nice people get to say hurtful things. She was, she repeated, concerned about the impression I am creating. I have always found that the word 'impression' is used when the facts do not quite fit what it is someone wants to say. I began to regret that I had brought chocolate biscuits to eat along with tea.

Apparently, she told me, there was worry hereabouts that I am bringing the 'reputation' of a very lovely school into disrepute. (That would be because of the blogging. Obviously, it is not the bullying bringing the school into disrepute. It is my jumping up and down.) She is a governor at the school; she admitted it was a 'difficult time' but said I was making it seem like a 'zoo of little animals'. I said I shared her high opinion of the school. That did not mean to say we did not have a problem.

I said I thought she should be more concerned with the bullying and my son's welfare than with my protests. Prompted, the Vicar asked about the welfare of my lonely child and what was being done. Went one better, said: 'And what about you?' I felt the tears come and bit my lip, thought: 'I will not cry in front of you.' I admit I was touched by her enquiry. Felt it a pity that we were not closer. A shame that the nice Vicar, sitting in her nice vicarage overlooking the beautiful sea and the spectacular castle, had at no point in the previous year and a half invited a desperately lonely mother of three, struggling in any number of ways, over for a cup of tea and some serious girl talk. I said: 'Are we all right?' as I walked out the door. She hugged me in a vicarly sort of way and said: 'Yes.' 'Do you still think I am the most difficult person you have ever met?' She said: 'No, not now.' I do believe she was right the first time.

## Wednesday, 25 April 2007

### Mother mine

My mother is with us for a few days because my father was called away to Ireland. My mother said: 'I can manage.' Words which put the fear of God into me. She cannot manage. I said: 'Of course you can.' Then we went to pick her up. She is sleeping in our bedroom; we are in the study. Last night, she got lost in our bedroom. I am not sure how long it took her to find the bed again. She said: 'It's very dark in there.' She is blind. I am sure it was.

I love my mother. I love her as my mother. I love her as my new child. When she visits, she still wants to do things for me. Folding clothes, washing up. Sometimes, I wash clothes so she has some to fold. I do not tell her that. Yesterday, I went to sit with her on the sofa. She said: 'I wish I could do more to help. You need help.' I said: 'Mum, I have help – I have Girl Friday and she's great. You don't need to do anything for me. You have done enough.' She said: 'I want to do more.' Her

173

face crumpled, pinked up, and her traitorous eyes wept out their salty frustrations. I do not expect my mother to help me any more. It is my mother who expects to help me. It is my mother who feels let down when she has to sit down.

It takes some time to realize when you are a child that your parent has become your responsibility. When we are out, I do not know whether to run after the four-year-old in case he flings himself into the road or stay with my hesitating mother for fear she trips and falls. I hover, equally useless, between the two of them. Today, I took the baby and the four-year-old to a little play park in sight of the castle. My mother sat on a bench and the children sat on the swings. When we finished, we walked past the cricket green and stood by the road. I am pushing an oversized buggy; the baby has refused to get into it and is clamped to my hip with my left arm wrapped around her. The baby's refusal to cooperate leaves me with one free hand. I realize that I cannot cross the road with my four-year-old, buggy, baby, mother and her white stick. I think about getting the four-year-old into the buggy, but I could not then manoeuvre it down the pavement and up the other side. I think about getting my mother into the buggy, but she would never get out of it again. I think about climbing into the buggy with the baby, dangling a leg either side, getting the four-year-old and my mother to hold on and straddle-walking it across the road. I decide that would kill us all. I abandon the buggy. I think: 'I will cross the road with everybody and come back for the buggy.' I start doing a complicated minuet. I hoik up the sliding baby, arrange my blind mother on my free arm and instruct the four-year-old to take granny's hand. Suddenly, a stranger waiting for a bus says: 'Let me help.' And I do. I let her help.

## Thursday, 26 April 2007

## Bluebell wood

Spring is haunting me. You think you have it down pat. This is spring: chicks and lambs, the pastel prettiness of an Easter card. Tulips triumph while cherry trees plant loud lipstick kisses on the sky and spindly, yellow rape washes through fields.

Now, now ... bluebells crowd the mossed trees, gathering in shady places. I am used to city lands and tales of dark and streetsome terror when a woman walks alone. In a bluebell wood, you hear a movement in the crisp and wintered leaves and turn your head to catch nothing. You move through the narrow purple lines of nodding bells and think you catch them whispering. Whispers crowding out the truth; no one is there. I have always imagined bluebells to be the colour of a broken heart. Not that my heart is broken. Not now. My heart has been broken in its day like all good hearts. I think it mended. At least, its odd and purple pieces have been pushed back together, the torn seams sewn with clumsy stitches, and it ticks on yet.

The country is full of seas. The prairie crops, grasses, bluebells on a wooded hillside move as the sea moves. This suits me. The feeling I have had most often since I moved here is much as I imagine drowning to feel: the struggle and the fear. Driving today, I gripped the wheel as you would if you were in an ocean and held on to a floating wooden spar. I understand her reasoning, but I find myself lowered and strangely hurt by the busy little vicar body who took it upon herself to tell me I am Not The Most Popular Girl In School; that I am the Mother Who Blogged and that I should know that this is not a good thing. The bluebells know it. Salt water fills my mouth as I slide beneath the heavy waves.

## Friday, 27 April 2007

### The sound of gunfire

I thought I had sensed a change in the mood, a softening after Easter, till the Vicar pulled me in. Was I fooling myself? My child was hurt and bullied. Fact. Hurt in a variety of incidents. Fact. Hurt when other children turned their backs on him. Fact. Not the sort of facts you want around you. But real, damaging and out there. Fact. Fact. Fact. When a child hurts, a mother feels the pain. More fact. She thinks: 'What can I do? My child is hurting. I must make it stop.' Shame on me. Shame. Shame. Shame to make such a blogging fuss. A mother will, of course, defend her child, but I could have been more British. Had a quiet word. It would have been sorted out. I thought about it. And then I wrote about it.

I blogged again, and once again. It got to be a habit. I made sure in my blog that everyone knew that staff had acted swiftly and with consummate professionalism. As keen to turn things around as they would be if my child was their child. In a way, my child *is* their child. They have introduced a friendship bench and buddies, more supervision in the classroom and directed play at break time. They are bringing in a behavioural expert and a new anti-bullying policy. I could not have asked for more. I am grateful for every moment of thought they have put into turning things around. I could weep over them with gratitude each time I see a casual kindness to my child, a word, a sticker, a small hand taken and held.

As for whether it will work, I hope so. It seems to be. In the last little while, my son has not said, matter-of-factly, that he spends his break time watching others play. I think, 'all being well', 'fingers crossed' and 'let's hope so', it should 'come good'. My son is too small to ignore his feelings of hurt when children do not want to play with him, or when some child kicks out.

Luckily, I am older. Old enough to enjoy certain ironies. To pretend I have not noticed a reluctance to reply to an everyday question, or snubs and coolness from women who would spend smiles on me quite happily before. That there are women who do not pass the time of day as they might have done. Among them, the Patient Mother, whom I thought might be a friend. I can understand that chill – I know she thinks very highly of the school for what it does for her daughter. As for the rest, luckily, I am a grown-up and not a child. If I were a child, I might tell my mother. Then there would be trouble.

## Saturday, 28 April 2007

### Gathering nuts in May

I do not think I will ever look a lamb chop in the face again without a frisson of guilt. Gathered in a corner of a field were the sheep and lambs huddled together behind metal hurdles. Texel-cross lambs. Born to Beulah and Cheviot ewes 'put to the tup' by Texel rams. I like that phrase 'put to the tup'. I may use it again. I may use it in my private life. I doubt my husband knows what it means. I may have to explain it to him.

The sheep knew something was up. Two men chivvied out the ewes and scooped up days-old lambs. They were not scooping them up for a cuddle and an 'Ah. Look. It's a likkle, itsy-bitsy sheep' moment. Those moments are rare in farming. I hope. In any event, you do not want to be there when they are happening.

A man would sit the lamb in his arms with its front legs held up and out of the way. The lamb, if it had any sense, was suspicious at this point. The Sheep Farmer then clipped its ear with a plastic tag. So far: not good for the lamb, but not particularly bad either. Then he would slide a rubber ring, held wide apart with a steel tool, up the little lambikin's tail. This ring cuts off circulation to the tail, which drops off about five days later. According to the Sheep Farmer, this is necessary, or the muck gets caught in the fleece around the lamb's bottom; flies are attracted to it, lay their larvae, maggots hatch and eat the lamb. Yuk. You would not wish that on your worst enemy. Occasionally, before he rings the tail, he has to snap it away from the lamb's bottom and rip a cork of muck out of some place you wish you had never seen. If you do not do this, the lamb can get blocked up and die. It is, however, a process that makes the spectator go: 'Eeeurrgh.' Or maybe that is just me. He nods towards the nugget and says: 'Fancy a toffee?'

It is not exactly the best day of the lamb's life so far, but it could be worse. Could be, and is about to be, very much worse. The Sheep Farmer looks at the lamb. The lamb looks at the Sheep Farmer. He slips another ring on the tool and forces the rubber apart. The ring widens. The eyes of the lamb widen. My eyes widen. He slides the ring over the lamb's nuts. He lets it go. The lamb's nuts are now caught in a ring which, like that around its tail, will cut off circulation. The nuts drop off, one to two weeks later. By the time the lamb is painted with the Sheep Farmer's mark and lowered to the ground, he is not the lamb he was. He trots away, staggers, lies on the ground and bleats. He bleats: 'Fuck. I knew this was going to be a bad fucking day when I saw that dog.' It takes him about half an hour to recover. You would think it would take longer. It would take some men I know a lifetime. It would take them a good thirty years to get over losing the tail, let alone the good stuff. It used to be even worse for the lamb. Years ago, instead of the ring, shepherds would use a special knife to cut through the scrotum skin and then extract the testicles. If it was difficult to get them out, the shepherd who really loved his job (frankly, you would have to) would clamp them between his teeth and pull them out. He would have to suck a toffee to get rid of the taste of sheep nuts. Occasionally, lambs would die if the

178

shepherd had a mouth disease. How unlucky can one lamb be?
You get castrated by a loner; he takes your nuts, gives you bad
breath and it kills you.

## Sunday, 29 April 2007

### RKO landscape

Idle, city cynic that I am, here I am constantly taken by a
shake-your-head-and-pinch-yourself surprise. Out and about,
I think: 'Beauty. Simply. Beauty.' Beauty will not be ignored,
despite my best and busiest endeavour, and I never said, could
never say, this was not a beautiful land.

There are days. There are places which are as if they have
been painted by a master. You want to reach out to touch
the bulked white cloud to see if it is still oil-wet. You think
that the mellow green of the grasses, the grainy sand, the ironed
grey of the sea – how do these colours know the exact shade
of a masterpiece? They do. Each time different. You breathe
in. You expect the smell of garret and wiped cotton rags, not
spring iced air. I drove across a moor, the Cheviot hills in
the distance; the heather, brown, burgundy tinted; the whole
tufted with straw grass. You would think a hand had moulded
the land, its curves caught with all the perfection of a sleeping
Eve. I slowed the car, then stopped.

An iron TV transmitter stood splayed in the emptiness. I
am sure I have seen a giant monkey climb it and roar out his
black-and-white frustration. I watched the skies. I started to
look across the perfect moor to catch a glimpse of angry ape.
No biplanes, no ape. My only companion was a white-
bottomed deer which turned to look at me, listened to my
Amy Winehouse and liked her. It listened a while longer to her
urban beat. Then, casually, leapt a fence to disappear back into
the painted forest.

## Monday, 30 April 2007

### Living and learning

Had another German lesson today. I like my German lessons. They make me feel as if I am twelve again. I am tempted to plait my hair so tightly my head hurts and blow bubbles with pink gum. I can now order beer. '*Ein Glas Bier, bitte.*' I do not drink beer; I had better not go to Germany this week. Next week, I will learn how to order coffee and white wine. Then I can go.

## Tuesday, 1 May 2007

### Birdsong

I wish I could name the birds as they spell out the season's songs. A fluted, chiming symphony of half-familiar notes. A trill, a chirruped melody from rain-drenched leaves, a brushed percussion coo half-hidden in soft and drifting air. They talk to one other as the mauve light fades. Then washes back, gold this time. Their voices lift, remark, keep time. Birdsong marks out a mellow soundtrack to my busy life. I have to stop. Awhile. I have to pause to listen. Then, it comes again. Sweeter for the silence that went before.

## Wednesday, 2 May 2007

### TV or not TV

The children lost TV. Note, I say 'lost TV' not 'lost the TV'. They lost permission to watch TV because of some dark crime they committed which I cannot now remember. It must have been a good one, because I unplugged the video and DVD player to ram home the point. I was not at all influenced by my mother's observation on her most recent visit: 'You let them watch a lot more TV than you used to, don't you?' I denied this and promptly issued my fatwa. I would have shoved the set itself into a cupboard but I might run mad if I lost BBC News 24, so I hid the zappers in case temptation struck.

The good thing about banning TV: you move straight to the moral high ground. I do not get to go there very often. It is pretty and I like it. You drop small shiny pebbles into conversation: 'Of course, the children aren't watching television at the moment. They're learning Latin.' In reality, my children would rather lie glazed in front of the television than do almost anything else. If you offered them a golden ticket to a green cheese, pitted moon, they would probably say: 'Great. When the programme is over.'

The bad thing about losing TV: they insist on making their own entertainment. If that is how they carried on in the past, I am amazed anybody made it to adolescence. I stumbled out of the bedroom to get the wailing baby. My husband is away again, which always helps to ramp up the morning mayhem. My six-year-old was hefting the baby along the corridor to me, staggering slightly, both of his arms wrapped around her sleep-suited body, unable quite to see over her head. This was kind and brotherly of him. Coincidentally, fishing the baby out of her cot had freed up her mattress. It could join the other three mattresses the boys had carefully laid, end to end, down the very steep staircase in our rented house. He handed her to me and trotted back down the corridor. 'Do not even think about it,' I croaked as he shimmied into his nylon sleeping bag. He perched himself at the top of the Cresta Run. Grinned and launched himself into outer space.

I am so ringing my Gay Best Boyfriend. I do not know how the boys were not splattered against the wooden door at the bottom of the stairs like Warner Brothers cartoon characters.

After all my concern about him bashing his head at school, I had this vision of carrying him unconscious, his head swathed in a knob of bandages, into class. The pyjama-clad four-year-old took my hand to comfort me. 'I don't go down in the sleeping bag, Mummy,' he said. 'I just go in my pyjamas.'

## Thursday, 3 May 2007

### The sound of silence

The first time the Patient Mother cut me dead as she walked past me in the car park, I thought: 'She didn't see me.' The second time, when I could not move the car fast enough for her, I thought: 'What's going on?' I went to pick up my six-year-old from school. She was standing talking to another mother at the gate. She did not acknowledge me. I crossed the road, my four-year-old's hand tucked in mine, the six-year-old close by, the baby on my hip. I put them in the car, sucked my teeth and shook my head in regret. I thought: 'Well, I know why you're doing it, but I don't like you doing it. Am I going to let this happen? I don't think so.' I strapped them in. 'Stay there,' I said. 'Sit tight. I'll be one minute.' I crossed the road again. She was still chatting in the sunshine. 'Can you call me please?' I asked. She looked at me. I said: 'You've got my number, haven't you?' Knowing that she had. She nodded, said: 'Yes, OK.' She smiled briefly and looked away. I turned around went back to the car. I thought: 'All right. Let's sort this out. I'll wait for you to call.'

## Friday, 4 May 2007

## Checking in and checking out

It strikes me there's always something. If I am not worrying about one child, I am worrying about another. If I am not worrying about the children, I am worrying about my parents. I knew I had to fly over to Ireland. My mother sounded forlorn and lost in her calls. She said: 'Your father's managing very well.' Then, later: 'We're too old for this.' They were staking out the sickbed of my eighty-six-year-old aunt in a nursing home. Holding her thin hand, saying prayers, doing what you do as someone you love fades out to black.

My little family was supposed to go away for the bank holiday weekend to a hotel. 'We will go another weekend,' I told them. 'OK? My aunt is ill. I should tell her goodbye and I have to go look after Granny and Grandad.' My six-year-old, phlegmatic: 'If she's your aunt, you should go watch her die.' My four-year-old, passionate: 'I'm coming with you.' The baby: disappointed. In me. Again.

At the airport, I take comfort in the fact that once I have, literally, shaken off the children, who make a last-ditch bid to smuggle themselves through to Departures, I am a World Traveller. I decide the new laptop I am carrying makes me look like the professional I once was. I might even be on a business trip.

As I walk through security, a guard who has used his X-ray vision to look into my handbag calls his colleague over. I wonder if he is admiring the shiny laptop. He points to something and a security guard walks back over to the belt. He nods to the bag. I say: 'Absolutely.' I want to be helpful and support the fight against world terrorism. Even in my handbag. He takes out and moves aside my laptop, two mobile phones, two notebooks, a black leather diary and a cosmetics bag. He puts in his hand and extracts a jammy knife. I had cut bread in the kitchen, brought the slices and a pot of jam into the car for our drive to the airport an hour away. I jammed bread for all three children before I lost the knife. I twisted and turned in my seat to find it but it had disappeared. It reappeared. In time to have me labelled 'the madwoman' at airport security. At Heathrow they would have taken me away to a little room and strip-searched me for the matching fork and spoon. As it was, the guard held up the knife for inspection. He looked at it. Then at me. 'Raspberry,' I said. His eyes narrowed.

I made it to Dublin. Being away from your husband and children is both gutting and empowering. These step-away moments make you remember there was a time you could cope on your own – obtain euros, hire cars, figure out how to reverse them. Particularly empowering is the moment on the motorway when you realize you are driving not so much a sluggish car, as a car with the handbrake on. It had its revenge. Arriving at the lakeside hotel, I shut the door. It locked. It would not unlock. I press the electronic key fob. (What is it with car keys?) Nothing. I had clicked a switch inside the car marked 'Lock/Unlock' before I climbed out. I did not realize that meant for ever. I try a different approach. I abandon electronics and look for a lock to put the key in. I prowl the car in case a lock magically appears. It does not.

I ring my husband. I say: 'I have a bit of an emergency.' He says: 'I'll ring you back.' He does not. I have to ring the car-hire company and explain. I try to explain without telling them I clicked the 'Lock/Unlock' switch. I have to ring the AA and eventually a nice friendly man with a garage rings me back. The young mechanic he sends shows me how to slip the tail of the key or a screwdriver into a small slit in the lower edge of the black plastic door handle to flip it off and reveal the metal lock underneath. I now have options; as a mechanic.

Or a master criminal. The young man says I am not stupid, I just need a new battery for the fob.

About this time, my parents arrive back at the hotel. My aunt died in the early hours. I am too late to say goodbye.

## Saturday, 5 May 2007

### The removal

The mourners fill the chapel at the nursing home to thumb their crosses on my aunt's cold forehead and tell their rosary beads, paying their respects before tomorrow's funeral. There is no table, chair, rock, stiller than the dead. You look into the coffin at the dead. You know there cannot be a breath, but part of you, the undefeated part, that part, searches for a glimmer. Something in you, looking at the dead, knows you are looking at your future. Your own contained stillness. That makes you look again.

I have been lucky in my aunts. I enjoyed a goodly collection whom I loved and was loved by in return. I still have a few. This one, however, escaped the net. I hardly knew this Irish aunt. No going back on that. She knew all of me through phone calls and photographs; school, wedding, children. Yet to me, she was hardly more than a name. A chapter or three in my father's life. A kindness at Christmas sending me Brer Rabbit storybooks past any interest in such things. I travelled to Ireland for my parents. Truth be told. If that does not sound harsh. Which it does, of course. Now that she is dead.

Even so, it is a shock gazing at this almost stranger as she lies in a ruched white satin and lace-trimmed cover, which drapes under her body, folds blanket back over long legs, then gushes over the coffin edge. I have seen the same satin and lace on the little girls that fill the hotels of Ireland, celebrating their first and holiest Communion. Little brides of Christ, as is my aunt.

Though bigger. This unknown and dead aunt wears a 'habit' of blue, a picture of the Virgin Mary emblazoned on her chest, pearly rosary beads wrapped around her bony fingers. It seems so intimate, this communion with the dead. But I do not think she would mind. She, after all, knows me through my father. In any event, she is in no state to complain aloud that I never visited, never called. I stand there, guilty, hearing the accusations in her silence.

## The cottage

My father wanted to visit the cottage where his sister lived. It is a place out of time. It cannot be today. This is no Celtic tiger. It is a sad and Irish Brigadoon. A time-forgotten land. You drive off the road and turn down a lane bordered with a mossed and tumbled wall. A broken-up yard, once neatly swept and with flowers, now laps at a string of falling-down barns. Their wooden doors, rotten; bolts and locks hanging loose. Poor guardians to emptiness. My father says there were chickens, a horse, cows and pigs. Today, spiders crawl through the black fissures that cut through gaping gable walls, and roof beams hang jagged in the air, held up by cobwebs and history. The loft has been sealed since 1920. My father tells how it was used by men from the IRA as a bolthole. Hearing the lorries of Black and Tan British soldiers rumbling along the lane, his father checked the loft to find weapons and ammunition, which he dumped down the well only moments before the soldiers pulled up in the farmyard.

Like my aunt, the cottage has been cleared of life but somehow the cottage remembers it. Dark air heavy with acrid peat smoke from an ancient stove. A Givenchy perfume on the table, more glamorous than the peat. A fierce warning shouted by a pot of pills resting on a shelf: 'Do not stop taking this medicine except on your doctor's advice.' Sacred Heart

pictures watching. A perpetually flickering electric flame burning, divine and neglected, on the wall. Newspaper pages from
14 August 1964 protect the kitchen table underneath heat-hurt
plastic cloths. A calendar with the leaves torn off from January,
February and March 1954 lies on an old seat. Another for 2003
hangs on the wall. I wonder, were these the years worth
keeping?

My aunt lived as no one lives now. Her mother dead at
thirty-three, left as a child of fourteen to look after five other
children and her father. Boiling up pans of potatoes and meal
for the pigs, selling eggs to buy flour and sugar, making
her own butter and bread. She waved goodbye to the young
ones bound for England, and grew old with a brother in a
two-bedroom cottage, she in one room, he in the other and
a smoky kitchen between. She brought in the cows for her
brother to milk and pushed a wheelbarrow with two milk-
filled creamery cans up the lane, then brought the empty ones
back again. She carried water from a spring to drink and
washed only in rainwater. Fifteen years ago, water was piped
into the house. Five years ago, the brother died. She did not,
and measured out the days left to her in prayer. Visited Dublin
just once, England, never. Then cancer. Death. Heaven. My
aunt. I never knew her.

## Sunday, 6 May 2007

### Dead and buried

My father hates to be late for anything. Consequently we
arrived an hour before the funeral and sat outside the church
in driving rain waiting for the dead. The Irish know how to
mourn, face up to death, shake the hand of the hunched
bereaved, whisper: 'I'm sorry for your trouble'. They bow their
heads in churched and wooden ranks and pray that their own

day will not come too soon. The rosary at the funeral mass is as the sea washing over shingle on a holy shore. Then back out into the driving rain to fill the waiting hole with womankind. Umbrellas covering my mourning father and his living sisters; wood keeping the rain from the face of the sister lost in death.

After the funeral and a lunch of soup and ham sandwiches, we went back to the cottage. Leaving the family to plunder damp holy pictures and wallflowers, I set off with a local farmer to brave a bull-filled field. One bull can fill a field very fast when you are trying to make it to the other side. I wanted to reach the 'fairy forth' and figured I needed a bodyguard. Across Ireland, there are small mounds or hills called fairy forths or ring forths. There is one on the thirty acres left behind by my aunt. One superstition goes that if you walk round it seven times, you get a wish. I like to make wishes.

The hills were probably lookouts or defence points in ancient times. Folks are wary because the mounds are surrounded by trees but nothing grows on the top of the forth. The superstition goes that you never cut down trees on the forth nor do you plough them under. Sinister tales abound. The man who cut down a tree and was blinded in his eye; the farmer who ploughed it under only for his twenty-two-year-old son to die in a car crash. 'Why risk it?' I thought as I walked my seven rounds. 'I hope the bull doesn't get me.' I thought too about my wish. Life is packed so tight, it can be difficult to make a moment to know what to wish for. If you do not make the time to catch the wish, you cannot hope to have it come true. Walking the fairy forth gives you a moment in space and in time to think what it is you want most. You can wait for the fairies to give it to you or you can go get it. It might be quicker to go get it.

## Monday, 7 May 2007

### Poster boys

I have made it back. I am lucky to be back at all. The general election is on in Ireland. I know that because I nearly joined my aunt in the grave on the drive back to Dublin airport. I was trying to read the election posters that hang off every other lamp post and telegraph pole. Somebody, somewhere, has told Irish politicians that the best way to bring out the vote is to become a major road hazard. It is a retro-chic thing.

Pink is the colour of my return. I came home to a kitchen table which has been tinted a lovely shade of deep-rose pink. My six-year-old said: 'You like pink. Don't you, Mummy?' I looked at the table, which was once my grandfather's. It is oak; you can see the grain through its pink glaze. I looked at the carpet in the kitchen of our rented house. Also pink. A 'no getting away from it' shade of pink. An 'I hope you are not expecting to keep your deposit' shade of pink. 'We were playing at being master chefs,' the six-year-old continued. 'We made bubbles.' He giggled. He kept watching me.

The master chefs knew what they were doing. They had tipped red, blue and yellow food dye into a bowl along with honey, syrup (maple), curry powder (madras), rice (brown), pasta (quills), ketchup (Heinz), baking powder, bicarbonate of soda and a bottle of vinegar (malt). We have performed a less ambitious variant on this experiment in the garden as Mummy explained the nature of a chemical reaction and the creation of a gas. At least, she pointed and said: 'Look.' During the master chef extravaganza, in the kitchen laboratory, Daddy was upstairs, trying to get the baby to go to sleep. 'You know that story of the magic porridge pot,' he said. 'It was like that. But worse.'

I was trapped. I encourage scientific experiments. I ban TV.

I left Daddy in charge. 'You do like it, don't you, Mummy?' asked my six-year-old again, anxious now. I caught back a sigh. I nodded, slowly. 'Pink is my very favourite colour.'

## Friday, 11 May 2007

### Totally unfunny

I am fed up. I am so fed up I do not think I can even be funny about how fed up I am. My 'home' is occupied by smiley, dusty men with big boots who have revealed they are four weeks behind schedule. We cannot move back into the cottage when we thought we could. It is not their fault. Two weeks went on slating a roof, which was not in the orginal spec; another two weeks replastering all the walls, when it was hoped they would just need repair. Both roof and walls look better; I feel worse. I want my house back.

I do not think the funeral helped. Death, I have to say, is a bit of a downer. Not just for the dead. Funerals give you the chance to catch up with those you love and never see, to meet those you like and will never see again. I met a deal of kindness there. Other people's kindness fills up an empty part of me. Someone who walked me across a field with a bull in it. He made me braver. An old friend of my father who said to me: 'You're a lovely-looking girl.' I am forty-two; I suspect he had cataracts. I am forty-two; I take a compliment where I can get one. There are times when I feel my life has no pause button. Something you could press for a few moments of silent, thinking time to ask: 'Where am I now?' I grope around. No button. The clock ticks on. Even this morning, I crawled back to bed after the school run. At least I tried to. My husband was downstairs, Girl Friday was downstairs, but my four-year-old came up to me three times within half an hour, hectoring, demanding, loving.

Yesterday, the boys had a spaghetti sword fight. Inch-long pieces of (uncooked) spaghetti, shattered over the kitchen floor. At bedtime, the six-year-old water bombed the four-year-old's bed. What am I going to do when the baby is old enough to join in concert with her brothers' mayhem? We are outnumbered. In twenty years' time, I am sure I will laugh at their antics. If I am not dead, I will play 'remember whens' with them. I will say: 'Remember when you flooded the bathroom? Twice in four days.' Today, today, I want to weep. I feel guilty that I work. Working at home, but still working. If I was more focused on the children, they would stop moving seamlessly from one outrage to the next. If I was more willing to make papier mâché piggy banks and take them on more forays to the beach, they would transform themselves. They would be Granny's dream boys. I am constantly the bad guy. I take treasures away, rant, drone on, endless and relentless. They must 'listen ... do as you are told'. They carry on, regardless. I am reconstituting the star chart (rewards and praise for good behaviour.) I do not want to draw up a star chart; I want to run away. I am just not sure London is far enough.


## Monday, 14 May 2007

### Splish splosh

Went shopping for a bathroom. There was a moment. The baby was crying, the four-year-old was demanding I attach his moulded red plastic Power Ranger to the rocket and my husband said if we went with the bath taps and showerhead I wanted, they would obscure the view out of the window. I thought: 'Do you know what? Fundamentally, I don't care. In a month or so, I won't even notice. Let's just decide something and go.'

We had already been bathroom shopping in one of those

shopping warehouses where you buy food in bulk and tele-visions that think they are cinemas. There were some very large shoppers in that very large shop. People so large you wondered whether they shopped in bulk because they ate in bulk. You wanted to point at their trolleys and ask: 'Ever wondered why you're fat? Stop shopping here. Shop in your local grocer's. It will cost more. You will eat less. You will get thinner.' I shouldn't scoff. I look at the boys some mornings. I say: 'Did you grow last night?' They are taller than they were when I put them to bed. There are other mornings when I look at my hips. I say: 'Did you grow last night?' They are bigger than when I put them to bed. Doubtless, there will come a day when I will heave myself, rippling and sodden, out of my luxury bath, abandon my village shops and insist we go shopping with a forklift.

## Thursday, 17 May 2007

### Hinged and hung

Newly carved window frames and doorways hang suspended by ropes from the rafters of outbuildings. They frame space and make you think of possibilities. You could step through the empty door to find a finer world, open a magic window on to a sunnier life. The frames hang like a promise and say: 'The future is walking through our doors any minute now. Keep faith awhile and see.'

I know I can relax. Where there was a wall along the back of the kitchen, there will be doors to a courtyard garden. One of the builders placed a penny coin, as shiny as could be, beneath the first stone of the door surround to wish us luck. Is that not kind and noble? A well-meant wish for luck. Can a house fail to be happy when founded on another person's kindess? He does the same in every house he builds. I could argue it is a new life we are building up here but mine is not a new house. Nobler yet, then, to wish me luck. He made an exception. Perhaps he thought we needed more luck than most.

## Friday, 18 May 2007

### The hardest word

The Patient Mother emailed me. She said: 'There's so much I want to say and most of it focuses on the appalling attitude I have recently adopted towards you. I haven't phoned you as you asked me to do because I was afraid you wouldn't really want to talk to me. I have behaved terribly, like a stupid spoilt child, not to mention ... sheep – following suit, if you know what I mean. I have never meant to ignore you, snub you or act coolly towards you. It's something I've never done to any-one before and believe you me it's preyed on my mind every day ... I actually feel quite disgusted with myself. Please forgive my rudeness. I am truly sorry for being so pathetic.' She ended: 'I hope we can be friends again and maybe even one day meet up for coffee (or tea in my case).'

I know that she considers her own and special child has blossomed in the school and I understood why she was angered by my words. I thought: 'Cor blimey – how cool is she to have the courage to say sorry and how brave of her to do it with such electronic grace?' I replied: 'Listen, honey. Fret not. Everybody is entitled to their opinion and all sorts of people thought I should not be blogging about the school. Various peeps got swept up in the scandalous fact I was writing, with-out necessarily absorbing what I was saying. I respect anyone's right to hold a different opinion from my own. 100 per cent. Truly. Re "the other girls in the dorm" not speaking to me: A) I am a grown-up and worse things have happened; B) long before your email, I had written you a "Get out of jail free" card for any number of reasons . . . So we are A-OK. Promise. And coffee or tea would be lovely any time that suits.'

## Saturday, 19 May 2007

## Beefcake

A London Friday night. Where would I have been? A chichi supper in a sushi restaurant, exhausted by work, distracted from enjoyment by a who-knows-why apathy of the soul? Maybe not. Maybe a just-out movie, alone or with a friend. Alone, I am likely to cry in movies, sit in crushed velveteen seats, eat tear-wetted popcorn, grope hopelessly for tissue scraps. If given the choice, I prefer company and laughter. But in the country. Tra la. Who goes out to dinner in the country? Some do. I don't, or only when the moon's shine is blue. Certainly not a movie. What's 'a movie'? Better, far, a stock-judging event, a fund-raiser for a good and rural cause. I can die happy now I have stared at a cow's backside all night. I asked myself: 'Does life get any better than this? Right here, right now, staring at this particular cow's arse?' I thought to myself: 'I bloody hope so.'

Then I thought: what is not to enjoy about a Charolais cow? Who needs a Hollywood star rising from the sea? Watch the muscle ripple in that young bull's rump. Admire the conformation of that heifer, set four-square and shapely. This cheeky Suffolk tup, a painted caramel and black-faced beauty, spray-tanned for the night. A city dweller – which, of course, is far from what I am – a city dweller might think one sheep looked much like a fleecy other. Might feel they would rather eat the steak than spend quality time at the weekend with it. That is not me, of course.

To judge the beast, a farmer told me you look to see if they are 'breedy' – that is to say, if they are a bright, attractive sort of animal. To be regarded as breedy, the animal's 'top line', which runs along their back, has to be straight and true and they should not be knock-kneed. Judges rank and mark the differences between the creatures in secret; contestants score them. Frighteningly complicated mathematics are done by frighteningly clever women sitting in front of an Aga. Calculators tap, there is a quiet scurry of papers and a winner emerges whose judgement matches that of the judge. I did not win; though, as it turned out, I am a good judge of bull.

They are cool customers, these farming types. They march you to the creamy bull, which is a thing of power and beauty. They flay it with their practised butcher's eyes, point and say: 'Under that, the fillet,' or 'The hindquarter's where the eating is.' Conversation is of bull semen in straws and the washed-out embryos of calves. Breeding and the money breeding is worth; £55,000 for one Charolais bull recently. It makes me think, when a farmer wants a wife, does he do as the rest of the world does? Catch a smile thrown by a pretty face? Buy her a drink? Cadge a kiss? Fall in love? Or, as he stands at the crowded bar with a note folded and standing to attention in his hand, does he watch the way she moves across the room? Listen for the knock of a knee? Check the brightness of her eye? Span with invisible hands the spreaded width of her hips? Does he ask whether money will be well-spent?

## Wednesday, 23 May 2007

### Scooby Doo, where are you?

I wanted a night away to take my mind off all the building work. Not to go down to London. I miss it too much when I come back. I had a seriously bad idea. I decided I would spend a night in one of the castles up here – not the King's but one that claims to be 'Britain's Most Haunted Castle'. Then I had an even worse idea. I thought: 'If I am going to spend a night in Britain's most haunted castle, I should do it on my own, otherwise it would be cheating.' Cheating who, exactly? The dead but not yet gone? A night away from the children. I could have spent it at a luxury hotel with a complementary spa treatment. I could have zipped down to London and spent it with a credit card. I could have found a lover in a chat room, made some excuse about the car running out of petrol and spent it in cyberspace with my hand on my mouse. Instead, I spent it in a cold apartment up a stone tower without another living soul in sight.

Before I went up to my apartment, a 'ghost walker' gave us a tour of the castle and its grounds, describing horrid, bloody tortures in the sort of professional detail I did not think entirely necessary. There were half a dozen of us on the walk. He shut us up in the darkness of the dungeon, described the freezing touch of a twelve-year-old girl dead from pneumonia and the heavy rose scent of a deserted and unhappy wife. He claimed that as he had sat in one room, a rocking chair started to rock violently, while on another night, a flag had dropped from the chapel wall to wrap itself round a visitor.

When he found out I was staying the night, he told me the little bedroom in my tippy-toppy tower apartment had a 'very oppressive' atmosphere. He predicted: 'I bet you won't sleep in that one tonight.' 'Not now I won't,' I told him. He said visitors often abandoned my apartment in the middle of the night after doors opened and banged shut and lights went on and off. I said: 'Feel free not to share.' Not one to take a hint, he claimed two staff would no longer work in it after they went into one of the bedrooms and the door 'jammed'.

Tour over, apartment cautiously entered, I made a cup of tea and poured a glass of wine. I poured two – I didn't want anyone thinking I was rude. I opened up the visitors' book. George: 'I a.m. Lying in bed, eyes open, wife asleep. A round ball of light flashes and is gone. Again a round ball of light.' A Whitby couple: 'Caught lots of orbs. How exciting. Just to warn others, one was in the sitting-room area of the apartment.' Orbs are considered by some to be the souls of the departed. Others think they are dust. The problem is that I am reading this book in the sitting-room area of the apartment in a chair that smells like it is trying to pass on a message. A message like: 'Don't sit here. Someone is sitting here already.' I think: 'Relax.' There is a knock on the door. I think: 'Bugger politeness, I am not answering the door to anyone who might be dead.' Then I think: 'I should stop reading this book and go to bed,' but I am slightly worried that if I stop reading, I will look up and a hooded figure will say: 'Boo.'

Eventually, I make myself look up and take stock. There are three bedrooms in the apartment: the little one I have been warned about, a twin-bedded room and one with a double bed. The little room is up a stone staircase and has a curtain across the entrance; the other two bedrooms both have doors. I am no sooner going to sleep in the oppressive little bedroom than fly. Neither am I going into any bedroom where the door 'jams' and the walls start to bleed. The ghost walker did not say the walls would bleed but it pays to think ahead. Reluctantly, I choose one and settle down, but for some reason I cannot quite sleep. I lie there in the bed pretending to sleep in case anyone is watching. I figure if I am awake, any watcher would presume I am in need of company. I am not in need of company. I am in need of my head examining. I do the metaphorical equivalent of stuffing my fingers in my ears and humming loudly. I do not hum out loud. I do not want to make any noise which would draw attention to myself. I do not want to hear anything more and I certainly do not want to see anything. I lie there as the hours crawl by, and wait for dawn, which arrives at least three hours late. I have brought Alpen and milk for breakfast and find a bowl and spoon in the cupboard. My heart is pounding so loudly as I open the box, I think: 'Do you know, I don't think I am that hungry. I think I will drive home now and eat my cereal there.' And on the way back, driving home along an empty road over the dew-drenched moors, my heart lifts and I think: 'I am alive. I am alive.'

## Saturday, 26 May 2007

### I have seen the future – and it might just work

I am impressed by the skill I see around me in the cottage. I enjoy the evidence of craftsmanship. I can appreciate a plaster-perfect wall; the subtle, creamy finish of a painted room; red clay flattened brick rescued from underneath the kitchen floor, cleaned and displayed in a newly opened-up hearth; a landing floor, quilt-patched with wood rescued from that kitchen floor, each piece eased in and nailed down by a craftsman. It is not just a matter of a job and a bill. I can appreciate the efforts of a man trying to steam, sand, scrape and burn whitewash and distemper clinging tight to the ceiling beams it has loved for years. I know his arms ache and his breath catches in the dust as he helps to build an idea of a house.

An American friend told me that I am in a conversation with the house. True. My house speaks to me of the past, the present and the future. In that corner of what will be my sitting room, a pantry stood; that windowsill by a greasy wall was where a woman made her butter; the hearth we have uncovered once held a kitchen range. I have listened and learned something of the house and those who lived here, in the rewriting of its rooms and passages. The present, of course, is around in all its brick-dusted glory, patterns keyed in the render, electric cables hanging from the walls, strangers who have become friends marking the rooms with their skills. But I can see the future better than the present. As I stood on the landing looking down the painted corridor through the house, I saw soft painted walls and light from mended windows. The walls pushed back to open up the route between what were two houses, knitting the divide with space. I thought: 'Perhaps this could be my home. Perhaps I could hang pictures along these walls.'

## Wednesday, 6 June 2007

### Bad hair day

My husband takes this land in his stride. He never seems to blink at it. I find the country odd in so many ways. Everywhere you go, there are animals. You do not walk down a city street to find it teeming with wild dogs. Not unless you are very unlucky. Here, however, sheep and cows are everywhere, while the roads hop with hares, but the animals are never left to enjoy their bucolic peace. Someone always wants something from them: their meat, their milk, their young. Yesterday, it was their wool.

I went to watch a gang of New Zealand sheep shearers in operation. Five hunky men with big biceps, torn vests and distressed jeans, sweating to the sounds of the Eighties. My Gay Best Boyfriend would have loved it, but any relationship, you could tell, would be abusive.

The shearer tumbles a fat, woolly sheep over a wooden gate. Whoomph! His buzzing machine shears hang from the metal gallows above him. 'Time to leave,' thinks the sheep. Too late. Pop rock from a dangling boombox belts out in time to a bleating beat. The sheep is sitting on her back end, black hooves waving in the air, when our macho shearer hero shoves her foreleg between his own ragged, muscular legs. Hunched over her body, he starts to strip her.

Down the belly and into the lower reaches, down the inside

of a hind leg and then up and around her tail end. One hand moves with the machine, the other stretching the skin; it is beginning to get chilly down there. Up and along her side to the spine; the flesh showing tremble pink underneath striped white fuzz. Down the foreleg and shoulder. He tilts back her head and holds it against his six-pack, pressing the vibrating tool up and around the throat; he throws the loose noose of fleece around and over her head and pushes her on to her back to reach round her bared shoulder better. Suddenly, her head is between his legs as he works down the second shoulder to the last leg.

It takes a minute and a half, maybe two, to strip a sheep of her dignity. The shearers straighten, only to haul out another sheep, clicking a counter to show they have a new squeeze between their knees. I cannot believe they do not dream of sheep at night. I do not want to know the details. I am certain that sheep dream of them; an electric barbers' shop from hell with Kiwi demons.

The gang spends around six weeks in Northumberland and Scotland, with each man expecting to shear around 250 sheep a day. At this farm, on this day, they were shearing Beulahs and Texel crosses. They shear twice a year in New Zealand and most of this group have recently arrived from Canada. Belly wool is taken off first and discarded. Aside from that, the fleece comes off in one piece. The gang also includes two 'wrappers', who throw the fleece on to the floor, clean side down, tuck in the neck end, fold first one side then the other and roll it into a bundle. The bundles are then tossed into a large plastic bag for one of the wrappers to stomp down, much as grape pickers stamp on grapes. The wool pack is then sewn up with cord threaded through by a large nail hammered into a needle.

Each fleece will bring around £1 from the British Wool Marketing Board; each sheep sheared costs the farmer around £1. Traditionally, the belly fleece and the little tufts of wool that come off during the shearing were all sold. Even muck on the tufts was cut off to allow those tufts to be sold as well. Now, the price of wool is low enough to mean the tufts are left where they lie. The Sheep Farmer said: 'Cash-wise, it's a useless exercise. We do it for welfare reasons or they are eaten alive by maggots.' I saw a maggoty sheep. Not pretty. He went on: 'The other reason is they get heavy with the dew, and they roll over on to their back and can't get up. Then a crow will come and peck their eyes out.'

The 'ganger' in charge, shouted me over to him as I folded and rolled a fleece, grease on my hands. I thought: 'Lucky me.' It has been a long time since a rugged New Zealander showed an interest in me. In truth, a rugged New Zealander has never shown any interest in me. He was called something indisputably male. It might have been 'Dave'. Perhaps it was Gnasher. I walked across and looked down. He had a sheep between his legs. I thought: 'Should I be here?' He gestured to me to throw a leg over. I thought: 'I am never going to get an offer like this again.' I used my knees to hold the sheep in place, holding the shears in one hand and a leg in the other. I think it was the sheep's leg. I was tense. It might have been Gnasher's. In which case, he should drink less and eat more. As Gnasher helped me push her head between my legs, I thought: 'I hope sheep don't bite.' This is not the thought you want to be having as a sheep stares balefully at your backside and you give her the worst haircut of her life. They don't bite; at least, she didn't. She would have had good reason. She was definitely having a bad hair day. The only good thing to be said about my shearing was that I did not actually kill her. That and the fact it brought me closer to Gnasher. I do not know which of us was the more traumatised by the end of my shearing, me or the sheep. Me, I think. It has been known for farmers' wives to run away with a tractorman or shearer. Strangely, he did not ask me to run away and join his gang. I could learn.

## Monday, 11 June 2007

## It's a duck, dammit

School is having an anti-bullying week. That is good. Let's start from me being happy. Look at me sitting in the classroom, see me smile. I am relaxed and 'happy' and prepared to listen, indeed participate, although I hate to participate in workshops. The only other workshop I ever attended was an anti-racism workshop at my son's previous school. Naturally enough, the only parents to attend an anti-racism workshop were those least likely to be racists. When I gently made that blazingly obvious point to the earnest and trendily multicultural woman in charge (sorry, 'facilitating' the workshop), I was told that we could feed back what we learned to the other parents at the school gate. That is to say, we could hazard which of the young mothers sported a Union Jack hip tattoo underneath her thong and white sweats, then engage her in conversation about her right to wear a burka. How exactly do you start that conversation? 'Hello, you look like you might be a Nazi. How do you feel about Islam?'

We were invited to a workshop on emotional literacy and bullying. The problem with politically correct workshops is they turn me into a raving fascist. I am, to all intents and purposes, sitting still. In reality, as I listen to the liberal drivel which is sold to you as fact, I feel my orange plastic moulded chair move further and further to the right, so far and so fast, the world starts rushing by me in the opposite direction in a hasty pudding blur of Jerusalem and fireworks.

The workshop started off: 'When I am included, I feel . . .' We took it in turns to fill in the gap. I said 'happy'. I could have said 'surprised'. Then went on to: 'When I am not included, I feel . . .' I said 'gutted'. That about covers it. I drank my tea while the nice lady wrote things on her large pad of paper hanging from the board. Alert. Alert. I picked up my ginger biscuit and put it down again, uneaten. I have to be seriously disturbed not to finish a biscuit. The people who might be involved in a bullying incident include a 'receiver'. 'Receiver'? Why not 'victim'? She said she would come back to that. That was the moment the chair started travelling really fast through space and time. I had thought that in a bullying situation there was a bully and a victim. I checked the handout to make sure I had not misheard. It is explicit. There is a 'person (or child) who is bullied' or who is a 'target of bullying (rather than "victim")'. It goes on: there is a 'person doing the bullying, using bullying behaviours (rather than "bully")'. It goes on: 'The reason for this choice of words is that bullying does not come about as a result of fixed personality traits in children, leading them to become a "bully" or a "victim" (both terms which can imply a permanence and resistance to change).'

The handout continues: 'In fact, research suggests that many perfectly nice and popular children use bullying behaviours on occasion, and many are unaware of the devastating impact which their behaviour has on the children they target.' Well, that's all right then. Because you can attach the words 'research suggests' to a statement does not make it true. I would also suggest that if a child is a 'target of bullying', I doubt very much whether the child doing the targeting is 'perfectly nice'. These bullying children are being 'bullies'. If any one of my 'perfectly nice' children used bullying behaviour, I would, without hesitation, call the little wretch a bully.

'It would also seem that anyone could become a target of bullying if the context allows this to happen.' 'Context' presumably means the enormous, jug-eared fourteen-year-old who insists on pinning you against the wall and thumping you repeatedly because he thinks you are gay. The jug-eared one is not a bully, he is demonstrating 'bullying behaviours' for his own reasons. Doubtless, remembering that would make it hurt less.

Then it asserts: 'For most children the roles will be dependent on a situation, and they will be, over time and in different contexts, target, witness and person doing the bullying.' That is to say, we are all bullies, passive bystanders and sometime victims. I have had therapy and I think this utter psychobabble. The nice woman assured us that in all likelihood, we had all been guilty of bullying behaviour or at least witnessed bullying. I wanted to groan out loud at this point; I wanted to clutch my face and shriek at her. When I dared warble: 'Not true' and that she could perhaps speak from her own experience but not for anybody else, certainly not for me, her answer was that perhaps I just 'hadn't realized' what I had been doing. I did groan out loud then. How do you answer that one?

My child was excluded by other children from activities and physically hurt. He was, for a time, a victim. Point. Par. Ends. The school acted. They did a good job. He is no longer a victim and I am an altogether happier mother. I was not happy sitting in that classroom listening to what I considered politically correct drivel, passed on as received wisdom. At the end of it, I was so angry, my hands shook as I gathered my papers together. I was not shaking for my child. I was shaking for the children out there whose lives are misery: fat girls and misfit boys who will hang themselves this year or next. They will do that because of bullies. Let's use the B word. When behaviour and actors in that behaviour are not given their proper names, the names everybody understands, it undermines faith in the rest of the strategy. The lady assured the parents and teachers gathered before her that we did not want a 'blame' scenario. Why not? What is wrong with blame? The flip side of blame is responsibility. Let's be sure and tell the kids. Accept responsibility for your actions. Own it. Say it out loud;

you are the only ones who can. 'I'm a bully and you can't touch me for it.'

## Thursday, 14 June 2007

### All aboard for the double decker

I am trying not to think of London as home – to think of it instead as 'London', a place I used to live. A while ago, driving the children to my favourite beach, we came over a hill, the narrow road falling away, cutting through the fields, out to the links. Tucked behind the golf club was a big red London bus. My first thought: 'There's a big red London bus.' I am nothing if not obvious. My second: 'Can I get on it?' Third: 'Will it take me home?' Tsk tsk. I mean 'to London'. I glanced quickly at my husband as he pulled the car tight over into the side of the hedged road. I thought: 'Can he see it? Can he see the bus? Or is it only me?' I am not sure whether I was disappointed or relieved when he said: 'Look, kids, a bus.' He turned off the engine. 'Make sure Mummy doesn't get on it.' I thought about running for it. I decided against it for fear the bus would pull away in a cloud of fumes and dirt just as I reached for the pole. I did not want to see the children's faces when I turned back to them having bungled my escape.

Yesterday, I was braver. I hopped on. The big red London bus rumbled down the A1. There is something about a bus journey. You think: 'OK, this time is mine. I am excused a little while. Now, where is it that I'm going? Why? And who is it that I am again?' I sat on the top deck at the front of the bus. You have to if you want to pretend you are driving. You could tell you weren't in London – little things like green fields and cows.

My conductor, a former management consultant, and the driver, a former miner, bought the Routemaster bus two years ago. It costs £15,000 to buy and do up a bus. It has done 3 million miles since it was first commissioned in 1966, and has carried an estimated 3 million passengers. They call the bus 'Kenny' after the mayoral man who sacked it from its city job. Now, instead of commuters and shoppers and metropolitan folk, it carries golfers and tourists up and down a thirty-nine-mile stretch of Northumberland's sandy, castled coast. I like Kenny. I put my hand on his metal bonnet and felt it throb. I could tell Kenny likes me. I rang his bell. Twice. We have a lot in common, the two of us. We're about the same age, we've been around, we've seen things, we're natural Londoners, we're probably both a bit too big, back-end-wise. Admittedly, no one points at mine like they do when he thunders past, but Kenny and I have a bond. If I return to London, I am taking the bus.

## Friday, 15 June 2007

### Billy the Kid

The boys have lost TV for a month. A month! That is to say until we move back into our cottage. I was about as happy as the children were. It is one thing for me to take TV away, it is another for Billy the Kid to take it away when I am out at my book group. For a month. I wanted to know why. Apparently, the six-year-old swore at his brother and then his father. 'Where the fuck did he get that from?' I asked my husband. 'I have no fucking idea,' he said defensively.

## Tuesday, 19 June 2007

### The moving finger writes

We were having a family day out when I did something to my back. I cannot quite stand upright. Periodically, I groan. I was squatting next to the children, pleading with them to choose something in a shop so I could go back to a cup of tea and a cheese scone in the café next door. I admit I was buying silence. I am not proud of it, but I was desperate for the tea. As I stood up, I thought: 'Oops.' It was so bad, I was clutching at the shelves. The nice shop assistant came over. I said: 'Having a bit of a problem standing up. I just need a minute.' He was about twenty-three; he thought I was seventy. The car was parked up a hill. As we laboured up it, my husband said to the boys: 'We'll have to roll Mummy down this hill like a pig in a barrel.' I was in a considerable amount of pain at this point, hanging on to my husband's arm with one hand and holding on to my six-year-old's shoulder with the other. I stopped walking in silent protest. My six-year-old said: 'I don't think you look like a pig, Mummy' – I smiled lovingly at my child – 'even if Daddy does.' I did not smile lovingly at his father.

## Wednesday, 20 June 2007

### Mrs Overall

'Gnarly', I think, might be the term for my body and mood. I am in such a bad way, I do not even know what to do about it. Every now and then, I crawl into bed and sob. Do I go to London to my own osteopath? Do I hang on and hope that someone can fit me in up here? My first instinct was to get on a train. Only the fact that I did not know whether I could make it from the train to the taxi rank at the other end stopped me. I think I could just about make it if I didn't carry a baby or a handbag. I might have to cry the whole four hours down there. Alternatively, I could get slightly out of it on anti-inflammatories and white wine.

I have been looking forward to going down to London to see some friends and take care of a bit of business; it does not have the same attraction if I literally have to crawl back into town. Maybe I could tell everyone: 'Fell orf the hunter. Damned shame. Had to shoot the horse.' That would also explain the reek of alcohol if I started drinking with my breakfast bap on the train. It sounds so much more interesting than 'Dicky back. Old crock. What can you do?' At one point my husband said: 'You seem to be walking better.' In what world does he live? My body is completely twisted and I am dragging a foot. The only thing I am missing is a bell rope. There are times when it is thoroughly demoralizing to live with an optimist.

A small part of me feels as if I should sort it out up here and that I cannot keep getting on a train every time I want a haircut or a newspaper. (Actually, I did get a haircut up here a few weeks ago. I hated it. It took the guy about seven minutes. Seven minutes. Maybe it takes my London hairdresser seven minutes and he spends another thirty crouched behind my head making scissor sounds, but I doubt it.) Another part thinks: 'Go to London. See your own back man. Make up some excuse and stay a while.'

### Thursday, 21 June 2007

### Crossing the Rubicon

I stayed and saw someone local. I have to say it was something of a Rubicon for me. Obviously, this was entirely because of my commitment to northern living and had nothing whatsoever to do with the fact I might not manage the journey without pulling the emergency handle for the guard to bring me more drugs. The osteo was very nice. He thought I had sprained a ligament which had put my muscles into spasm. He happens to be tall, dark and handsome. He hugged me. I like it when people hug me, especially when they look like he does. He stood behind me, wrapped his arms around me and stretched me. He asked: 'Does that hurt?' I felt like saying: 'Yes, but I don't care.' He pulled bits of me. Luckily, nothing came off. Nothing I needed, anyway. Maybe I am taller. That would be nice. It might take me some time to figure that one out, because I am still walking with a stoop. It is a shame about the stoop because my figure is lovely now I have a bad back. I have to say that it is not entirely my own work. I had to put a Wonderbra on because stooping makes your breasts dangle and I did not want to graze my nipples. I also struggled into a pair of enormous elasticated knickers that promise to smooth away all your lumps and bumps, and go all the way up to the bra and all the way down your thigh. They are the sort of knickers you buy to go with a particular silky outfit. As soon as you get home and take them out of the packet, you hold them out in front of you and think: 'I'm married. I don't have to wear these.' They do provide useful support when your back gives out, though.

I liked the osteopath, but he seemed to have a hidden agenda to change my entire life. Among other things, he advised I drank less tea and more water. Luckily he did not ask me whether I had a Chablis habit. He also said I should suck my abdominal muscles in. I did not want to tell him that I was already sucking my abdominal muscles in. Apparently, sucking in your abdominal muscles makes you think about your movements more and protects you from momentum (which is a bad thing). Finally, he said I should lie on my left side, curl myself into a foetal ball, stick a pillow between my legs and stay there.

I said: 'I can't spend my entire day in the foetal position, much as I'd like to.' But apparently, that is exactly what I should do whenever I feel the need, which will probably be just about all the time.

## Saturday, 23 June 2007

### Outside looking in

I was invited to Girl Friday's thirtieth birthday party. I never go to parties. I do not work well in large groups. Frankly, I do not work all that well in small groups either. The theme was fancy dress of the Sixties, Seventies and Eighties. I was in a weird combination of Sixties and Seventies in an old orange smock dress and orange silk blouse, black and white tights, red ankle boots and a wig of long, dark, wavy hair. The thing I most resembled was a dog's dinner. My husband took one look at me and pleaded work, so I set off on my own. The girl introduced me to her bewigged time capsule of a family lining the ballooned walls of the community club. The disco blare made it impossible to hear anyone. She brought me over to her girlfriends of pink ladies and Marilyn Monroe. I shook some hands. One young girl laughed as I glad-handed. I must stop myself shaking hands. I said to the party girl, a picture in a massive wig and platform shoes: 'You go mingle. I am going over to the bar.' I thought: 'I don't want this poor girl feeling like she has to nursemaid me at her own party.' My back was still bad and I stood alone at the bar for what felt like three hours but was probably thirty minutes. Occasionally a boy would look across at me and I would think: 'I am way too old for you, mate.' He would think the same; not even a Blues Brother came over to chat me up. Eventually I skulked away. Apparently I missed the party games.

## Monday, 25 June 2007

### Baby talk

I tell my baby girl 'I love you' one hundred times a day. The thought as natural as a breath. I chase and catch, hold her in my champion arms and kiss a rounded cheek. I shout out 'I love you' as I whirl her round in celebration of my dazzling prize. Later, as we play, she sucks in her cheeks to moue a kiss, then, distracted by a brother or toy, walks away. Disappointed in my loss, forlorn, I say 'I love you' to her back. Sitting on the kitchen floor, with infinite and tender care she tears the paper edging from a teabag, peers into the heart of her gift and pours it into her lap pot to join the rest. I, as ever, notice too late. Sigh, scoop and hug, whisper 'I love you' and pull her from the dried tea sea.

She walks now among our words, one small and trusting hand in mine. Unsteady still, sometimes she totters and then falls, plump on her behind. Unperturbed, she sits blank a while and then clambers up to try again to reach her goal of understanding. She says: 'Mama. Loves. Loves me.' True and sweet. Her mother loves her. She does not say the words she hears. She does not say 'I love you', though you would think she might. Might hope she would. Instead, she wraps herself entire in this one and truest certainty. 'Mama. Loves. Me.'

## Tuesday, 26 June 2007

### Sweet home

I am not sure what my builders think of me. I like the fact they take decisions. I just like to know the reasons behind the decisions. 'Why have you put the pantry door on that way round?' 'Why can we have a flat floor when we couldn't a week ago?' 'Why have you knocked down that wall?' Whichever one of them I am cross-examining will look at me for a split second. Sometimes, I think he is constructing his answer. Sometimes, I think he is thinking: 'Why ... do you ask all these questions?' They are very patient with me, but they like to talk to my husband. I suspect he provides them with answers rather than questions. Maybe they just feel sorry for him. Maybe they think I ask him: 'Why do you want sex with me tonight?' Anyway, they do not have long to finish off the job and give us our house back. It will not be entirely finished. Work will continue on the arches when we move back in, but I do not mind that. Frankly, I will miss the builders when they leave.

We are supposed to move back in two weeks. Again. I really want to move back. I feel adrift. It has been nice to be in a village and I think it has helped me feel as if I belong, but I want to get on with my life. I want to have the space to stretch out and breathe. There is a pond in the garden of this rented house. We carefully covered it up. The boys equally carefully uncovered it. I want to open the door and let my sons out to play in the garden without worrying about whether they will drown. I want to fill my pantry with fancy tinned stuff that looks like art and glass jars of fruit we will never eat, not even at Christmas. I want to keep vanilla pods in sugar and have everything just so. For a day at least. That will be a very good day. One to remember. I want to go home.

## Thursday, 28 June 2007

### It's my party

Terrible night. My six-year-old woke up at about 1.30 a.m., complaining of feeling sick and had to come into my bed. I think I managed about an hour of sleep after that. If we weren't traipsing to the bathroom, he was asking for water, tapping on the wooden bedhead or moaning: 'Mummy, I feel sick.' 'Me too,' I muttered into the pillow. I can virtually guarantee that one or other of the children are sick whenever my husband is away – usually the four-year-old. It is as if he says to them: 'Remember. Be good for Mummy and be sure to vomit lots while Daddy is away.'

I do not know whether it is sleep deprivation, but I cannot decide what to do tomorrow. Tomorrow being my birthday. In London, if I could get the day off work, I would often spend it alone shopping, seeing an exhibition or a movie and then out to dinner with my husband in the evening. I do not know where to go here. Can I replicate the birthday I would have had but in a different place, or is that a dangerous thing to do? Will I compare, contrast and find my northern life too different for my taste? Will I end up buying a saddle for no better reason than I fetched up in the saddle shop? Or do I do something entirely different? Go for a bone-drenching beach walk alone? (Happy Birthday, Billy No-Mates.) Take the four-year-old and the baby to a castle? (If I was counting, I would estimate I have visited two castles this week.) Perhaps I will buy a birthday cake and share it with the builders.

## Friday, 29 June 2007

### Prayers

My four-year-old came in with a tightly folded piece of paper. He said: 'Happy Birthday, Mummy.' Bleary, I pushed a pillow underneath my head. I said: 'Darling, how lovely.' I unfolded the A4 paper to admire the coloured pencil scribbling. I unfolded it some more to reveal the words: 'To Granny and Grandad, love.' I said: 'This says it's for Granny and Grandad.' 'Yes,' he nodded, 'but they can't have it. It's yours.' I kissed him. When I came down to breakfast, my six-year-old had marked the occasion by peeling a satsuma and making plate faces with it for his brother and sister and chopping up an apple for me. He must have been awake for some time because the apple was brown with deep scars; it looked like it had been in a knife fight and lost, badly. Technically, he is not allowed to use knives when I am out of the room, but since there were no fingers among the slices, I pretended not to notice. The only injury of the morning was in fact mine when I was helping to dress him for school and an arm shot out of his sleeve and he socked me in the eye incredibly hard. I thought: 'No one's ever given me a black eye for my birthday before.'

Once the older boy was at school, my four-year-old and I went to the local ice-cream parlour, which has a long counter with stools that you draw up and occasionally fall off. This year, it finally recognized Britain's membership of the European Union and introduced cappuccinos and lattes. Before the arrival of the big glittery coffee machine, I asked for a cappuccino and was told: 'We don't do cappuccinos, pet. We do coffee and hot milk.' I love this café. It serves milkshakes in glasses whose sides bulge with pressed glass fruit. Next to the frothing trophy of pink, bubble-popping milk, an aluminium vat stands with more shake; ready, when you drain the glass, to fill your life again with thick and chilly sweetness. Here, bar flies, stuck fat and happy on their stools, eat bacon sandwiches and watch cold tourists buy colder ice-cream cornets at the window. Hands wrapped around your coffee, you think: 'I live here. I know you do not have to stand at the window. You can come in and sit awhile.' But you do not call out an invitation to the strangers.

My birthday was all the better for being spontaneous. I like the idea of spontaneity, I just find it difficult to work it into my schedule. But as soon as I decided to stay put, it was make do and mend and all the better for it. My four-year-old and

I bought a blue marbled plastic bucket, a red spade and a fishing net, snatched up the baby and headed for the beach. I was a silent soul before I became a mother; silence was easy for me. I could hold my peace and never felt the need to chat and chatter. Then children come and you think: 'I have to talk. I have to teach or my child will grow as silent and grave as his mother, which would never do.' So you talk and do not stop. You say: 'Look at that ...' Whatever it may be. You say: 'Did you see ...?' and 'That's because ...' till any sensible child blocks up his ears with peas. Then, children leave. 'Bye, Mum.'

There is silence in the kitchen and the car and everywhere. But there cannot be silence in her heart. I think, in her most secret places, a mother's chatter plays out, regardless of the emptied nest. An old woman, shabby in a mac and slippered feet, holding a shopping carry-all; her hair, tousled; her mind, worse. The words escape again, she calls long-gone children to her side and loud-mumbles to them of birds and trees and passing marvels that she sees.

I have not yet become that ghost, but as I watched my son walk ahead of me, intent on the sea, resolute in his wellies, his net in one hand, his bucket dangling from an arm, the spade gripped in the other hand, I thought: 'This is how the man will be: looking out to the horizon, armed and ready for his task, his mother hardly more than a memory. This is how I will be: trailing behind him, hoping he will stay safe, that he is happy, will turn round and remember me.' He found his spot in a wash of water running across the beach while the baby girl and I squatted down, gathering seashells and pressing them into sandy walls of small castles. I got older. Despite that, it was a good day.

## Wednesday, 4 July 2007

## Good cop, bad cop

It is a week till we move back into the cottage. It is difficult to believe it will be ready. I do not think I helped when I asked the builders to move the bath they had installed. They went off me a bit. I walked into the bathroom and the roll-top bath was pressed against the wall as if it had a crush on it. It looked terrible. Admittedly, the builders had asked me whether I wanted it to stand away from the wall or against it. I might have said: 'Against it.' I did not mean obscenely pressed against it, right against it, up against it. I did not mean for the bath to make a show of herself. I meant more of a casually, in the vicinity, if you happen to be passing then feel free to call in 'against it'. It is, in fact, not just the bath which is up against it, but the builders too. I thought about not saying anything. I always think about not saying anything. Then I climbed into the bath and realized you could not rest your elbow on the side or put your hand on the bath to lever yourself up. I thought: 'Every time I have a bath I am going to think: 'This over-priced bath is far too close to that newly plastered wall in a bathroom I have just paid good money for and which I hoped would be perfect because it is costing enough to be perfect.' I said: 'Slight problem.' The builder was incredibly calm about it, bearing in mind the plumbers had only just finished plumbing it all in. Sometimes I think my husband should have these conversations without me. The mixer tap arrived bent and the taps arrived without their 'Hot' and 'Cold' buttons. My husband said: 'You ring them.' Unlike the bath, the Aga was installed surprisingly far from the wall. My husband said: 'You talk to them.' I say: 'Why do I always have to be the bad cop?' He looks at me with puppy-dog eyes. 'You know how I hate confrontation,' he says, throwing down the nice-guy card and sweeping up the chips. I confront; the situation changes for the better. He hands me a bullet for the gun, hands me a bullet belt for better rat-a-tat. I fire, and between their ragged, bloody gasps the wounded think: 'I don't know how that nice bloke puts up with that stroppy baggage.' My husband will kindly smile down upon their suffering faces, uncork his canteen of water to wet their dry and cracked lips, straighten up, beckon over his armoured wife, point, smile again and say: 'This one's not dead yet.'

## Thursday, 5 July 2007

### House about town

I am trying out a new café in the nearest market town. It has armchairs. This may sound like nothing very much, but believe me, an armchair to drink a decent cup of coffee in is right up there among my priorities, alongside 'Bring up the children to be decent human beings', 'Stop my mother getting any frailer', 'Make friends' and 'Learn German'.

Perhaps I will not need the armchair. I have an idea. The newly refurbished kitchen – at least the half-refurbished kitchen – has a high window. I have decided to buy two bar stools and acquire one of those large china coffee mugs that want to be a Starbucks paper cup. When particularly desperate, I could ask the nice man who drives the big red bus for golfers and tourists to come round and park in front of the kitchen window. I could stare out, pretend I am back in the city. I have it all planned. I will do the school run in the morning, buy the newspapers and head for my little piece of London. I will turn on the Gaggia coffee maker, perhaps I will queue up by the sink for a while and leave some money in the children's toy till. I think that would work. The other advantage to my sill café is you do not need friends in Starbucks. If you sit there on your own, you feel not odd, but urban and busy. 'Too busy for friends right this minute. Too busy thinking of romance. Too busy planning my career. Too busy writing this screenplay. I only just have time for this latte and one more piece of caramel shortbread.' Alternatively, if my lonely coffee stop palled, I could always say to another mother: 'Come round for a coffee. I will meet you at my windowsill. Ten-ish.'

God knows, I need more coffee these days. I blame the osteopath for telling me to cut down on caffeine. If people stopped telling me what to do, I would not have the urge to go out and do the opposite. I also blame my caffeine cravings on the fact that we are due to move on Wednesday. We were due to move on Tuesday but pushed it back a day to buy our way back into the builders' affections after making them shift the bath. I went up to the cottage this morning. In fact, I went up to the cottage three times within five hours. I suspect the builders have started hiding when they see me coming. The plumber moves more slowly than they do. Or perhaps he cannot fit. I said to him: 'Thank you for moving the bath.' He did not say anything in return; he just looked at me. He could have been thinking: 'In this light, when she stands like that, she looks like Kate Moss,' but I do not think so.

## Monday, 9 July 2007

### Indefinite futures

We were supposed to move house the day after tomorrow. Yesterday, it became blazingly apparent it was not going to happen. Today, the builder described it as 'imperative' we put the move back. Unfortunately, we cannot get hold of the removal man to tell him the move is off. Again. And would he mind moving us next week, or possibly the week after that, or maybe sometime never? I knew this would happen, as an old teacher of mine used to say. I have this vision of a large removal van turning up at the crack of dawn only for us to say: 'Not today, thank you, Milky.' Maybe if I stopped wanting it so much, it would all come together. As it is, every time I walk into the cottage, I look around and think: 'This is not going to get finished in time.' But you do not want to seem like a panicky, depressive girly. You do not want to stick a finger in your mouth, twirl a curl around another and giggle nervously as a sweating man tries to reach the finishing line. They do not like it.

I was right, though.

Builders step through their own personal landscape of debris and chaos. They say: 'I am really looking forward to getting stuck in to that problem with the drains.' They like banging their heads against brick walls. That way they get to knock them over. I am trying to keep it in 'What's another week between friends?' perspective, but I am desperate to stop squatting in the rented house. Ever since the boys dyed the kitchen carpet pink, I have not been able to relax. The whole process of getting back home is just taking so much time: packing, or at least thinking about packing; endless fannying on about bits and bobs of furniture we have managed our entire lives without but which have become critically important to our happiness. Glamorous stuff like pan stackers and trivets. I mean, 'trivets'. How have I managed all these years without a trivet? There was once a time when I did not even know what a trivet was. Ah. The innocence of youth.

Then there is the Aga. My husband's idea – not so much a cooker as a cast-iron anchor roped to my ankle. Not so much an anchor as an advertisement to all and sundry 'Look, we're middle class and have come to live in the country.' All sorts of rituals appear necessary when a new Aga is installed. Not least signing over a large amount of money. This afternoon, I spent several hours mopping down the sweat from the hulking brute.

Normally, I would quite like that. But there was little return. I took up a slightly soapy cloth and washed it first. An hour later, the sweat was running from it. I tell you, these things are very demanding. I expected something that would clean itself and do its share of the ironing. What do I get? A traditional 'Mop me down and worship my size'. It doesn't even have any conversation. Still, it is on now and will keep the builders warm while they work through to the bitter end.

## Thursday, 12 July 2007

### Alpha male

Tore down to the city to chose tiles with my husband. Tore back up again to get to a Christian supper at the local United Reform Church. The Oyster Farmer's Wife completed something called an Alpha course, and the graduates celebrate with a supper to which they invite guests who might also want to do an Alpha course. She invited me. We were unusual among our London friends in that we went to mass. Being a 'believer' has no novelty value here at all. My 'belief' is a pretty ropy affair of feminist hesitation, personal doubts, general embarrassment and a cultural legacy from my mother, but other people's certainty impresses me. I looked at my prayerful friend, thought: 'I am about to move house again – look what happened last time. I need God on my side. Why not?'

As a Catholic, I do not have to talk about God. I hardly have to talk *to* God. The priests and my mother can do that for me. I have hardly been to mass since we moved up here. I hardly even pray to God these days. I figure he is busy, what with Iraq and all. But I tell a lie – I do. I regularly, head in hands, say: 'God, give me strength.' Or 'Lord, give me patience' or sometimes 'Fucking Hell.' Does that count, I wonder? Does he hear these Mother's Prayers and answer them? I have not yet fallen to my knees and wept. Not recently anyhows. So perhaps he does give me pause and succour so that I do not explode in geyser ways, spouting anger and hot and bubbling mother blood.

We had supper in the church hall. Sausages and salad, pavlova and wine. I had brought the wine. I was not taking the chance of going through it entirely sober. The Oyster Farmer's Wife is charming and very skilled socially. She does that thing with your name and an interesting fact to give you something to latch on to when you are introduced. I half expected her to say when she was introducing me: 'This is Wifey. She's probably going to Hell.' The meal finished. We watched a DVD, a man preaching in a London church to the young and beautiful who would not be damned for all the world. They too had eaten their supper and drunk their wine and now listened with intent. Trainee doctors, lawyers and accountants. Shiny hair and painted lips. Serious expressions as they listened to the pastor's tips for the top. They closed their eyes in prayer. 'I am the way, the truth and the life,' the man said on behalf of the Lord. I am wondering as I look at the youthful screen beauties whether any of them have known the grief and loneliness which has you reach for faith in the hope of peace of mind. When the DVD was finished, the URC forty-something minister said: 'Anyone who is interested in the course can tell me as I stack the chairs away.' And I said: 'Did you notice how beautiful and young they were? Are we supposed to feel that way?' I think: 'If Jesus wants me for a sunbeam, I could save a fortune on cosmetics.'

## Wedding blues

I know the feel of my mother's wedding dress. Her first one, that is. As a girl child, I would slip it over my plaited head and feel the scratch of net at my throat, the rippled waves of lace; drop pearls and rainbowed sequins catching beneath my nails as I clawed, vain, at the too-tight zip. Bride for an hour, I would gather up the skirt in frothing handfuls, preen and whirl-twirl before the glass. Dressing in my mother's past and my own future. I wonder, will my daughter do the same in my ivory and satin empire line? Will I let her play dress-up? Or will I say: 'No, darling, Mummy wants to be buried in her dress. Won't she look pretty in the box? She'll finally get her money's worth anyhow. Here's a cowboy outfit. Wear that instead.'

I have seen black-and-white photos of that special day, my mother's happiness with the groom who did not stick around. Who had to be replaced with something that smiled and was more durable. 'You may kiss the bride and make her cry,' the priest must have said to this groom who fathered a child and then cavalierly, cancerously, died. Job done. But I never knew until today that my mother's bouquet was of golden yellow roses with a white ribbon bow. Now I know, I can smell the yellow from here.

Black and white; the day seems far away. In the hectic pink flush of my mother's cheek, I am there – or at least the idea of me. My uncle just JPEGed me a colour photo of the day. Double click, double click, open and OK: my parents' wedding, 24 August 1963. A windy day. My mother's lace dress with its hooped petticoat, lifted up and hurled against her own proud sentry mother in a sky-blue two piece. Dress and coat with matching 'I'm looking for something for my daughter's wedding' daisy-petalled hat. 'He loves her, he loves her not.'

He loved her, just not for long enough. And my gran, my gran who liked an orchid, exotic in a clear plastic box; it was burgundy. A nice contrast, we all thought, against the blue.

The huddle then, from left to right, my father (now deceased, in a dove-grey silk tie), his hatchet-faced mother (my other grandmother in a dark-blue suit), my sky-blue gran and the pink-cheeked bride. My mother is the only one to smile. I cannot tell if his mother is trying to smile and unaccustomed to it or whether she is thinking: 'This will not end well.' A groom then, two widows and a bride. I think he should have guessed how it would end. The way it often ends for men. Dead. And gone. Did I mention he was gone?

Still, I am glad I went to the wedding, stood with them in the breeze awhile, smelled the flowers, admired my gran's hat, the sheen on my first father's tie. I magnified his face to a pixelating blur. A blur the size of a daughter's hand. I know this to be the case. I pressed my hand against his glass face and measured it. Taking it away and looking hard, I thought I saw him smile.

## Saturday, 14 July 2007

### Galloping Gordons

I spent the afternoon dressed as a Victorian to sell cakes at the school fete and the evening in a gown at the hunt ball. The hunt ball. It is worth repeating. 'How was your weekend?' 'Oh, y'know, busy. Did the shopping. Trip to the beach. School fete. Went to the hunt ball. On at the castle.' I was slightly disappointed because I had thought we would eat dinner on horseback, but they insisted we sat on chairs at a table. I had thought we would eat roast fox, but it was braised Northumberland beef. I also thought we would burn an effigy of Tony Blair before the dancing started; instead, we were entertained by white-fleshed belly dancers. It could have been a chartered accountant's annual thrash had it not been for a couple of clues like the chaps in red tailcoats who are the masters of the hunt and the raffle prizes which included an £80 voucher to 'buy new tack for your horse (saddles, bridles, bits)' as well as a pallet of 'haylage (which) provides the ultimate in high nutritional forage . . . sweet and appealing to even the fussiest of horses.' I was so disappointed when I did not win the haylage.

My Best Friend From School came up and we went with the Accountant, the Sheep Farmer and his wife, who is pregnant with their third child. The Sheep Farmer said to my Best Friend From School: 'Mind, she made a hell'uva bad job of shearing that sheep.' I did not think he was joking. He went on: 'Look out the window on the A1 and you'll see it. It's the one that limps.' After dinner, there was dancing. I am not sure what these hunting types are like on the field, but they are bloody dangerous on a dance floor. Gusto does not cover it. Hooves pounded the ground, sweat flew from flanks; they leapt over 'Come on Eileen'. The hounds scented their prey and they thundered on past 'I Predict a Riot', ploughing through the mud, the blood beating in their ears. Women in silk and beaded frocks cantered around the dance floor on high and skinny heels; occasionally they whinnied. I had decided against high heels. This was possibly a mistake. The organizer is particularly beautiful. Another very tall woman, like my Riding Pal – perhaps it is the Viking blood. Her legs are as long as I am; the top of my head is about level with her midriff. I looked up at this Hunt Ball lovely. I said: 'Well done. Everyone is having a fantastic time.' She smiled brilliantly at me, a vision in bronze and black satin. She said: 'How nice of you to say that.' As she turned away, she patted me on the head. I wondered briefly if she was going to offer me a sugar lump.

## Wednesday, 18 July 2007

## Moving mountains

We eventually managed to get hold of the removal company and arranged it for today. It was grim. It usually is. We did at least have a removal company this time rather than three mates and a horsebox, but I almost wished we had stuck to the horsebox. There was some mix-up in communications. I said to my husband: 'Are they sending a pantechnicon?' I am not sure what a pantechnicon is, but it sounds big. He told me they were sending three vans. It sounded odd at the time, but I thought: 'OK.' They did not send three vans, they sent one van and two men. Two unhappy men who took one look and did not like what they saw. They immediately started talking about their tachograph. I do not know what a tachograph is either, but it sounded a lot less helpful than a pantechnicon. They had only just arrived and were already grumbling about getting back in time and needing four men instead of two. Not even bacon, egg and mushroom sandwiches from the village bakery quietened them. And they are particularly good sandwiches.

My only consolation was that I could not entirely make out what the gaffer was saying. He had a very thick Scottish accent. He would hold out a box and say something like: 'Eurrrgh rrrrrrrhhing khhhhheeeargh?' Occasionally, he would say: 'Eurrrgh rrrrrrrhhing tachograph.' When he said something like that, I did not want to understand him.

I could not even make the point that they had been sent an inventory and it was their decision to send the one van and two men, because we were so very much in the wrong for not putting every last fork in a large cardboard box of its own. I had to accept responsibility for that one. For some reason, I had to bail out for an hour yesterday, walk up through the woods at the back of the Accountant's and go lie on my own on the wooden bench to look at the castle and the lighthouse and the sea for a while. I could not tell you whether I was low because of the grinding boredom of moving again or because I was thinking: 'OK, this is it then. I really have moved to Northumberland. No more coxing and boxing and renting. I will have a proper home. It is time to start feeling like I belong.'

Girl Friday offered to stay and help, but I did not think that was fair. By midnight, with some way to go on packing, I had entirely lost the will to live. My husband kept going but I went to bed. I decided the children's toys could stay in their own unlidded plastic boxes. I asked myself: 'Why unpack drawers when you can put a piece of paper over them?' I told myself it was entirely reasonable for my husband to unhook the computers and pack away his office paperwork in black bin bags and suitcases while the removers were shipping stuff out of the house. It did not work well. It certainly does not make me a pin-up as client of the year back at the removal company depot. I also decided I had gone off my husband. Communication is the key to a successful relationship. He said: 'Do you resent me for making you do this again?' I was barely speaking to him. This was our third move in two years. I said: 'To be accurate, I resent and dislike you in equal parts.'

I should not have stopped putting my life away in cardboard boxes. I was totally in the wrong. Apparently, everything needs to go in a box. I am the only person in the world who does not realize you break the social contract with your removal company when you fail to put your plastic boxes and carrier bags in their cardboard boxes. It is something to do with stacking them one on top of the other and squaring them off. I thought the boxes were optional extras, like those small bottles of shampoo you get in hotel rooms. You are not actually obliged to use them to wash your hair. One of my builders has moved seventeen times in sixteen years. He has an infinitely more patient wife than me. I said: 'When you move, do you put everything – I mean everything – in cardboard boxes?' He said: 'Yes. My wife is very organized.' The upshot was they did two runs between the rented house and the cottage but did not quite finish the job. My husband said I am not allowed to go back to the rented house and see how much has been left behind. I think I will sneak in like Bluebeard's wife when he is busy elsewhere. It is possible the village might hear my scream.

## Monday, 23 July 2007
### Things fall apart

Every now and then when we think he might be fighting off a stomach migraine, we put the four-year-old on medication. The intermittent medication works well, but yesterday he came down with his stomach migraine again. Watching *Scooby Doo* in the sitting room, he threw up all over the new beige, textured three-seater sofa we had just got out of its plastic wrapping. I had not even sat down on it unwrapped. He also threw up over a new wickerwork chair, the new oaked floor and my husband. Later, the child in bed, my husband said: 'Is this all a huge mistake? Are you sure you still love me?' 'Is what a mistake?' 'The move, all this. The three moves' – he gestured to the cardboard boxes of who knows what, toys spread across the floor, burgeoning piles of paper, black plastic sacks of clothes. 'Too late now,' I said. 'We're here. We'll sort it out. It might take a while.' I do not know when my husband asks me this if he needs to hear that all is well, how he would feel if I raised a hand, said: 'No, stop the wagons. Turn back. I've been far enough away for long enough. This adventuring is not what I was looking for. Let us return to what we know.'

Then, 150 miles away, my mother fell. 'I'll just give the carpet a vacuum.' Trip and tumble. Crash and bang. On to the fake coaled fire and the spiked metal grate. At least the fire was not on. 'Ooops' and 'Ow'. Tears and 'Shouldn't haves'. Old-lady preoccupations and old-lady consequences. Vacuuming a carpet she cannot see to pick up dust of no consequence to anyone but her, she tripped over the wire. Her arm grazed by the spikes and bruised by the tumbled-out coals, she lay there a while with the white marble hearth like a gravestone beside her. That is what old ladies do, the etiquette of an aged person's fall. Lie there and play dead. Lie there and wish you were young again. Lie there and wait for Christmas to come or someone to walk through the door to pick you up and dust you down. Not on to the carpet – it is important to keep your carpet clean at all times. My father was out shopping. She remembered, flat against the woollen twist. She had turned the key in the back-door lock. You can never be too careful. Always lock your door to keep wolves and bad men out. You do not want wolves in the kitchen, they make such a mess – blood and crumbs everywhere. Minutes passed; the shining gilt and glass carriage clock made tick-tock turns around the garden. Slowly, she levered herself up to grasp the handy sofa arm, struggled upright and wobbled to the door to turn the key again. A blessing the sofa was so close to her, pulled away as it was from the walls, for a better and more thorough clean. It goes to show you should never cut corners when cleaning. Without the sofa there, she would never have got to her slippered feet.

She wobbled back to find the phone and speedy dialled a number for a neighbour. Shame she had put in the number wrong. Instead, she rang her brother, miles away, who said: 'Put down the phone and try again.' She tried again. No joy. She really must be more careful with her speedy dial-ups. What use else? She rang her niece and talked awhile, of the rain of which there is too much, and of me, of which there can never be enough. 'Stay with me on the line till he comes back,' and so she did. Kept my mother company while the old lady cried awhile, waiting for her shop-gone husband.

## Monday, 30 July 2007

### Roll up. Roll up

Ran away at the weekend to a local agriculture show. There was a climbing wall, studded with stones. My motherhood is filled with fear: that the children might go to sleep and not wake up despite the bedtime prayer; that they might ride a shiny board through salty waves and be taken by a rip tide or a shark; or that the bizarre and snaggle-toothed might snatch them in a supermarket aisle as I turn to pick up beans. I looked at the wall. I thought: 'You and your like. You are my enemy.'

My six-year-old, buckled in and harnessed to a rope, set off in a pilgrim scramble up the stones. I thought: 'If you do not climb that wall, you will not fall off it. If you do not climb that wall, you will not climb a mountain when you are twenty. You will not climb another and another. You will not die, young and brave and foolish, caught out by the weather on a mountainside.' He climbed and climbed; one foot slipped and then the other to leave him hanging by his arms. I caught my breath to see his white face look down at the ground as his body peeled his fingers from the rocks. He fell. He swung of course. He did not plummet then to hit, bang smash, the ground. He reached out once again, caught a rock, clung on, pushed on and scrambled higher, then still higher, taking my heart with him.

## Wednesday, 1 August 2007

### The knacker's yard for me

Yesterday, as time folded itself down into the twilight, neat and away, a golden wash lay across the sea and half the fields. Beasts grazed in the last of the sun and thought: 'You know, I am a lucky cow'; unlucky cows preferred the grassy gloom of the departing day, said: 'My life is skimmed. Soon it will be the knacker's yard for me.' Cotton-rompered babe in arms, I looked out beyond the glass to the shadows and the light. She looked too, said: 'Night night, cows.' Then turned away to the rocker and her bedtime books. I sat, rocked once, tipped her in to lie against my chest, picked up the nursery rhymes and said: 'Shall we begin?'

## Friday, 3 August 2007

### A stitch in time

I am not a woman with a veil, a distaff and a wheel; I have no pet sheep to shear and fleece to spin out yarn, then weave it into cloth. Unlike my mother, I do not sew, knit, purl or craft in any kind of way. I do not ice tall white colonnaded cakes for grateful niece brides or snip-snap and glue mauve butterflies on to get-well cards. A few years ago, this craft art stopped for my handy, never idle mother who could not knit another pair of eyes when hers gave out. She could not see to find and buy a pattern. Sometimes she might weep, but I have never heard her grumble. Instead of a craft knife and a rubber stamp, my mother holds a white stick and découpage smiles.

I found a half-complete field of tapestry sunflowers caught up in a frame. Bundled wool skeins hang from card: lemon, whites, khaki green, dark moss green, pale apple green, dark olive and light tan. You hold up the hole–punched card and a meadow of wool falls from it, ready for the harvest. She sorted, mounted them and named them for their colours. On a card-board scene, she spelled out the wools that she should use: this line here at the heart of the sunflower, dark brown; around it medium brown, then tan. The petals, yellow, dark, medium and light, the background ivory and white. The borders round the flower and falling leaves, medium air-force blue. She has sewn, half cross–stitch, four sunflowers to top and tail the bordering, winding leaves, mallow backdrop clouds, trees and grassy slope. But the rest, the rest is empty painted canvas, waiting to be stitched.

Her sight lost, hope for remedy lost, she stuck the needle tidily in the canvas, swept up the half-completed masterpiece in wool and said: 'Here, you take this. Finish it for me. I've worked so hard on it. I want it finished. Will you finish it instead of me?' I looked at it, the complex graphs with crosses, dots and spots of colour, numbers walking up and down the lines. I thought: 'I've no idea. I'd never have the patience.' I looked at my mother, who hates to leave a job half-done, and said: 'Yes. OK. I can't say when.'

I wrapped it in a pillow case, along with daughterly and good intentions, and put it in a drawer. This week, when I unpacked, I found it. Took it out and read what I should do. Keep the tension even, the canvas taut, never start or finish with a knot: decent rules by which to live your life. I thought: 'I'll never do this.' Picked up a length of lemon, then threaded it. Sewed a line of sunflowers in the distance underneath the trees, one arm wrapped around the canvas, the needle pushed, then pulled, the stitch complete. I thought: 'This will take me till I die. My mother's work all done.'

## Saturday, 4 August 2007

## The quest

The Yorkshire Mother came back from the sun with her four boys, man, van, people carrier, table and six chairs. They set out with hope, travelled over a continent and found oranges, not money, growing on the trees. Her boys gobbled up the fruit and the sun bleached out their hair while café businesses unwound. Earning has its season and winter beckoned. The couple had not earned enough to make it through the quiet months, so they shook off sand, repacked the van and people carrier, stuffed them full of furniture and golden boys, drove back over land, sleeping while ferries ploughed the seas, to a county they called home. They arrived without a house, or jobs, or cash – what money there once was spent on the hope of a better life. They have begun another quest – to find a home to rent, new jobs, cash – enough at least for oranges. And peace, of course. I do believe that when you lose a child as my friend did those years ago, that peace may be the hardest thing to find. That after suffering such a wrenching loss, it is difficult for a mother, even if she cooks, to make life taste as sweet as once it did, to rest quiet after supper, close her eyes in bed and think: 'That was a day well-spent. That was happiness. I am content.'

They are going to stay with us for a while while they look for somewhere to live.

## Wednesday, 8 August 2007

## Inside out

When London Diva visited with her family, my house was perfect, pretty much, give or take the odd builder or odd box. Houses are one thing; lives are more difficult to primp.

The King said they could look round his castle, so we went to smell its ancient stones. The baby decided she did not want to walk around a castle; she lifted up her arms: 'Carry, carry, Mama.' I picked her up, carried her awhile, then put her down. 'Carry, carry, Mama!' This time mildly outraged I thought that she might walk. I hefted her anew. The six-year-old clung to my side. 'I don't want to be here. What about the ghosts?' Suicidal soldiers and a small and long-dead little girl, he had heard tell of. 'Can we go now?' he pleaded. I put the baby down to rest my back. 'No, darling,' I said, 'we've only just arrived.' 'I feel sick,' my four-year-old informed me as the baby began to weep again. I reached across his brother's head to stroke and pat his cheek, said: 'Do you, darling, never mind,' and stooped to pick the baby up. I calculated the distance from the entrance, where we stood, to the exit. Far too far away. We staggered on past china plates, photos of the King as a small, curly-haired prince, armour, and still and waxy dungeoned gore. 'Look, children: history. No, don't look there.' I put the baby down; she wailed again. She did not like my habit. Maybe it is here that ghostly stories start: a weeping child, a desperate screaming mother around a corner and out of sight? Climbing down some steps, my six-year-old barked his shin; his face crumpled. I put the baby down to kiss him better. He cried. She cried. The four-year-old said: 'Don't you care that I feel sick?' London Diva, walking ahead with her husband, her pair of beautiful teenage and near-teenage girls, turned back. She paused a moment to consider the family snap we made and said, reaching out a hand: 'Is this your life?'

## Thursday, 9 August 2007

### One thing and another

An outing to a city hospital to look into my six-year-old's nut allergy. Breastfeeding is supposed to reduce the risk of allergies. He was breastfed for thirteen months; I feel like suing my own nipples. A nurse covers his arms with solutions and pricks them through the skin. It turns out he is also allergic to cats, dogs, horses and grasses. I tell my husband if he was allergic to sand and bad coffee, we could all go back to London.

Children's Outpatients is busy with intent artists carefully sticking sequins on to cardboard silhouettes of children who run and jump for joy. Next to them, small boys gaze rapt into virtual reality, only their fingers and eyeballs moving as the game plays out. Pretty girls wear golden princess frocks while others storm a grey and plastic castle with battlements and an orange slide for a quick getaway if small barbarians make it through the gates. As my sons played in and around the castle, I noticed an engraved and silver plaque, its shiny brother hung on a different wall, each hardly bigger than a matchbox. They said: 'With love from The Family and Friends of Katie Grant, Aged 2'. I wondered who she was, this lost child whose parents thought to gift a toy to others. I asked a nurse. Asking, I thought: 'I hope she is remembered and not just in a plaque.' She was. As she cleared away the glitter, the nurse said: 'Ah yes, Katie.' The nurse said people were so kind – a fire engine, a doll's house. Each toy to mark a missing child. She said it was a shame: the slide was broken, the castle, it would have to go. But Katie's silvered name will not lie among plastic and forgotten ruins: the plates will be unscrewed from castle walls and fixed to something else. I thought how right to keep her name; right, too, that a toy should break from hard and eager play. That is what toys should do.

## Monday, 13 August 2007

### Plagues upon houses

Have been visited by plagues, several and diverse. A plague of boils. Maybe not boils, spots then. It is fair to say I have not had spots like these since I was sixteen when I spent a considerable period of time staring at my nose thinking: 'How spotty can you get?' Not only spots: a skin rash has reappeared which I have not seen since I was locked in a job at the BBC which I hated and which hated me back. When I went to a cosmetics counter in the nearest city last week, I explained I needed the magic potion I had once used to get rid of the stress rash — oh yes, and I had spots. The woman found the magic potion, then said: 'Try a pore-minimizing serum.' A pore-minimizing serum? That is to say, I have spots, a rash and enormously large pores. Do they train these women to say things like: 'Well, I think you are beautiful as you are but perhaps you would like to try this shaving foam?' or 'I hardly noticed the adult acne because I was so taken by your enormous blue eyes.' Managers must go on the same courses: 'On the one hand, you make a lovely cup of tea; on the other, you have cost the company £32 million and you're fired.' I want to know whether these women ever look at their sisters and say: 'Do you know what? I think you are just too ugly for me to help.'

It is not just the boils, we have so many flies in the cottage, it is difficult to think we are not damned. They drop from nowhere into your tea cup or on to a half-emptied plate. I sprayed and closed doors; stalked with tea towels and newspapers. I bought two plastic fly swatters. Two on the off chance I might get to keep one when the boys discover them and take them out to the garden to hit each other with. I also bought an electronic tennis bat you swing at them; hanging, after all, is too good for them and tying nooses that small can be very time-consuming. Finally, I bought a poison pen to wipe round the windows and doors, which I feel is rather Agatha Christie. I also have my doubts whether they can read. I wrote a note on the window. It said: 'Dear Flies. Go away or I will kill you.' I signed it 'Lady of the Flies'.

We are also a house of pestilence and disease. Not only did my six-year-old, my husband and I all fall to vomiting and bile, but the Yorkshire Mother's seven-year-old and nine-year-old came down with it too. They moved out yesterday into a rented house a couple of miles away. There was a moment of quiet, then last night my baby girl caught it. I moved a mattress into her room, right by her cot. She would say: 'Feel sick' and we would play catch into a plastic bowl. Say: 'Wata' and I would hold a sippy cup. Vomit and I would say: 'I'll be right back, OK?' and she would lie there, nod and I would go wash an unlucky panda, or fetch another towel or sheet. We lay together on the mattress and she pressed her apple face into the dark place between my cheek and cotton pillow. I said: 'I love you, darling one.' I do not think there is a word, nor ever can be one, to catch and paint the all-at-once rush of a mother's love. It is as if you catch a leaky boat to ride the rapids, tip and swirl around the rocks, gasp to see the rainbowed, unmapped waterfall, then plunge – not downwards into the white and foaming water rush, but up and up and up.


## Sunday, 19 August 2007

### Happy holidays

The week has been mad; then again, every week is mad. My Clever Cousin came to do complicated things to my computers. He was supposed to come on Wednesday and leave on Thursday at noon. Every time he fixed one program, another unravelled. He ended up leaving on Friday at 6 p.m. He does not have kids. He has fish. I said: 'What do you think?' He said: 'It's chaos.' I would have asked him why he thought that, but someone screamed, interrupting my thought process. It might have been me.

Summer holidays mean that we have neighbours again in the other cottages along our row. Small children play complicated superhero games in the shrubbery. My six-year-old's part demands he spends every waking moment in a John Deere tractorman boilersuit and his cycle helmet. Even when he eats. When the boys and their friends do things I do not like, I throw them out of the garden. If it is good enough for God. Following a bad experience with a room being trashed, which would not have shamed a Seventies rock band, I also have strict rules about playing inside. On Friday, as I was talking to a builder about the next phase of work in the arches, my six-year-old asked: 'Can we go upstairs, Mummy?' I said yes, noticing too late the tribe of children with him. As soon as I had finished talking to the builder, I ran upstairs to bring everyone back down. There was a young boy I had never seen before in the room. I said: 'Who are you?' I suppose I should really have said: 'Whose are you and where are you from?' I still do not know. Later, when I asked my sons, they shrugged.

At some point in the morning, my Riding Pal drops by with her friend who has the Exmoor ponies. They are both on large horses. My friend says: 'I'm really hungover. Can I have some water?' I go get her some water. I say to my Clever Cousin: 'Come and meet my friend.' He stands up, eases past the builder (although we have moved back in, the builders are still with us), steps round a workbench at the door and comes outside to meet her. I say: 'She is on a horse.' I probably did not need to say this. We chat awhile about the fact the other rider is on a horse with a glorious, glamorous name. She says: 'But I think she looks like a Matilda.' I look at the horse. I think: 'What would make you think your horse looks like a

Matilda? What would make you think your horse looked like anything but a horse?'

They trot off. A couple of hours later, the Evangelicals arrive with their three children. I say to my cousin: 'Come and meet my friends.' I realize I cannot even offer them a biscuit because I am completely out of food. I own an Aga and I am completely out of food. They probably take your Aga away if you do not dedicate at least one day a week to baking cheese scones and fruit cake, let alone if you run out of food.

My Clever Cousin finally made a successful break for freedom. Then on Saturday morning, we had to get out early to visit a farm shop to buy wooden gates for the access road outside the cottages. The boys pestered me for two small padlocks. I gave in. Within an hour of getting home, my six-year-old had padlocked a friend to a knotted rope tied to a tree, which they were using to let themselves down into a nettled strip of field. As the boy dangled from the rope my son realized, a little late, that he had lost the key to the padlock. I had hoped this habit of losing keys would skip a generation. My husband managed to haul the boy up and unlock him with the spare key I had kept (you live and you learn), but not before the struggling had snapped the branch of the rowan tree. I threw them all out of the garden for that one. Pointing to a small tear in his trousers, the boy said: 'Look! He did that when he padlocked me to the rope.' I thought: 'I am so not explaining what happened to your mother.' I said: 'Well, next time he offers to padlock you to something, say no.'

## Wednesday, 22 August 2007

### The ghost of Hamlet's father

Before I went out last night, the Yorkshire Mother rang to say she had been offered a job cooking in an old people's home.

A house, a job now, piecing her life back together. I was going out to the haunted castle again. The Patient Mother wanted to go on the ghost tour and stay overnight in one of the apartments. The Hunt Ball Lovely was going too. I was willing enough to keep them company on the tour, but I cannot say the idea of another sleepless night appealed. Before the tour we ate dinner in the apartment they were staying in – spaghetti bolognese and After Eight chocolate mints.

The castle is supposed to have any number of ghosts, as is the way with castles: a miserable lady, a blue boy, a suicide. What struck me was the way we carry our own ghosts with us. The Patient Mother said she had brought her bunny. A floppy brown and greyish-cream rabbit whose worn ears she still strokes and strokes again then feels against her cheek. Ears once cut off by a brother, sewn back on by mother. Whose paw she had to finger-touch before she slept; whose smell was as familiar, if she were to hold it to her nose, wetted by her breath, as her own grown woman scent. Her companion, then, since five, he has never spent a night away from her: not in honeymoon, childbirth, grief, sickness or any kind of joy. Insisting instead that she must take her nightly refuge in the comforts of childhood.

She sipped a glass of wine and said she would not contemplate a night away from her old friend, would not give the rabbit to her own child. I asked: 'What does she mean to you, this rabbit comforter?' She said: 'My childhood. My father.' Her father died at fifty-eight, six years in the ground. She will not let him go. Not one whit of him. She said: 'I like the fact he visits, watches over me. I like the fact we talk.' And the rabbit, it lies yet on this grown woman's pillow; blue button eyes, once brown glass, alert to every sigh and turn. I said: 'What do you think would happen if you did not take the rabbit into your bed?' She said she did not know, would not find out. When darkness comes, she said she does not, cannot turn her back from her old friend at night, keeping instead her face turned towards the rabbit's own. I said: 'And any other toys?' Two bears, two sheep. A crowded bed, then, hers. A wife, a husband, all the toys of girlhood and her father's ghost watching over all.

The Hunt Ball Lovely, too, brought ghosts, or one at least. She said that driving over she had thought of one young true love she had known. A boy she had grown up with, dated, loved, then drifted from. At twenty-one, he had travelled through Australia and died there in an accident when he fell from the cab of a lorry. She said: 'I thought if anyone would be my spirit guide, it would be him – he loved life so.'

And me? After supper, I sat alone on a damp bench within the walled courtyard in the cold, torchlit darkness while other ghost hunters toured the rack and spike elsewhere. I thought of my ghosts – the dead and gone and lost. Some I grieve for yet. As I grow older, I find longing pains replace youth's growing ones. Love and loss; thread twinned tight, twisted, bound, one with the other, impossible to tell apart so close they are in shade, both deep. I easy summoned up my missing; they stood around in pale, grey ranks, admiring stone walls and flags. I said: 'I've called you here to say. I love you all, miss you still and thought you'd like to know.' I strained to catch a murmur. Failed. A few nodded before fading entirely away; all among them smiled. I think one old lady in grey pin curls and soft wool cap, cradling a babe, raised a hand and waved. It is difficult to tell in the dark with the dead.

## Tuesday, 28 August 2007

## St Aga-tha

I am no longer an Aga virgin. I know this for a fact. Firstly, I burnt my chic black and cream Aga oven mits; scorched, singed, crisped at the tip of the right hand. I laid it down on the top to reach over to a pot. I peered into the broccoli and thought: 'Hmm, that doesn't smell good.' Only to realize the oven glove was smoking. On the upside, I did not have to eat it and the burn does make it look as if I occasionally cook. The Aga, I have discovered, is a tattle-tale. My husband was the one who wanted it. I did not. The expense made me feel bad. More than bad. The expense made me feel sick. I gave in and I was warming to it up to the moment I put the kettle on to make a cup of tea. The Evangelicals came round for supper; I had fed six children, then four grown-ups. I had cooked sausages and baked potatoes and beans alongside a vegetarian option. We had eaten in the garden, which entailed a fair amount of scurrying backwards and forwards carrying things. The pink kitchen table was on the grass since we do not have any garden furniture. This meant I had one surface too few in the kitchen. Things got moved about. My guests left. I thought: 'Before I put the kids to bed, I really want a cup of tea.' As I say, I put the kettle on.

Now, this was not my fault. I told my husband when the Aga arrived that we would have to use it for warmth (tick), for cooking (tick), for drying clothes (tick), for ironing (tick-ish), for making toast (slices of bread pinned in a mesh bat contraption then pressed to death (much as a Catholic martyr might have been) between the hot plate and the chrome lid: tick) and for boiling the kettle. Well, that is what I do. He, however, got the electric kettle out of a packing case and put it on the side. I put it away again. I said: 'We have an Aga. Use the Aga kettle. Fill it up and put it on the hot plate. We are wasting enough power as it is, without plugging in a kettle.' He got it out again. On Saturday, I put it on the Aga. What can I say? It had been a long day. The Aga kettle was not where it normally was. I wanted tea badly. I looked at the electric kettle as the black plastic started to wrinkle as it sat on the hot plate. I looked at the red switch you use to turn it on. I thought: 'That is so not supposed to be there and it is so not supposed to be melting.' I wrenched the kettle off a little late for the black toffee bottom and my hot plate, which now has the face of a clown imprinted on it. Unless, of course, it is the face of a Catholic martyr.

## Tuesday, 28 August 2007

### Foot and mouth

Glendale. Some people wait all year for the right agricultural show to come around. OK, they may flirt a little with another agricultural show, but when you know you have found the agricultural show for you, a strange peace steals over you, that hard, coiled part of you relaxes, thinks: 'Perhaps this is how life is, should be, will be for ever.'

Alternatively, we have lived here too long. We arrived early, and as we settled by the main ring to eat bacon sandwiches and watch the horse jumping, I thought: 'Oh good, horses to watch.' Events here are a little like wallpaper: you glance up and there is a horse. I have never looked that closely; maybe it is wallpaper. But it moves; maybe that is because I have been drinking the water. Anyway, they had the moving wallpaper trick going while we ate the bacon sandwiches, and I gasped when a stray hoof knocked off a pole. My husband said: 'I think you are going native.' I said: 'I don't think so. Make sure we are back in time for the hounds. They're on at three.' He muttered something. I did not ask him to repeat it.

Courtesy of foot and mouth, there were no cattle, sheep or goats. Sign of the times, there was a 'chief livestock and biosecurity steward'. Presumably he has links with the United Nations. Without beasts, I had to find comfort in the horticultural and industrial tent. In the vast marquee were baked products, flowers, and the fruit and veg of entrants striving for unnatural glory. Onions the size of a three-year-old's head; cabbages the size of a ten-year-old's. Leeks as long as an arm, spilling over the table and reaching for the floor. I am not sure I could eat anything that reminded me of a body part. When I was a trainee reporter, I covered a leek show. A man who was languishing in a coma won first prize. He was in the local hospital after being knocked down by a car late one night. As he lay ill and all unknowing, never likely to recover, his twin brother carefully tended his leeks, watered, fed, talked to them. The mother was old and frail. She visited her lost son every day, sat by him, held his hand. She was there when they announced he had won first place with his leeks. Tribute to a brother's tender love. I remember she cried.

One of my favourites yesterday was the competitive potatoes. Without wishing to malign the potatoes, I could see very little difference between them. Perhaps the winner had a little more muscle tone. It was also a very slow race, I stood there for some considerable period of time and I could hardly see them moving. It must have been a relay, because they were in teams of four. No team dropped a baton, and I'm confident no team failed a drugs test.

The competitive ethic was everywhere. Potatoes, cabbage growers, horses in fancy dress. I was slightly disappointed because there had been talk of me judging the horse fancy-dress competition, but when I arrived, someone else was down to judge it. I had been practising by shaking my children's hands for the past fortnight, looking them straight in the eye and saying: 'Well done. Jolly good effort,' which was slightly confusing for them at teatime or indeed when they got up on a morning. But in a way I was relieved, because I was not sure which hoof I should shake when it came to the horse. Did you perhaps shake all of them? Or more if it was a male horse?

The fact that I once thought that I might judge the fancy

dress meant I sat and watched it with a particular interest. Two horses came as walls. That is to say they were covered in brick painted sheets. On one wall a little Humpty Dumpty sat with two King's Men in bearskins riding behind him. A woman next to me muttered: 'I'm sure Humpty Dumpty comes out every year.' I thought that harsh, but as I say, they are very competitive up here. Even the potatoes. The other wall came as Hadrian's Wall, complete with a Roman soldier in a red tunic and helmet. Other Roman soldiers followed on horseback and two little Romans in togas tried to keep up behind them. Needless to say the Roman 'man' had to pull a reluctant Roman woman behind him. She was probably saying: 'But Gluteus, I like Londinium.' The audience liked the little Romans and their horses. They love Hadrian's Wall in Northumberland. I have found, when there is a pause in the conversation, if you say: 'So, that's a fabulous wall, you've got up here,' it gets you quite a long way. That and: 'So, do you ride?' If all else fails: 'So, do you farm around here?' Aside from Hadrian's Wall, there was a teddy bear's picnic — lots of children dressed as teddy bears, some poor bear girl pushing a bear baby in a buggy round and round the main ring, which will probably put her off motherhood for life. The horse was dressed as a picnic blanket.

Hadrian's Wall won, which was a safe choice, but you had to give full marks to the parents who blacked up their children. Blacked up their children. Just one more time. Blacked up their children. I watched the cavalcade across the field as they walked on. A rider in a black hooded cloak, another with a Arabian scarf wrapped around part of his face. Each rider pulled along a blacked-up child; one wearing a large black Afro wig, the other a black Mohican with a ponytail. I said: 'Oh my God,' as they came by, 'are those children pretending to be black?' At that moment, one of the children raised a placard with the words: 'The Abolition of Slavery, 1807.' That was a yes, then. Full marks to parents who attempt to be political at an agricultural show. I would have made them my winners for sheer front. On the other hand, cor blimey. Cor blimey. I nudged my husband as the slave trade came by. I said: 'What you said earlier ... I don't think that's true.'

## Monday, 3 September 2007

### Heartbreak Hotel

My husband has spent more time with us this summer but is due back in the office. An hour before he left, he said: 'I am so ready to go back to London.' Then he said: 'But I'll miss you.' And he went, waving cheerily as he pulled away. Cue massive tears from the four-year-old due to start full-time school on Wednesday. The six-year-old said: 'You have to stop because you're making me sad now.' While my baby girl stretched out from her high chair to lay across the tea table, gaze into his sodden little face and tell him: 'Don't cy. Don't cy.'

## Tuesday, 4 September 2007

### Lady of the Flies

Summer, then, has been insane. Not a little mad, but full-blown, lollopy, lollopy insane with builders and moving and more builders and children everywhere. Today was particularly bad – for a start, the flies came back. Often one fly is on top of another. Having sex. I said to two of them: 'Get a room.' Then remembered they had: my kitchen. I make the pancakes, pick out the flies and feed the children. The Dairy Farmer's Wife is expected at ten, so I tidy round furiously. She is slightly late, which means the children have time to untidy everything by the time she arrives.

Halfway through lunch with the Dairy Farmer's Wife, the builders arrive. I was not expecting builders this week as they are technically on another job. My builder puts into my care his teenage apprentice, who is tasked to strip out my en-suite shower, which I want tiled. This means I now have no sanctuary. The apprentice is at that age when every word he utters has to be wrenched from him. He makes me think to the future, to how my sons will be when they are grown. The noise level with my outlaw boys after six weeks of summer is horrendous. If we had neighbours, they would be drawing up a petition to get us rehoused. I said to them tonight: 'Boys, the noise has to stop.' I do not think they heard me. In ten years, if the builder's apprentice is anything to go by, I will be pleading with them to speak to me at all.

After lunch, the Dairy Farmer's Wife takes the children down to her farm and I arrange to meet up with them in two hours' time at their swimming lesson. I had wanted to do some work but realized instead I needed to spend the time finding things for school tomorrow and writing names on clothes. I have always suspected parents are forced to write names in the clothes so that when teachers get the children mixed up, they can haul up the collar and read it. Some of the clothes these days have a space for the child's name and his class. I put 'aspirational middle' but I got bored after the gym kit. I do not have to bother finding my four-year-old's new school shoes because he had already told me he is not wearing them. For some reason, I can find no blue airtex tops for the six-year-old and no school trousers for the four-year-old. In the midst of this, the Yorkshire Father drops by with his five, seven, nine and eleven-year-old boys. Within ten minutes, the nine-year-old has killed fourteen flies and the eleven-year-old, twenty-eight. They line up the bodies for me on the floor. When they leave, I put away all the clothes and calculate that I have exactly, to the second, five minutes to drink a cup of tea and eat expensive chocolate to make myself feel better about everything. I spoon a fly out of the tea. At that very moment, the Evangelicals arrive with their three children. I make the grown-ups a cup of tea (two minutes), chew a large piece of chocolate (one minute) and chat (another two minutes); I leave them finishing their tea outside the cottage.

I am very stressed as I drive to the swimming pool and think about how to persuade my four-year-old to fall in love with school. During the complicated transfer of child seats in the car park between the Dairy Farmer's Wife and myself, I manage to reverse the car with the back passenger door open and scrape the car next to me. I leave a note. I want to leave an amazingly complicated rationale for why I parked where I did, explaining why the door was open, that I had not noticed, that at the very moment I did notice and turned to check, a child shouted out for me and I stalled, the door swung out, scraped and did damage, and what a bad day I am having. I settle instead for a 'terribly sorry' and 'my apologies' and 'please call me and let me know the cost' sort of note, sign it with my name and weight it down with their windscreen wiper. I am aware that I have not done anything to improve that driver's day either.

After we get home and have eaten tea, I go upstairs to check on the children to find the six-year-old has given the baby girl a piece of paper, a squeezy bottle of red paint and a paintbrush. The baby girl is painting the paper, and my newly sanded floor, pillarbox red. I am not happy. I explain why I am not happy. I know I should say: 'Thank you for looking after your sister and for being so creative. Shall we take the paintbrush away now and give her this nice wax crayon?' Instead, I say: 'What were you thinking of?' among other things. By the time I push, bully, plead and cajole everyone into bed, I am fit for nothing more than killing flies and drinking wine while I do it. Around 9.30ish the phone rings. A woman on the other end says: 'Hello, you left a note on my car . . .' I want to cry. I swallow and say: 'Yes, I am so sorry. I was trying to fit a child seat and I didn't realize the door was open and ...' She is lovely. Coincidentally, her car is going in for other paintwork jobs and she tells me her husband is a mechanic. She does not want any money from me. More importantly, she does not shout at me. She thanks me for the note and says she has got children too. I put the phone down before I cry. I think: 'How about that? The day just got better.'

## Thursday, 6 September 2007

### Say cheese

I dropped the boys at school. I remembered to take the camera to capture my four-year-old's first day. In most of the shots, he is looking unhappy but reconciled to his miserable fate; in one, he hides behind his six-year-old brother, but that might have been because he wanted me to stop taking photographs. He was brave, which made it more bearable; he wobbled only once when the teacher drew him away from me, but righted himself. I was holding it together until the moment it was time to leave him to it and I was handed a packet of tissues and a teabag wrapped in a white silk ribbon. 'Go home. Have a cry and make yourself a cup of tea,' a teacher said. Really, I was fine up to that point. They might as well have erected a billboard outside the school gates with the words: 'He's not your little boy any more, Mummy.' And in very small letters underneath: 'He'll forget your birthday, make excuses at Christmas. Eventually, he won't call and when you're really old, he'll put you in a home and never even visit.' I looked for the billboard when I came out. I thought: 'I don't want a cup of tea. I want my son back.'

I could not bring myself to drive home, so the baby girl and I drove in the opposite direction to a market town. Not the nearest market town, another one. One further away, so that I could kill more time. I told anyone who cared to listen that I did not live in the town, I was not supposed to be there, my son had started school and I did not want to go home when he was not there to fill it with his noise. Even my baby girl was looking embarrassed by the end of it. The nice lady who sold me blueberries and red exotic flowers knew how I was feeling. She had a six-year-old boy who did not like school, did not want to go back, felt he had no one to play with. She said: 'I would watch him in the playground without him knowing. I had to stop. It was making me ill.' I almost gave her my tissue-teabag favour. I thought: 'Been there. Done that.' Instead, I said: 'I know. You worry, don't you? I hope it goes well for him today.' She smiled at me and said: 'Yours too.'

## Monday, 10 September 2007

### Tory knockers

The other night, I got an offer from the Accountant I could not refuse. A ticket to a fund-raising ball at a local castle for Conservatism and cancer. Who thought up that combination? Not one that Conservative Party spin doctors would rejoice over. This is real politics out in the real world. Forget the obvious dangers of associating the party with a nasty disease that might kill you, let's just get on with it and raise some money. Quite right too. Conservatism. Cancer. There is a difference.

I caught a lift with the Accountant. Unfortunately, I had also asked the Oyster Farmer and his wife for a lift. They arrived at my door about twenty minutes after I had left. I blame sleep deprivation for every brainless thing I do. The children have a rota going as to who will wake me up at night. Monday night, it was all of them. Tuesday night, they let me sleep through to give me a false sense of security. Wednesday, the four-year-old woke up at one in the morning, sat up in bed, called for me and when I stumbled in, told me: 'It's dark. I can't find the bed.' I said: 'You are sitting on the bed.' Then he insisted on coming in with me and lying awake for an hour and a half, occasionally stroking my face with infinite tenderness which meant I could not even shout at him. Thursday, 3.10 a.m., the baby girl started screaming: 'Wata. Wata. Wata' as if I had her on a salt diet. Friday, 2.20 a.m., the baby wailed madly and collapsed back into sleep just as I got to her; about forty-five minutes later, the four-year-old woke me again because he said he was having a nightmare. Then, on Saturday morning, my six-year-old complained he had also called for me during the night and I had not come. I said: 'I didn't hear you. What was wrong?' He said: 'I couldn't find the duvet.' I said: 'Well, where was it?' He said: 'The bottom of the bed.' I said: 'Your duvet was at the bottom of the bed and you tried to wake me up in the middle of the night to get it for you?' 'Yes – and you didn't come. Where were you?' The consequence of this extreme sleep deprivation is low brain function, a distinct lack of amiability and periodic, acute stupidity such as arranging for a variety of lifts for the same occasion.

Anyway, I was running late owing to the fact I had meant to lay everything out for the ball the day before, but had not had the time. I also had to go with my hair half done because my hairdryer decided to cut out right in the middle of blow-drying it. I contemplated sticking my head in the Aga to finish the job, but thought it might traumatize the children if they saw me. I do not want them telling me in twenty years' time that their earliest memory is me lying on the kitchen floor with my head in the oven. Which is electric. When I left the house, it was without jewellery, gloves or the right handbag because I could not find any of them. Luckily, I found my long frock which I was convinced had gone to the textile bank or the charity shop when we moved house the last time. My husband is in London and Girl Friday has been on holiday, but she came in to babysit for me. As I walked out the door, I told her: 'Don't let any of the children in the bathroom, because when I tried to empty the bath, the chain came off the plug and I can't get the plug out.' She said: 'OK.' I suspect she thinks we live in chaos. I walked up to the Accountant's house, trying to shake off the thought that: A) my hair looked a mess; and B) there was a slightly scummy pond in the bathroom and the baby might throw herself in it reaching for a rubber duck while I was out. The headlines would read: 'Baby Drowns in Bathroom Pond as Champagne-Swilling Ma Jives with Tory Boys. Devastated Mother Blames Cameron and Cancer.'

The Tories may be the traditional party of low taxation, but this does not hold true for fund-raisers. We had no sooner sat down than demands for money started in the form of strange party games. There was also a 'Grand' auction and a silent auction. In the silent auction, you wrote your name and the amount you were willing to pay underneath the particular lot you were interested in; later on, as excitement built and the auction was about to close, you told a girl and she wrote it on a board for you. The lots included a 1994 Subaru Legacy Turbo 4×4 Estate (which fetched £810); the funds for this were to be shared with the campaign to stop the wind turbines on the Sheep Farmer's land. (They are very political, these people.) I think Cameron would have preferred to see a bicycle in the silent auction rather than something that boasted 'wide boy spotlights on the front'. You could also bid for 'a day's hunting for two' with two different hunts; a hacking jacket; a gundog workshop for four handlers and dogs; and a carriage driving lesson. I was tempted by the gundog workshop; presumably you throw a gun in the air and the dog is taught to fetch it; I decided instead to bid for a day's stalking on an estate in the south of the county. With just a minute or so to go, a bid for £275 came in over my head for the stalking and the girl started writing in the new name. I turned to complain. I said: 'You just beat my bid.' I did not add: 'You Tory bastard.' I thought that would be unsporting. I was glad I did not. He was very charming. He said I could go stalking with them and to call. I shall take him up on it. I am hoping we might see George Clooney.

I found myself looking round, saying to myself: 'So this is what Conservatives look like.' They still wear dinner jackets and lurex. I do not think they do this when they are knocking on doors for votes, but I could be wrong. I hope they do. There was a blonde girl in a black corset with the most enormous pair of breasts you have ever seen. Mesmerizing. I found myself wondering whether one would ever grow larger than the other. The skirt of the dress was scooped at the front on either side to reveal legs, but no one was looking at her legs, which I am sure were shapely, or her face, which I am sure was lovely. Wherever this girl went, her fellow Tories turned to stare at the passing and fabulous breasts. The Accountant said: 'That girl is gorgeous – the best-looking girl here.' I said: 'Excuse me.' I felt like saying: 'Take my word for it – my nipples are bigger.'

## Tuesday, 11 September 2007

### A pirate's life for me

Yesterday morning started off in the way all mornings should – in fancy dress. School wanted the children to come 'dressed as a character from a traditional tale or nursery rhyme. My six-year-old dressed as Captain Hook. My four-year-old as Shere Khan from *The Jungle Book*. I think we were pushing it. Then the baby girl wanted in. She demanded the red satin-look coat of Captain Hook. I had to bribe her with Superman's red polyester cape and a Santa Claus hat to be Red Riding Hood.

I admire her taste. Hook's red satin coat was my best dress ever. I wore it in the Eighties; hence the shoulder pads. The V-neck promised glories if you would only watch it long enough, while every time I took a step the skirt split wide open to reveal taut, shiny thigh. The entire dress was held in place by two buttons at the waist. As I looked at it in the cheval mirror, I would think: 'If I undo those two buttons, just those two buttons, the entire dress falls to the floor.' Sometimes, I would watch myself undo the buttons to see the dress shimmy from my shoulders, feel its brief caress before it folded itself into a flimsy heap at my pedicured feet. I do not think I ever looked better in a dress, but the days of taut shiny thighs and shoulder pads are long gone. There came a moment, a couple of years ago, when I thought: 'The days of this dress are over and I have a boy desperate for life as a pirate.' I laid it out on my bedroom floor, took a large pair of dressmaking scissors and scythed into my vamp past. I remade it: tightened up the waist, shortened the skirt, blanket-stitched narrow sleeves from the scraps and attached them to the ex-frock with white cotton. I did not think my son knew what it was I did. I thought he watched me cut and sew because he was anxious to be a pirate king. Yesterday morning, he hauled out the dressing-up trunk and dug around among the soldier's armour and green clown curls for the crumpled red coat and a battered black hat with a broken red feather. He pulled on the coat and said: 'You made me this. It was your best dress.' I picked up a black and wetted paintbrush to colour in his piratical moustache and beard; I took his chin in my hand and tilted his beautiful boy face to the morning light; I said: 'Once upon a time.'

## Wednesday, 12 September 2007

### Autumn

Honeysuckle, spindly pink and cream amid the white trumpets of bindweed, russet hawthorn beads and brambles. 'Summer,' the hedge says, 'ah, summer that was. Gone now. Almost never here. But we shall take comfort in the autumn that is come among us.' Over the hedge, cotton reels and cubes of straw mark the season's shift. Fields worked; already green shoots of rape and wheat haze the ever-restless earth. One or two late and golden fields of oats rustle with embarrassment, still to be standing there, while the wind pushes away the skinny warmth of the day.

## Friday, 14 September 2007

### Lady of the Flies 2

Ding dong, the flies are dead. Not all of them but most. Since I have effectively been living in the Australian outback of the nineteenth century, I am quite happy with a couple of dozen hangers-on who do not yet know the party is over. It was bad. I would make a cup of tea and as I poured in the milk, a fly would bob to the surface. Often it would still be swimming. Sometimes it would have an inflatable toy. I bought geranium oil and burners along with geranium incense sticks. The geranium oil got a bit much. It did not kill the flies; instead they retreated to the corners of the room to talk about me or sank to floor level. They swirled around my feet. I think they were doing that commando-like crawl you are supposed to do in the event of fire, pulling themselves along by their elbows to avoid the stink. I braved the nettles to get down to the sandpit and ladled sand into a glass mixing bowl and brought it back to the house. I slid in four incense sticks and lit them. My six-year-old came in. He looked delighted. He said: 'Mummy, you've baked a cake.' I said: 'No, it just looks like a cake. I'm killing flies.' He sighed and walked away. At the doorway, he said to the four-year-old: 'Don't bother asking. It's not a cake.'

## Tuesday, 18 September 2007

### Dirty dancing

I had put the children to bed after the usual two-hour performance involving baths, books and bollockings. I had lain next to the six-year-old and said: 'You make me so proud and I love you so much. Do you know that?' And he said: 'No. How much do you love me?' And I said: 'I love you brighter than the stars.' He said: 'Do you love me more than Daddy?' I said: 'Yes. That's just the way it is.' He said: 'More than Granny?' and I said yes and thought: 'Don't tell her though.' 'More than television?' No contest. 'More than your make-up?' More than that even. Once I had lost him to sleep, I came downstairs to the kitchen. I pushed the table against the hearth and cleared the chairs to one side. I thought: 'I can sweep the floor. Clear it of crumbs, mop off the dirt and wait for it to dry, or I can dance.' I pressed eject to open up the CD drawer on my laptop, fed it and thought: 'It has been an age since I went to a club. Will anyone buy me a drink?' Acoustic guitars and fiddles gushed out into the warm air to catch in the gobbets of crystal hanging from the chandelier. Folk rock spun me one way then the other. I like to dance, always have. I closed my eyes a while. My Gay Best Boyfriend cool-shimmies on the dance floor, hands behind his back, dandy hips asway. He and I do this thing. On the dance floor. We step around and round, twirling to face each other and then away. Anyone watching who did not know I am his hag, he is my Gay Best Friend, would think we have hot sex and oftentime. But we do not, will not, cannot think of such a thing. Instead, we dance, caressing with a smile, loving each other in the beat. I danced with him last night. I could not tell him so. I wonder, later, in his London bed, if he dreamt he danced with me.

## Wednesday, 19 September 2007

### Dinosaur roar

Last week, a retired child psychotherapist and a consultant psychotherapist were holidaying in the cottage next to us. I made a mental note to myself: 'Do not shout at the children. If you do want to shout at the children, remember to shut the windows.' I was doing really well until the phone rang just as I was putting everyone to bed. Usually, I let it ring but I thought it might be my husband so I dashed downstairs and answered it. It was the Tory 'bastard', who said he would not be able to take me stalking because of foot and mouth restrictions. As we were talking, I saw my pyjama-clad four-year-old and the six-year-old tear out of the front door and into the garden carrying cleaning products. When I put the phone down, I swept up the rompered baby and went out. I was careful not to shout. I called loudly: 'Boys.' I called slightly more loudly: 'Boys!' They emerged; the four-year-old, beaming. He always beams when he has done something that will drive me to distraction. I said: 'Right. I want the washing-up liquid and the washing powder tablets back. Now.' The six-year-old looked pained. 'How did you know?' he wailed. 'I know everything,' I said. 'I know everything you think. I know everything you do. For ever.' I thought: 'I really hope the psychotherapists can't hear this.'

We opened up the wooden gate and stepped down into their garden paradise. The four-year-old went one way, the six-year-old the other. Realizing his tactical mistake, the four-year-old veered over to his brother. He beamed at me again as he ran past to join his ally in all misdeeds. We peered over the stone wall at the bottom of the garden. The foaming bottle, the box and its contents were nowhere near where we were standing; they were laying among the trodden-down nettles, over where the four-year-old had been heading. I said, through tight lips: 'I want them picked up. Please.'

Babe on hip, I cut across the grass to the point the four-year-old had been aiming for originally – a patch of garden close to the greenhouse. Here, a narrow entrance squeezes you between glass and golden privet leaves to a garden room, a private place, curiously attractive to my children, enclosed by thick hedges on two sides, a greenhouse and a stone wall. Or what was a stone wall.

It is a superhero den, with a tree which the boys use to scramble into their other den in the nettle patch. The boys, with help from two small friends, had used sticks to scrape out the lime mortar and carefully pull and tumble out the stones. Aghast, I watched the four-year-old scrambling back through the hole with the washing-up liquid. Stones arched above his egg fragile head, resting on nothing but neighbours and innate goodwill. I said: 'You are kidding me. What were you thinking?' They wanted 'a shortcut'. While they worked with their sticks, they were pretending they were in the mouth of a big dinosaur taking out its teeth so it couldn't eat the little dinosaurs.

Later in the adult twilight, children in bed, disgraced, the consultant psychotherapist assessed the latest outrage. She said: 'You realize this is all about boundaries, don't you? You didn't say no to their other den when they wanted you to, so now they have pushed it further. They have literally pushed through the boundary. They want you to say no.' I said: 'I say no to my kids all the time.' So much for keeping a low profile, I thought. I told her about the dinosaurs. She said: 'Hmmm. So they think

257

there is a monster in their life somewhere.' I changed the subject. To their thieving. Bad choice. They have slipped into a habit of stealing biscuits, chocolate, sweet stuff. I had thought because they did not get enough sugar in their little lives. The retired child psychotherapist hazarded: 'Perhaps they feel they are not being nurtured enough.' I groaned inside. I said: 'What about the cleaning products though?' 'Yes,' she said, 'that's an interesting one. They are stealing what they think is important to you, they are stealing a piece of you.' I said: 'There is no way they associate me with cleaning products.'

I boy-banned them from my Eden.

## Tuesday, 25 September 2007

### Baby toast

I said to the baby girl – and I know you should not ask such questions of children – 'Who do you love the most?' She stared back at me, her face all truth and beauty; hazel-blue eyes and her mouth which looks like mine at the corners. I whispered again as I bunched her to me, settling in to the rocking chair: 'Who do you love the most? The best? Who in this world?' She lay back into me, raised up her plastic cup of milk as if to make a toast. 'Granny,' she confided.

## Tuesday, 2 October 2007

### My old china

My mother is much better than she was when I first moved here when she was so very fragile – unless you catch her on a morning when pain binds her limbs to bed. She ages with grace and bravery, my father matching his step to hers. They take pills, make jokes, hold hands on the sofa, talk about me all the time, I think; my father, a gentle man caring for her with resolute tenderness. They love the fact they are about to get a home from home, but as yet the arches are not ready and they cannot manage stairs so they are staying in the Accountant's holiday cottage down the road. I say they cannot manage stairs. This is their first visit since we moved back in. I showed them round the downstairs and said: 'I won't show you upstairs because you won't be able to manage the stairs.' I completed the last bit of this sentence to their backs as they disappeared up the staircase they cannot manage and down the landing. I trailed up after them. I said: 'You can't manage stairs. Remember? That's why we're having the arches built. So you can have a downstairs bedroom and a bathroom.' 'Yes, that's right, we can't manage stairs,' my mother said, pushing me gently to one side as she went to inspect the en suite.

Everything measured up to their high standards so I do not have to move again immediately, thank God. My mother said: 'It is everything I ever hoped you would have.' This is not entirely true. At one time, she would have liked me to marry Prince Charles and she would have preferred me to be a doctor. She sat back in my cream leather sofa in the kitchen. She said: 'Would it be a good idea if I gave you a china cabinet?' 'No,' I said. She got tougher. 'But there is a china cabinet sitting in our front bedroom's bow window and it doesn't belong in there. There isn't room for it.' I said: 'Have you just looked round my nice empty house to find where I can put all your old tat?' Her game was up. 'I do not want a china cabinet. I do not want that little head of a Scotsman in a glass with a fly in his eye.' She changed tack again. 'But if you don't want it, I shall have to give it all away.' She had been in the house less than thirty minutes before she put the knife to my throat: take the tat or lose your childhood memories. I cannot remember all that is in the china cabinet. As a child, I thought them marvels and would extract them, one by one, to carefully, and with clean hands, admire them: the silver model of the shrine of Lourdes which plays a hymn to the Virgin Mary if you wind a key, a little clockwork Russian doll with red bobbles on her hat who does a goosestep and at least one flamenco dancer, complete with castanets. My mother is a firm believer in decluttering providing she is the one doing the decluttering. I wonder, too, whether she wants me to carry the past into my future. She can rest easy on that one. I shall take the china cabinet and I think when the arches are complete, I shall find a place for it in their bedroom.

## Wednesday, 3 October 2007

### Mothers and daughters

I saw them walk away from me, my mother and my daughter. My mother in her slippers with her stick, head bent to listen, best she could, to my girl's burble. My baby girl beside her, pushing a buggy with a pink and brand-new dolly along the road outside the cottages. I thought: 'Engrave this on my heart: my mother walking, talking with the little mother next to her.' 'Shall we go in?' I heard her granny ask her. 'No. Walk again.' And walk they did. I thought: 'When you are all grown and a mother to more than just a doll, when my mother is no more, will something in you recall this golden autumn morning promenade?'

## Wednesday, 10 October 2007

### Samaritan city

The Dairy Farmer just broke his hip in a fracas with a cow and a large amount of slurry. I always suspected cows were dangerous. I buy walnut whips and pineapple chunks and set off for a visit to the sick.

I pull off the A1 on to a country road. I check I do not have the handbrake on. I check I have enough petrol. I think: 'The car is going to break down' and realize I have a flat tyre. Thinking about it, it must have been flat for a good ten minutes, maybe longer. I climb out of the car to stare at the smoking tyre. It smells bad and it is pouring with rain. I am in the middle of nowhere and have given up on mobile phones as there is never a signal or the battery is flat. I have been happier.

I think: 'Right, well, it could be worse. The boys are at school, the baby is with Girl Friday and it can't be that hard to change a tyre.' I open the boot and find a jack, screwdriver, dirty nappy, pushchair, large amount of children's clothing, two teddy bears, banana skin, spacegun and underneath it all, a tyre which I cannot lift. I go back to the front of the car with the jack. My husband has always maintained that if you use a jack in the wrong place on a car, your car will break. I slide it next to the wheel. A car goes by in the rain. I leap up and wave at it frantically and a nice man stops. He lends me his mobile phone so that I can call my husband (who is of course in London) and he can call the RAC. I think: 'I can't call the RAC direct because it may take too long and I don't want to keep the man waiting for his phone.' I have to ask the driver what road I am on. It turns out he is another local farmer and has heard all about the broken hip. He drives off. As he pulls away, I think: 'I really should have asked you to change the tyre for me.' It is too late.

I go back to the car and cautiously try turning the screw in the jack while working out whether the car could kill me if it falls off it. I decide I am reasonably safe as I am not underneath it on a trolley but kneeling next to it in a muddy puddle. I go back to the boot and pull out a few other pieces of metal that are lying around the spare tyre. I realize that rather than lifting the rear end of the car off the ground in a bid to extract the spare tyre from the boot, it may be easier to unwind the bolt holding it in place. I feel inadequate. A car drives by and I try to attract its attention but the driver does not see me. I contemplate putting on some lipstick and undoing some buttons. I am glad I have not done this when a little red runabout draws up and a white-haired old lady peers out. I say: 'Hello.' I do not want to frighten her. I crouch down. I say: 'Do you by any chance have a mobile pohone I could borrow?' I wonder if she knows what a mobile phone is. She says no, she is driving to see her daughter and had not wanted to drive by me. I know she is wishing she had a toffee she could offer me. I say how kind of her to stop and thank you. She drives on.

I go back to the car and look at the wheel. The tyre is still flat and I am getting wetter. I look at the signpost at the junction. I am about four miles from my friends. I wonder if they would hear me if I shout very loudly. Another car draws up. I think: 'For the back of beyond, you get a fair amount of passing traffic,' although the hands on my watch stopped going round some time ago. I say to the elderly man driving the car: 'Could I borrow your phone?' He hands it to me. His elderly wife looks at me with deep suspicion. I ring my husband. He tells me the RAC will not come as I am not named on the cover for the car and the AA cannot find me. While I am trying to explain where I am to him, despite the fact I have no idea, the elderly man goes over to look at the wheel and says he can fix it. I tell my husband I will ring him back. The elderly man, a caravaner, digs around his own boot. He pulls out a walking stick cum Zimmer frame and then a wheel brace. I wonder if he is carrying it in case the Zimmer ever gets a flat. We spend some time trying to find a place for the jack to go. He is incredibly game but is now wheezing very badly. His breath is so laboured I am seriously worried he is going to have a heart attack while he changes the wheel. I suspect his wife is sitting in the car rightly having a hissy fit. He has to give up when the jack refuses to go up any further. I shake him by the hand and thank his wife for lending him to me. I do not think she likes me.

I go back and have another go. I pull the jack out and slide it further along the car and turn the screw, but the wheel remains resolutely on the ground. I am not sure I care by now as I have no idea what to do once the wheel is in the air. Another car draws up. This final chap (who spends half his year in Australia and used to do something with trucks) cracks on with the job in hand. It takes him about five minutes. My tyre has a lengthy gash in it. He pours scorn on my spare wheel and implies I will die horribly if I go any speed at all. He says I must go straight to a garage and get a new tyre. I have the impression it could abandon the other three wheels and roll away from the car at any moment. He drives away. I open up the walnut whips.

### Wednesday, 17 October 2007

## What am I bid?

I went to an auction in the village. I took a little time to figure out my bidding strategy. A couple of lots had come up: a tent and a blackboard. Tucked away at the back of the bidding, panicked by the auctioneer's song of 'DoIhearfiveIhavesix-onmyleftsevensirthankyoudoiheareightninetenonmyrighttenten soldtotheladyonmyright', my nerve failed me and I ducked out of the bidding. I decided on the 'I want it' approach for a map of the shipwrecks off the Farne Islands. I stood at the front and nodded decisively at every opportunity. I thought it might psyche out any opposition – I may have been bidding against myself at times. I got the print for £50.

It is a work of art, put together by a lifeboatman of twenty years who doubled up as the local funeral director. The map has a little scroll in the bottom left-hand corner telling you his name: 'For Those in Peril, John Hanvey, 1976'. I rang him. Life is like that in Northumberland. I said: 'I love your map.' He told me he spent seven years researching the wrecks, using information from the logbook of the Longstone lighthouse keeper as well as from RNLI records, Lloyd's, a local museum and newspaper. He said: 'I carried around a pocketbook. Any old fishermen I met up and down the coast, I would say: "I have the name of a ship I suspect was wrecked, what do you know about it?"' When he had put the information together, he drew up around fifty of the maps, each one taking him a week at a time. Later, he had the prints made up.

The names of the ships and the small hand-drawn crosses remind you this is a map that charts bravery, smashed hopes and the graves of drowned men. The earliest wreck: 2 November 1462, 'Two French caravels' in the area off Bamburgh sands. Another early disaster ('vessels foundered ... positions doubtful'): November 1774, when six ships and '100 souls perished in one night'. Some of the losses are more recent. East of Longstone, 25 January 1940, the steamship *Everene of Latvia* was sunk by torpedo with nine drowned. Cobles, sloops, ketches, tankers: the hungry sea will take what it can. Occasionally, it will lose its grim and salty battle and the ship can be refloated. More often, they are lost and there are deaths such as those on 11 October 1840, when the steamship *Northern Yacht* foundered with twenty-two passengers and crew, or again on 20 July 1843, when the steamship *Pegasus* sank with fifty-four passengers and crew (both around Goldstone Rock, midway between Holy Island and the Farnes). In the worst cases, they are lost with 'all hands'.

The map of the wrecks is in blue, with the rocky islands brown and lapped by a dangerous and broken green. The sober columns of dates and black-inked names are broken by the picture of a seagull aloft – to some, a seagull represents a sailor's soul – a ship in full sail and a lifeboat breasting stormy waves. Underneath the lifeboat are the words of the sailor's prayer: 'Oh! Lord the sea is so large and my ship is so small.' These lost ships and sailors are not forgotten: their names still sail on a paper sea. John Hanvey made it so.

## Monday, 22 October 2007

### Boxes and blues

Ever since we moved up from London, we have had 'stuff' in cardboard boxes hanging about us. First, we kept the boxes in our own house; desperate for space, we stored them in Number 1 before eventually moving them into the metal container in the barn. The King of the Castle is about to demolish the barn and build a new one, so this weekend we opened up the container and emptied it. Straight into the bin for the most part – or the brazier, the tip, or for recycling. I cannot believe we wrapped it, moved it and kept it all for so long.

One box was worth the waiting. As I unwrapped the newspaper from the cut-glass candlesticks, I thought: 'Ah, home.' A wooden bowl from a hot and dusty place and a blood-red vase with a golden glass stag, once my grandmother's; a doll from my childhood, all smile and shiny blue trouser suit. Photographs, too: my husband, absurdly young, holding a glass of champagne and looking out into his future; my mother in hyacinth blue, more radiant than the bride, on my wedding day. Two small and rose-strewn hearts capturing the exchange of rings – not the congregation's laughter when the wedding band would not slide on to my finger. A picture of my eldest the day after he was born, and in folding pine, my wrapped-up boys fishing and laughing hard. Memories, my most sparkling things; no hallmarked value, no antiqued glory, precious only to me. But I grew sad as I unwrapped my loot, which had once sat on the mantelpiece of a black stone hearth against sunshine yellow walls in London. 'I do not have a mantelpiece,' I thought, 'and now my walls are cream.' Still, I polished them and scattered them about, sat back and thought: 'My memories about me where they belong. Now, am I at home?'

## Wednesday, 24 October 2007

### Through the looking glass

I became quite desperate to go down to London. Maybe it is because the end-of-year deadline is approaching when we decide whether we stay or go back. We have been up here more than two years now. If I think about London, I miss it. Therefore I try not to think about it. Try not to picture myself living there. I find it easier that way. My last few visits I found so difficult I stopped going, but I had to come back for half-term. For a few days. To see if it was all still there. It is the first visit for a long time when I have been willing to risk haunting the old neighbourhoods and arranging to see a whole parcel of old friends, all crammed together in a week. I decided to take the children to the dinosaur museum. It was such a good idea, every other mother in London decided to have it too. Utterly heaving.

The very worst moment was in the picnic area, where we were waiting for friends to join us. It was crowded. I had wrapped four salami baps in a tea towel, popped in three satsumas for the children and a bottle of mineral water between the four of us. I was entirely happy with this as a lunch until I sat down at a table with a woman, a baby in a pushchair and a little girl. There was a reason this table was the only one with free seats. Every other mother in the place knew that this woman was going to make her look bad. My children ate their

266

baps watching the banquet opposite with wonder. I knew I had made a mistake as soon as I saw the first Tupperware box, but it was too late – we had already sat down. Sandwiches, hummus, carrot sticks, raisins, yoghurt, chocolate soya dessert, sliced melon, green grapes, juice. There was probably more, but my mother has advised me that you can only use your peripheral vision for so long before your eyeballs drop out of your skull. The woman opposite made endless 'happy chat' with the little girl; the more happy chat she made, the more silent my own children became. Having watched for long enough, my baby daughter decided she had no intention of eating the substandard fare I had provided; she emptied out her salami on to the floor, picked apart the bread and then dropped half her satsuma segments. My six-year-old immediately handed her what was left of his. The Picnic Queen took pity. 'She can have some melon if she likes,' she said and pushed over the left-over melon. This was so humiliating, I blushed. The boys leapt on the melon as if they had never seen an exotic fruit before in their lives. I said: 'Thank you; that's very kind' as you do when someone has just shown you up in front of your children as a mother who cuts corners. She then compounded it by telling me: 'You worry too much.' I 'worry too much'? I felt an incredibly 'British' locking up of those facial muscles that were not already in spasm from the humiliation of the pity fruit. I wanted to say: 'If I worry too much, it is because mothers like you make me feel bad.' She was the sister of that irritating stranger who accosts you in the street with 'Cheer up! It might never happen.' I hate people who tell you to cheer up. I hate mothers who feel sorry for my children. I stopped hating her as they left the table when I heard her say to the little girl: 'I told your mummy . . .' I thought: 'Oh, you're a nanny. You should have said. That explains the carrot sticks in their own Tupperware box and the expensive fruit and the relentless chat. That's all right then – I'll stop worrying.'

## Tuesday, 6 November 2007

### Mapping out the past

It is a cold, gold, old time of year as autumn readies itself for winter. Trees which flared like brands plunged into the earth have lost their claim to flame; embered leaves, dead and dusty now, tumble over their roots while spindly hawthorn twists and turns in the low-slung sunshine thrown splendid across the fields. I thought: 'I live in the country. I'll go for a walk.'

I have a copy of a map from 200 years ago, the fields named: Wheat Riggs, Bottle Banks, Gin Quarter, Old Cow Pasture, Kings Chambers. Wells and a windmill, limestone quarries where once men gouged out the land, all etched in ink. I thought: 'I shall walk into history, around Barley Close to the pool where marsh grasses grow and deer drink and once there was a ford.' I walked down the winding lane, past the green-stoned barn soon to disappear and over the rough ground edging the fresh sown crop – land sliding out to the horizoned Cheviot swell – till I found the blue-green pool water, bullrushes and reeds swaying in the picked-up hurly-burly wind. I walked around the pool, its leaf beach empty of deer, slender grey trees and dead nettles guarding the privacy of a lost and ancient Britain. My way blocked, I scrambled on to a lichen-painted fencepost to better clear the strung-out barbed wire. I paused, considered, jumped; my ankle turned on the rutted ground and I thought: 'You just cannot trust the countryside.' I limped slowly back to the cottage and the present. I think I may have sprained my ankle.

## Thursday, 8 November 2007

### Somewhere

This morning, the sky was bruised blue yet the light was gold and true. I had dropped the boys at school, was driving home and saw an arc of splintered light as bright as I have ever seen. Years ago in London, I once saw a prism, a stripe, when a child I loved died, and I thought: 'That gleam in this gritty dirty sky, that gleam is meant for me.' Today, between the hedged gaps, we glimpsed the rainbow's fall to earth, scattering its colours in the grass. I said to the baby girl: 'Look, look, there are two' as the other, shadowing, pastel bow appeared. I looked back to the road, a car approaching. I braked, swerved slightly, hit the only curb on the country lane and my tyre blew. Again. I thought: 'Bloody hell. Bugger the tyre. We're getting home this time,' and drove back slowly, my road ahead ribboning through the coloured 'Welcome' arch.

## Tuesday, 13 November 2007

### Bang bang bang

Had three bang bang bang nice things happen on one day. I dropped the car off at the garage in the village to get the new tyre put on and went round to have tea with the Little Old Lady. I had been a couple of days before, but she lives near the garage so I walked across and rang the bell. She came to the door and she looked so pleased to see me standing there on her mat. That is it. That was the first nice thing. The tea and cake and chat were all good too, but it was her smile when she first saw me. I put it in my pocket and I am keeping it.

When I went back to pick up the car and pay, the garage owner told me I had done for the tyre 'good and proper' driving it home after I knew I had a flat. I shrugged. I said: 'What can you do? I was in the middle of nowhere. I had the baby. I didn't have my phone. My husband is away in London, so he couldn't have done anything. I had exactly the same thing a couple of weeks ago and it took for ever until someone passed by who could help.' With oily fingers, he rifled through some paperwork and pulled out a couple of business cards and said: 'Keep them in the car. You can always call us and we'll come and get you sorted.' I mean, how good is that? Last time, the RAC would not even come out to me and the AA could not find me. I am tempted to have a microchip embedded in my ear and let him track me with satellite technology 24/7.

Then I got home and rang the King of the Castle about the map. I wanted to know whether he used names for the fields and, if he did, whether they were the historical ones. As it turns out, some of the names are the same and some of them have changed a little in the past 240 years: what was Dinner Flatts is now Dundee Flatts; Garner Flatts, Gardiners; and Wheat Riggs, Wheat Ridge. He told me this and then said: 'We're away for a couple of days, but when we get back, we'll ring you and come round for supper.' I think I live here.

## Wednesday, 14 November 2007

### All my sons

I love my children. All four of them: there is one I cannot hold. Not true. I hold him in my heart. I just cannot hold his hand in mine. He would be eight today.

Two days before he was due to be born, he stopped moving. I did the things you do: ate vanilla ice cream for which I had no appetite, climbed awkwardly into a hot bath, dribbled water on to my still belly, fell silent, thought: 'Fuck and buggery.' My husband drove me to hospital. I spoke. 'I'm sure it's fine, but I can't feel the baby move.' The midwife took me in, laid me down, wired me up, turned off the light. She cold-gelled and swept the veined mound with ultrasound. I thought: 'Now's the time to wave, baby.' No wave. She could not find a pulsing beat in the grainy black and white. I thought: 'I shan't ask for a picture then this time.' She said: 'I'm going to get someone else to have a look.' I thought: 'That's not what you'd call a good sign,' as the door shush-closed behind her. A brief pause before an older woman came in. Kind. Experienced with bad news. Sweep and look again to find death, tragedy, horror and desolation. She leaned in towards me, said her prayers for the dead: 'I am very sorry to have to tell you . . .' My husband and I clung together as if our world had ended. Our world *had* ended. I can tell you the exact sound a heart makes when it breaks. It sounds like a wolf. Both of us heard it.

If you have a stillbirth, they do not cut you up, rip out the babe, sew you up and send you away, almost whole again. Lick split. Instead, they say: 'Don't swallow this,' and hand you a torpedo, connect you to a drip and 'start you off'. They say: 'This isn't going to hurt,' and lie. 'We'll break your waters,' and take up a crochet hook but not to make a table mat. 'Let's give you morphine. Usually, we don't do this.' The morphine helps but not enough. 'Not long now' and 'Push' and 'Stop' and sixty hours later: 'Well done,' and you see how your life could have been.

My baby boy was beautiful. These babies often are. My baby boy was dead. Stillbirth can be like that. Lying on a paper blanket, the bones in his skull all pushed around, misshapen. The dead, they do decay. Yet, when I felt his head push out from me, he had felt wet, warm and wonderful. Don't look now. The skin, already flayed from his neck, came off at a too tender touch. I do not know the colour of his eyes, but his fingers, tips tinted in scarlet, folded to hold my finger. The first and last time I held his hand in mine. My hand splayed on his chest, his left hand curled round my little finger; my thumb tucked in the other. I felt along the Babygro for his feet, the curve of his calf, the better to remember his body. We had time with him, but not enough; I kissed his rosebud mouth, but not enough; I showered him in tears, too many.

I know how death smells. We lit candles in tins. One for vitality. It did not work. We took endless photos of a subject who never moved. As my husband slept for an hour through the London night, I sat with my baby, told him about Christmas and birthdays and jungle animals and Northumberland which his father loved and where we holidayed each New Year. I swear he heard me. Then the smell got too much and we buried him. I have the bill yet. Keepsakes are hard to come by when a baby dies.

Supply of a small white coffin and transport:

Fee: £150

Extra mileage: £80

Gravediggers: £60

They were toothless. The gravediggers, standing too close and anxious to get on with the job, leaning on their spades as we buried our future. In his coffin we put a teddy bear (cruel of us to bury a teddy), a photo of a kiss, a crucifix (I have its mate), a tulip and a letter. Hardly room in there for the baby. We printed the letter on the order of service for the funeral. It said: 'We knew you before you were born and we wouldn't have missed a moment of our time together as a family. Wherever we go in life, you will be with us and part of us. You will always be the little blond-haired boy running alongside us on a Northumberland beach and the sound of your laughter will always fill our home.'

No reason for the death. As the hospital report said: 'No malformations or obvious infection.' Often the way. His heart weighed 19g. Not a heavy heart. Mine weighed more. No medic in rubbered hands can weigh a mother's love, though. The fact my husband touches me reminds me not to die and he pulls me through the anguish of the days and nights and days. And we whisper a promise to each other that we will not compromise; we will think differently, do what it takes to strive for happiness together.

## Thursday, 15 November 2006

### Hard road

Bad day yesterday. I went for a walk on the beach at one point. I do not know if that made it worse. My husband was in London – unavoidable – and it was the first time we have been apart on the anniversary. I clambered down the dune path and on to the shore. I walked along to where the earth has pushed up a curved rocky road through the sands and into the sea. I looked out into the water and the clouded sky and shouted out my son's name as if to call him in from play and to my side. I thought: 'Can you hear me? Do you know I'm here? That I still love you?' and called out to him again, this time louder. I do not know what made this year so very hard – my husband's absence, or perhaps the fact that every year since our first son died there has been a pregnancy, a baby, a prospect of another baby and another redemption but that time is over. Our family is done – no more babies. I looked out to the moving mirror which is the sea. My salt tears falling, more mirrors dropping into the sand, smashing into the white water foaming over my boots, I thought: 'I wish I could be pregnant again. Pregnant with him again. Do it all differently, have it end differently for him. Make a better job of it this time,' and from the pain

I would say that my scarred heart tore and bled awhile as damaged hearts occasionally do.

## Friday, 16 November 2007

### Call for help

My daughter cried out the other night. She had not been well and I staggered out of bed and grabbed my dressing gown. My husband had only got to bed in the early hours because he was mired in a work crisis, and I had carefully left the bedroom door open because I figured she would wake up. It was indeed much easier to hear her with the door open. Only problem was I forgot it was there and walked straight into it. This has given me a large lump on my eyebrow and a cut lip which immediately swelled up, so that I looked like Marge Simpson, only without the blue hair. Naturally enough, as soon as I had whacked myself nearly insensible on the door she stopped crying. I crawled back into bed, having inspected the damage, and I lay there whimpering, thinking: 'I am going to wake up in the morning and look like I have been walloped. People are going to say: 'What on earth did you do?' And I am going to say: 'I walked into a door' and they are going to think: 'Yeah, right.' But by the morning it had gone down. Now all I have left to show for it is a sore eyebrow and an ulcer on the inside of my lip from the cut.

## Friday, 23 November 2007

### Down and out

I went down to London on Tuesday. I had a business meeting arranged for yesterday and thought I would go down early to see the Islington Beauty and get my hair cut. She has two boys only a little younger than mine, yet manages to stay slim and utterly lovely, unlike me at the moment. I admit I have been 'letting myself go' a little. I wash, obviously. But in the past year I have gone up a dress size and now my only question when I look at clothes is: 'Will it keep me warm?' My lack-adaisical approach to appearance got so bad about a month ago that I cut my own hair. Not just my fringe. All of my hair. Not entirely off. Not like Britney, but a pretty thorough scissoring trim down both sides. Not long ago I would have cut off my own hand rather than do such a thing to myself. Anyway, I got the London haircut, which is a start at least, and have decided to make more of an effort.

Despite the haircut, the trip was a vaguely uneasy one all told. I was supposed to spend both nights with the Islington Beauty. When I arrived on Tuesday, she was hideously stressed by a work deadline, a poorly child and the fact she was due to go away on holiday a couple of days later. She was so stressed it became blazingly apparent I could not stay there two nights or I would pitch her over into insanity. There was nothing I could do about the first night, so we had dinner and I said I would stay somewhere else on Wednesday. Morning comes around and I kiss her goodbye. She says: 'Are you sure this is OK?' I say: 'Absolutely,' and as the door to her Georgian townhouse closes behind me, I think: 'That's it. I'm homeless in London.' I cannot go home a day early because I still have not had my meeting. I could ring London Diva or the Perfect Mother, either of whom will then feel like second best, or I could stay in a Travelodge. I seriously contemplate the Travelodge option but decide it would be so miserable I might throw first the white plastic kettle out of the window and then myself.

I start heading for a tube station and it is at this exact moment I run into the Accountant, who is also down in London on business. I know the Evangelicals would think this was the work of Jesus. There I am, homeless in the Big City, and I run into my best friend from the country who happens to have a flat there. Do I tell him my problem? Of course not. I cannot possibly tell him I am homeless in London and do not know where I am going to sleep. It sounds as if I am so dull that the Islington Beauty has asked me to leave. It would also sound as if I am inviting him to a night of illicit passion. Instead of explaining my predicament, we drink coffee and eat French pastries at a pavement table of a chic café, discuss the relative merits of city and country, and I say 'See ya' and wave merrily as we part.

I am very aware that my husband sent me down to London on the strict understanding I did not spend any money – aside from the haircut – because we have not paid our last set of bills from the builders. It is a very middle-class sort of broke – big house, no money sort of thing. Despite that, after the Accountant disappears into the London sunlight, I contemplate checking into a posh hotel in the centre of town. I only have a handbag with me. This is because I travel light when I do not have the children. The handbag has everything I need in it – purse, toothbrush, change of underwear, change of silk dress, lipstick, powder, mascara, novel, newspaper, notebook, pen, tube map and, astonishingly, a mobile phone which works. I wonder whether hotel staff would think I was a prostitute if I check in for the night with only a handbag. Would they presume it contained baby oil and handcuffs? I decide I am prepared to be considered a prostitute for the sake of knowing where I will sleep that night. I use the mobile phone to ring the posh hotel. The receptionist tells me it will cost £250 to stay the night. £250? I would have to take up prostitution to be able to afford £250 for a night in a hotel. Prostitution seems like too much trouble. I ring the London Diva. I say: 'Hi, it's me. I'm homeless.' She listens to my story of scruples and inhibition. She laughs and says: 'That's fine. Come stay with the B team.'

On the train back north after Thursday's three-hour business meeting, I decide it is OK to have lunch in the restaurant car. I have a table. I do some work. I drink some wine. I sit there till Durham, then move back to my original seat in the buffet car. When I get back, I find a man sitting there who looks vaguely bemused as I ransack his coat and go through his newspapers searching for the Waterstone's bag I left behind to mark my place. The bag has vanished. I search the floor and the overhead compartment and the luggage storage behind the seat, but it has disappeared. It has my favourite brown hat in it from Germany and nine new notebooks. I curse. I had been searching for exactly these notebooks for three months, and despite my husband's strictures about money I had bought them.

I go back down the carriage to look for the guard. The guard is not there. I tell the steward who is leaning against the bar chatting to his colleague that my bag has disappeared and he asks me when I checked on it last. I tell him about three hours ago. He is not impressed with such a cavalier approach to my belongings. He says: 'Things get stolen every day on the train.' I say: 'Right.' He says: 'There are 400 people on a train. Would you trust these 400 people with your stuff?' Patently, yes. He asks me whether I still want to talk to the guard. I say: 'No. Not if that's GNER's reaction to something getting stolen – there's not a lot of point, is there?' The steward says: 'Well, if you tell me what I can do about it, I'll do it.' My opinion of him by this point is not a lot higher than my opinion of whoever took the bag. I start walking up and down the train trying to spot it. I even check the toilets. I see a Waterstone's bag on an overhead shelf of a luggage compartment and immediately rifle it. A mildly irate middle-aged man tells me: 'That's not yours.' He obviously thinks I am trying to steal it. I tell him my bag has gone missing, but I am not convinced he believes me. I do indeed look as if I am reconnoitring things to steal as I walk slowly past everybody's tables, my eye snagging on their mobile phones and shiny laptops. I am thinking: 'Why would anyone want my notebooks and hat when they could have your stuff?' The steward pushes his tea trolley past me and as he sees what I am doing, he says he will keep a look out for me. I think: 'It's a shame you didn't volunteer to do that in the first place.'

I decide to risk the guard's scorn and report the bag missing. The guard is called Terry and does not pour scorn on me. He says things do get stolen but not every day. He is genuinely concerned. He is sorry that my bag has been swiped. He tells me the Darlington to Durham and the Durham to Newcastle stretches of the journey are particular hotspots because they are such short journeys. He says a thief can come on, steal something and be off again with his swag within minutes. Sometimes they stand on the platform, duck in, take the nearest item and are off again without even the price of a ticket. I say pathetically: 'I know you can't do anything.' He says: 'I'll have a good look for you,' and he takes my number and says whatever happens he will call when the train gets to Edinburgh. When his first call comes in later that night, he has found nothing. About an hour later, he finds the bag as the train starts its journey down the line again. I do not know who is more pleased him or me. He tells me the bag was near the kitchen. We wonder if someone has picked it up mistakenly thinking it was theirs – this seems unlikely. Or whether a thief had hoped for a bag of expensive hardback autobiographies for Christmas and got a bagful of blank notebooks and a funny hat and dumped them. Terry asks me which station I want the bag left at. He even rings me a third time to say he handed the bag over to station staff and they will keep it for me. I decide my adventures in London have a happy ending: I do not slide into prostitution, I get my bag back; the thief, as yet, has to buy his Christmas presents; and Terry travelled back down the line knowing he made a difference.

## Heads or tails?

I did the silliest thing yesterday morning – fell from the top of the stairs to the bottom. I believe my lambskin slippers must be haunted. I had just started to walk down the stairs and suddenly my feet flew up in the air, I crashed down on to my backside, thought 'Bugger' then continued to travel, bump, bump, bump, down the entire length of the stairs. My head slamming on to every stair as I careered down, screaming. When I reached the bottom, I lay there sobbing. Luckily my husband was in the kitchen so he ran through and held me while I wept into his chest and drooled all over his shirt.

I am definitely concussed. I was left with the most terrible headache. I went to bed early and this morning my husband said: 'I woke you up every two hours to make sure you weren't dead.' I think he expected me to say thank you – I was too exhausted. I also feel periodically nauseous. Forget the con-cussion – what is wrong with me? Can you get late-onset dyspraxia? I have turned into a klutz. In the past three weeks, I have sprained my ankle, walked into a door and now fallen down the stairs (for the second time this year). Perhaps I need to try doing one thing at a time. When I jumped off the fence, I was thinking about history; when I walked into the door, I was thinking about the screaming baby; and when I was coming down the stairs, I was thinking about my six-year-old's reluctance to do homework and whether he would go to university in twelve years' time.

I would not mind but I have one of those phone interviews with insurance companies later this afternoon where they try to figure out if you are a safe bet to insure. I have had one before, and aside from asking you a variety of highly personal medical questions which immediately make you feel like you are about to die from some horrible disease, they have a whole section on dangerous pursuits – do you rock climb . . . scuba-dive . . . rally drive?' I hope they do not ask 'Can you walk and chew gum?'

## Thursday, 29 November 2007

### Still in La La Land

Went to the doctor's yesterday as I still felt so poxy after the fall downstairs. Nauseous, headachey and zip brain activity. He peered into my eyes with a torch, which always makes me want to shriek with terror, then made me walk in a straight line, which I can never do anyway – drunk, sober, concussed or entirely sane. As a finale, he peered down the back of my pants. Usually I would quite like that, but I knew it was black and blue down there. He said the body needed time to recover and to rest after traumatizing it. On the way out of the surgery I picked up some accident prevention leaflets aimed at the elderly – then again, who would pick them up if they said 'For klutzes of all ages'? Apparently you spend forty years trying to minimize your cellulite, then you hit sixty-five and have to climb into a 'hip protector', which is a giant pair of knickers with concrete pads along each side. According to the leaflet: 'Hip protector underwear cuts down the risk of a fracture if you fall' and you are advised to wear it 'day and night'. I am not sure how my husband would feel if I started wearing it at night, although I quite like the idea. I got home and said to Girl Friday: 'I am thinking of getting hip protector underwear.' She said: 'Why don't you just wear a cycle helmet when-ever you're at home?' One pratfall and suddenly everyone's a comedian.

## Thursday, 13 December 2007

## Postcard from London

Spent a few days in Frankfurt visiting my friend who is recovering from an operation. I flew back into London rather than Edinburgh so that I could go to a Christmas party last night.

My husband met me at City airport. We were to do a very daring thing – leave the children with Girl Friday and have a night away without them. This was the first night we have spent together and away from the children for three and a half years. My husband said: 'We don't need a cab. We'll walk.' I did not think that boded well. He took my laptop and I pulled my little case on wheels along the narrow pavements, past the parked cars captive behind metal railings and underneath a flyover for the Docklands Light Railway. My husband pointed to a neon-lit sign some way ahead – 'Travelodge'. I stopped to consider our journey's destination. I said: 'So we are staying at the Travelodge?' He said: 'Yes, you said you wanted somewhere convenient and it's only £70.' I tugged my wheely case off the pavement and towards the brightly lit entrance. I said: 'We've been together for nineteen years and sometimes I don't think you know me at all.' He said: 'Well, this is what I do when I come to London.' I said: 'And whose fault is that?'

He checked us in; I walked across to the vending machine in the foyer, put in a pound coin and a diet coke slammed into the drawer. I thought: 'I think I need more than a diet coke.' We took the lift up to the room and pushed open the door as a plane taxied past the window. I heard a roaring noise. I think it was a plane. There is a chance it was the blood in my ears. I put down the case on the floor beside the wardrobe and my handbag on the table in front of the mirror and cracked open the diet coke. It did not make me feel better. I put the kettle on and made a cup of tea. It did not make me feel better. I pulled the pillow lengthways so that I could lean against it, and sank into the bed. My husband lay down next to me. The weight of his body tipping me into him. I thought: 'Could the bed be made of sponge, I wonder?' I thought: 'It is not so much the wallow in the mattress or the sound of planes or the fact its location seems so desolate – it is more that he thinks that this is what I am worth, what I deserve.' I said: 'This is our first night away together in three and a half years and you have brought me to City airport's Travelodge. The thing I want to do most of all right now is cry.'

I started getting ready for the party and he slipped out. I thought: 'Maybe I'm tired from travelling. Maybe it's all right. I'll get drunk at the party and when I get back, it won't seem so bad.' My husband came back into the bedroom, his phone in his hand. He said: 'OK, I've booked the Savoy. Shall we go now?'

## Friday, 14 December 2007

### Some kinda dame

The Savoy is due for a refurbishment and is auctioning its furnishings next week. Staying there on Wednesday night felt slightly strange. Perhaps it was the fact I should, by rights, have been at the Travelodge, or perhaps it was the sales tags hanging from the furniture in the room. We were in Room 662. It felt entirely authentic, as if you had ratcheted back in time. I looked out of the window, half-expecting London to be in black and white. I thought: 'Any minute now, a man in a fedora is going to come in with a gun in his hand and a crooked smile. He is going to make me hate him. Then he is going to make me love him. Finally, he is going to walk away into the shadows and never look back, even though his heart is breaking.' I threw

myself on the bed (Lot 2117, a pollard oak and ebonized bedroom suite in the Art Deco style, comprising a double bed with
headboard, a bedside cabinet and a dressing table 196cm wide:
£800–£1,200) to wait for him. I got up again and went across
to Lot 2119 – a pollard oak circular occasional table in the
Art Deco style, 60cm diameter and 65cm high (£100–£150).
I slid a cigarette from a silver case, pursed lips any man would
be happy to call home, and sat down in Lot 2120 (a grey uphol-
stered tub chair: £100–£150). I crossed my long slim legs,
the silk making the kind of noise silk makes, thought 'Daiquiri'
and got up again. I sashayed across to Lot 2118 (a pollard oak
and ebonized cabinet in the Art Deco style, 80cm wide × 60cm
deep × 171cm high: £300–£500). I opened the lacquered door
and a fat man's body toppled out. I screamed. My husband came
in from the bathroom, tousled and slightly damp. He was not
wearing a fedora. He did not notice the bullet-ridden body on
the floor or the writhing cigarette smoke between us. He said:
'Happy, darling?'


## Saturday, 15 December 2007

### 'How lovely are your branches'

In London, we used to go to a flower market, buy bagels, drink
coffee and pay a nice coster man for a six-foot tree 'guaranteed
not to drop its needles eva'. Last year, we drove out to a farm
and looked round a barn where dozens of trees dangled from
the rafters and all I could think of were hanged men swaying
gently in the breeze. Quite took the edge off the festive jollity.
Today, my husband went in the Saab with the four-year-
old and I went in the Volvo with the six-year-old, the baby girl
and a neighbour; we drove alongside hoar-frosted fields to a
forest, where we stumbled around avoiding savage animals and
looking for the perfect tree. I was slightly worried we might all

freeze to death or get eaten while my husband decided which one he was willing to take home with him. (Choosing a tree is one of those things he takes an inordinate amount of time over. Rapt, he will burble endlessly about size and symmetry and the straightness of the trunk – it must be a male thing.) With a whole forest to choose from, I thought that if the weather and animals did not kill us first, we risked being there till Easter. Time for decisiveness.

'That one looks lovely,' I said, pointing to a tree. (It was a tree – how different can one be from the next?) My husband eyed it with some scepticism but it was straight and true and did not run away. We took turns to saw it down with a handy jagged-toothed hacksaw and, in between, sang carols. I could not hear other families singing carols, but I thought I could add it to the collection of Christmas memories I am determined my children should have. Memories like 'Do you remember how you always used to embarrass us by singing carols when we chopped down the Christmas tree? By the way, why couldn't we just buy a tree like normal people?' We dragged it back to the car, paid £15 to a chilly-looking man in a metal container who bagged it up for us in a large net before strapping it to the car with twine. It was dark by the time we had done. We broke down on the way home – I swear to God we are going fibre-optic next year.

## Tuesday, 18 December 2007

### Joyful and triumphant

When we got the car to a garage and the tree home, it turned out it was twelve feet high. It did not look that big in the forest. We left it outside for a couple of days – I think my husband was hoping it might shrink in the rain – and brought it in today. As my husband manhandled it into a stand and screwed it into place, he said: 'I'm so glad you chose this tree and not me.' Luckily we could squeeze it into the sitting room in the arches where we have a sloping vaulted ceiling. It is so large it reminds me a little of the one they have in Trafalgar Square; I keep expecting to walk in and find the Salvation Army gathered round it singing 'Oh Come All Ye Faithful'. It is beautifully decorated halfway up and pretty much naked at the top apart from the fairy, which my husband strapped to two brooms and levered on. Moral of the story being if you have a very tall Christmas tree, it pays to decorate it when it is lying on its side.

## Wednesday, 19 December 2007

### Poop poop

My Riding Pal set me up with a friend of hers who runs a local shoot. I knew I needed some gear, so today I called in at the 'country outfitters' near the castle. The charming man who owns it is a keen fan of shooting. He obviously approved of my decision to give it a go – I do not think he was influenced by the fact he was about to earn a walloping amount of money. He held up a pair of knickerbockers, or 'breeks' as they are technically termed. They are supposed to finish just under the knee. This pair finished at my ankles. I must be shorter than the average 'gun'. He found me a smaller pair. When I say smaller, I mean leg length. Silk-lined, tweed knickerbockers feel fabulous on, warm and roomy, but they do nothing to minimize your backside.

I also needed a checked shirt and fitted Barbour jacket because my only outdoor alternatives are my fabulous floor-length coat or a very scruffy tan suede jacket which is falling apart at the seams. The Barbour belts at the waist. I did not think this would be a brilliant idea bearing in mind the knickerbockers underneath, but amazingly it worked very well. It was slightly Second World War (the Nazis, not the good guys). I thought I was done until he handed me a tweed Gainsborough cap (same tweed as the knickerbockers). I looked a picture. I said to the outfitter: 'I don't want to look like I'm cross-dressing, you know.' He laughed. He said: 'Not at all.' I am not sure if he realized what I meant by 'cross-dressing'. I think it is possible he thought I meant it made me look mean.

I bought the lot and at home climbed into my gear, not forgetting long green shooting socks I had borrowed from the King of the Castle which tied under the knee and over the cuff of the knickerbocker with a tasselled yellow gaiter. I thought there was a chance I looked like a Principal Boy (absurd, cute, sexually ambiguous) and there was a chance I looked like Mr Toad (tweedy, green and fat). I came down to the kitchen. My six-year-old said: 'Mummy – you look stupid.' My four-year-old could not speak for laughing; the baby girl said: 'Where's Mummy?' and began to wail. My husband looked me up and down. He said: 'Exactly how much did that lot cost?'


## Friday, 21 December 2007

### Once more into the breeks

Walked into the pub where 'the guns', that is to say 'the men doing the shooting', were meeting. There were about a dozen, along with a gamekeeper and deputy gamekeeper, 'beaters' (who flush out the game) and 'pickers up' with dogs (who find the birds which have been brought down). Walking into a pub full of men when you are wearing tweed breeks that make you look like you ate a rhino is daunting – the daylight equivalent of that dream where you realize you are naked in the office. The shoot starts with coffee and bacon sandwiches and much shaking of hands and making of introductions before the alcohol comes out at around 9.30 a.m. It is my belief that country folk have larger livers than townsfolk owing to the amount of alcohol they consume while still remaining sober. Ideally the more dangerous the pastime – hunting, for instance, quad-biking or shooting – the more alcohol is consumed.

There was an administrative reason for the early Percy Special. Thinking about it, there often is a reason for a drink in the country, reasons which include 'I'm here' and 'Well, if you're offering.' The pewter cups extracted by the captain of the shooting syndicate from a tan leather 'field bar' were all engraved with numbers on their bottoms. The chap knocks back the drink and turns the cup over to read its number, which tells him where he is standing in the line of guns. Anyone impatient to know his number raises the cup high in front of him as if to make an extravagant toast and peers underneath it. If it were not the first drink of the day, I imagine a lot of them might get rather wet.

After the number draw and the safety lecture from the game-keeper, which included strict advice to 'keep plenty of blue sky under the target', we all piled outside into the 4×4s and headed off into the cold and misty morning for the first of four 'drives'. A drive is where the chaps with the guns stand in their line across a field while the beaters walk along, making a terrible racket, and chase out the birds. The captain explained that the 'sport' is to shoot the bird high in the sky – about thirty yards up. I would have thought there would be more sport if the bird had its own gun, but I did not like to say as much in case he shot me.

At one point during the second drive, I looked across to the gun next to where I was standing – a local dentist. My own dentist is an hour's drive away. I watched him fire into the sky and a pheasant cartwheel down to land close to his feet. It fluttered up from the ground, collapsed, attempted to fly again and fell back in a flurry of beating wings. He stepped across, leaned down and broke its neck. I thought: 'I am so not having you as my dentist.'

To fire a gun, you stand with it tucked tightly into your shoulder. You slide off the safety catch, look along the barrel for the brass bead at the end of it, sweep the gun around, aiming ahead of the target, and pull the trigger, still following the direction in which the bird is flying. It makes a boom noise. During the third drive, my host let me hold his gun. I did not know how my husband would feel about me holding another man's gun, but he was not there so I did it anyway. The captain stood close behind me to stop the recoil knocking me to the ground and I fired his Beretta twice. I missed. I swear the partridge laughed as it flew away.

The cock pheasant is a riot of colour, a blue and green head, red circle drawn around his eyes, white neck, bronze and copper-brown body with a duck-egg blue close to the wings. Partridge are a more discreet grey and buff, while woodcock are small birds with long beaks. Back at the cars, a hen and a cock pheasant are lashed together as a 'brace' with green string, then dangled from the cross-hatched iron bars of a trailer. Their heads knock together in consolation.

I can see the attraction of shooting. It is sociable, outdoors and there are bang-bang toys. Of course, I am not a bird. As a bird, I would be less keen.

### Saturday, 22 December 2007

### Home is where the heart is

My parents arrived yesterday while I was out shooting. It is just as well the Christmas tree is so big, it may take my mother and father's minds off how cold it is in the arches. Their own house is so warm you could grow orchids in it. They have roaring artificial fires and central heating, which they like to use at the same time. They are careful to close doors after themselves and have double-glazed windows which are sealed so tight that in the event of a nuclear war, they would be entirely safe from radiation sickness and would hold out just as long as their tinned products. I wanted them to be equally as warm here, but the underfloor heating in the arches is not working as it should be. There is nothing more we can do before Christmas. Meanwhile, we have shipped in four heaters to take the worst of the chill off the air.

I am irritated it is not perfect for them. Last night my husband lit a fire. They sat together on the new sofa, the lights glowing on the Biggest Christmas Tree In The World, my mother drinking tea. I said: 'I'm sorry it's not warmer in here.' 'Actually,' she said, and in the dazzle of the fairylights I could not see if she shivered slightly, 'it's just right.'

### Monday, 24 December 2007

#### 'Peace on earth, goodwill to all men'

We went to the village at the foot of the castle for the Christmas crib service with the children and my mother. My husband took the children in one car and I took my mother in the other, dropping her by the church gate so she did not have so far to walk. My Riding Pal was just going in, so she gave my mother her arm. I felt like saying: 'Trot – don't canter.' (My father did not come because he thinks he will go straight to Hell if he sets foot in a church that is not Catholic. Either that or he hated my mother's hat.) Early on in the service, the Vicar got all the children sitting on the floor at the front of the congregation and had them place the china figures among the straw. My six-year-old took a king, my four-year-old as yet too shy, my girl more interested in the chocolate Santa she found in the pocket of my wax jacket than Baby Jesus in his manger. I had to perch on a kneeler with her at the front, and the Vicar beamed at me when she saw me hunkered down among the little ones before her pulpit. I smiled back. I said: 'That was a very lovely service' at the end as she waited by the oak door giving out balloons to excited children.

Outside, the Yorkshire Mother was there with her husband and boys. Her son is buried in the churchyard, and the younger boys were going to let off their balloons at his grave. I hugged her. When you lose a child, simple things about Christmas can be hard. A hopping robin – you think: 'Is that him come to say hello?' Open a creamy envelope, gilt-winged seraphim revealed, you think: 'Can he play the trumpet now, my lost and angel child?' Wrapping in paper penguins her other children's toys, a mother takes a moment – he would be such and such an age and there is no stocking she can fill with tangerines and chocolate coins, nothing she can buy for him, cover in foil stars and scrawl: 'Merry Christmas, love from Santa Claus.'

## Tuesday, 25 December 2007

### The Story of Christmas

Unusually, lunch was indeed at lunchtime, after the children had opened everything – the hit being a helicopter which flew on and off for three hours, after which the rear propeller was damaged in a head-on collision with an enemy table leg. As my mother and father came through from their sitting room and we all sat down for lunch, I allowed myself a cat lick of happiness that the house was doing what it was designed to do and that they were with us.

Later, we went for a walk on the beach by the castle. The boys tore into the dunes, disappearing then reappearing as I began to worry they had been eaten by sand rats. Soft mauve and pastel blues filled the vastness of the sky behind the castle, soft pink and apricot above a mercury sea touched with white gold; yet the small waves which stood up before throwing themselves to break against the sand were as green as bottle glass. My daughter staggered to the water's edge. 'Not too close,' I warned, and she smiled at me, a small triumph to let the sea cover over her pink-flowered boots. 'She's fine,' my husband said. He reached for my hand. 'Merry Christmas.' He stopped walking, pulled me back to him and kissed me.

## Sunday December 30 2007

### Auf Wiedersehen Pet?

London Diva and the Godfather arrived last night with their girls and a teenage pal. The Accountant let them stay in his cottage because my parents are still with us. We went across to Holy Island with them. You drive across a causeway which is flooded depending on the tides, cutting it off from the mainland. Occasionally tourists try to make it and the sea rushes in, stranding them on top of their cars or in the wooden hut on stilts at the midway point, from which they are airlifted to safety. Presumably, once they have been hauled on board, the helicopter rescue crew uses a rolled-up newspaper and hits them round the head, chorusing 'Duh!' You just hope the same tourists never have to drive over a level crossing.

There is a very small settlement on the island, a beautiful castle and the falling-down ruins of a priory. A monastery was established here in the seventh century and monks sent out from it to convert the Anglo-Saxons. It is still considered to be a place of spiritual retreat. For some reason, it always makes me feel acutely uncomfortable. Perhaps my inner demons feel anxious about so much Christianity surrounding them, or perhaps it is the feeling I might be trapped on the island and burnt in a wickerwork effigy of a London bus. As we walked through the jumbled-up streets, my husband said: 'It is lovely here – so peaceful.' London Diva nudged me. I said to him: 'Don't even think about it.'

When we got home, the Diva said: 'Are you all right? You don't look all right. I don't think I have ever seen you look sadder.' I said: 'I'm fine – I'm just a bit tired' – and I am. In one of my periods where I do not so much sleep as lie back in the dark with my eyes open. Most of all, though, I was thinking about whether we stay or go back to London. If we go back, we return to old friends and the place I love most in the world, but can you ever really go back, and could I live with the guilt of dragging everyone along with me when we have made a life here for all of us? Would I be a fool having spent all this time and money creating a great house for us to live in only to walk away from it? But if we stay, is this life enough for me? Would I live for ever more on the boundary of things and, if so, am I content to live as an outsider? I am not sure I will ever really belong. After all, I do not farm, I do not ride, I do not own a castle.

## Monday, 31 December 2007

### Old Year's Night

Luckily it was the four-year-old's birthday, so I could divert everybody's attention from the grinding noise coming from my head, still busy with 'Do we stay or do we go now?' with birthday cake and the information that in this part of Northumberland, they do not call it New Year's Eve but Old Year's Night. We all had dinner, roast Northumberland lamb and chocolate pudding, and around 11 p.m. the Accountant came along, closely followed by the Consultant and her husband, and we drank champagne and watched the fireworks display in London on the television.

I always review my year then write my resolutions in the sand – I figure you might as well start as you mean to go on. Last year when the Oyster Farmer and his wife were round for dinner, I gave it a mark – four and a half out of ten. This year, a review slipped my mind – why was that? Is it that I do not care about the past any more? Unlikely – I am Catholic and have been in therapy: I virtually live in the past. Do I think there is no room for improvement? Obviously a far more difficult one to answer. Maybe I was too busy still living it. Now I have a moment, the year.

Bad things included:

* tears and fears that my elder son was not happy at school

* anxiety about my younger one's stomach migraines

* intermittent loneliness and the blues about where I was and what I was doing

* missing London, London, London

* the suspicion I am getting really old and likely to get older.

Good things included:

* the children

* my mother's health rallying

* writing this account of my life

* moving back into the cottage and finally having the space to swing a cat. (Shame my cat did a runner pretty much as soon as we arrived in Northumberland.)

* giving things a go and seeing the good things about my new life in Northumberland, such as quite how beautiful it is

* recognizing I had, despite myself perhaps, made friends here.

Resolutions:

* more patience

* more sleep, which might help with the first one

* be happy and keep trying.

As for the decision about whether we stay in Northumberland or return to London: Time is up – it is made – I just do not want to say it out loud yet.

# Postscript

We decided to stay. My husband never shifted from loving Northumberland, the boys love school and their muddy, sandy outdoors life, my girl loves horses and I love all of them. The house, too, is set up to accommodate my parents as and when they need it, which gives me comfort and a sense of the possible. The decision to stay was not an easy one and part of me will always yearn to be back in London. I am still a Daughter of the City – but it is time to grow up and leave home. Every day I find myself surprised by a suspicion that I 'belong' more than I did the day before, that I am being claimed somehow.

The past two and half years have indeed been an adventure, during which I made friends and intend to make more, learned country ways, tasted at least the beauty and power of this place and grew to appreciate the kindness and warmth of those I now live among. Best of all, I have not been eaten by bears. Perhaps now I will always be pulled between Northumberland and London, between heart and soul, between the wife and mother I am and the memory of who I was. I will visit London and miss it as long as ever I am away, but, for the moment, this is where we stand. Who knows? Things change. Not long ago, my husband said: 'Let's face facts. If I was dead, you wouldn't be here.' I looked at him. I picked up my coffee cup and held it in both of my hands, slightly obscuring my face. I said: 'Let's face facts. You're not dead.'

# Acknowledgements

I would like to thank my agent, Patrick Walsh of Conville and Walsh, for his unflagging enthusiasm and support, as well as his colleagues Jake Smith-Bosanquet and Rob Dinsdale. Venetia Butterfield of Viking saw potential in my blog, www.wifeinthenorth.com, and her insights and friendship helped me turn it into a book. The team at Penguin were a joy to work alongside and I am also grateful for the advice, guidance and generosity of friends and family during the writing process, in particular my technical wizard, Michael Reilly-Cooper. I owe a debt of thanks to Tom Watson MP, Iain Dale and Andrew Sullivan for first linking my blog to theirs, as well as those who take the time to read me in cyberspace. Finally, I would like to thank my beloved parents and of course my Husband in the South.

# He just wanted a decent book to read ...

Not too much to ask, is it? It was in 1935 when Allen Lane, Managing Director of Bodley Head Publishers, stood on a platform at Exeter railway station looking for something good to read on his journey back to London. His choice was limited to popular magazines and poor-quality paperbacks – the same choice faced every day by the vast majority of readers, few of whom could afford hardbacks. Lane's disappointment and subsequent anger at the range of books generally available led him to found a company – and change the world.

*'We believed in the existence in this country of a vast reading public for intelligent books at a low price, and staked everything on it'*
**Sir Allen Lane, 1902–1970, founder of Penguin Books**

The quality paperback had arrived – and not just in bookshops. Lane was adamant that his Penguins should appear in chain stores and tobacconists, and should cost no more than a packet of cigarettes.

Reading habits (and cigarette prices) have changed since 1935, but Penguin still believes in publishing the best books for everybody to enjoy. We still believe that good design costs no more than bad design, and we still believe that quality books published passionately and responsibly make the world a better place.

So wherever you see the little bird – whether it's on a piece of prize-winning literary fiction or a celebrity autobiography, political tour de force or historical masterpiece, a serial-killer thriller, reference book, world classic or a piece of pure escapism – you can bet that it represents the very best that the genre has to offer.

**Whatever you like to read – trust Penguin.**